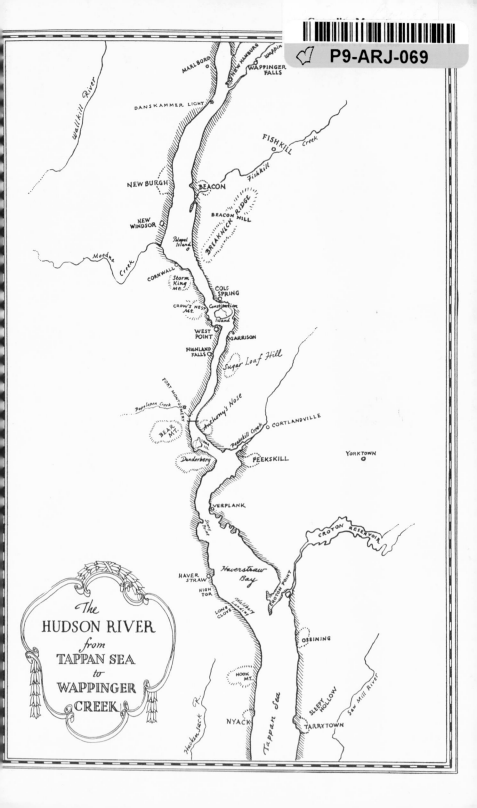

The
HUDSON RIVER
from
TAPPAN SEA
to
WAPPINGER
CREEK

HUDSON RIVER LANDINGS

THE MOUTH OF THE HUDSON RIVER TO-DAY

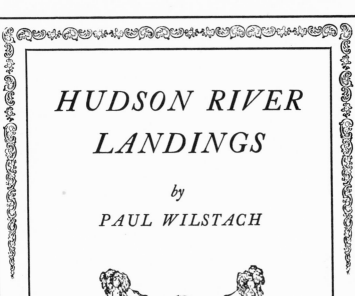

HUDSON RIVER
LANDINGS

by

PAUL WILSTACH

Illustrated

IRA J. FRIEDMAN, Inc.
Port Washington, L.I., N.Y.

CONTENTS

CONTENTS—*Continued*

CONTENTS—*Continued*

CONTENTS—*Concluded*

ILLUSTRATIONS

ILLUSTRATIONS—*Continued*

HUDSON RIVER LANDINGS

HUDSON RIVER LANDINGS

CHAPTER I

LEARNING THE RIVER

Hudson River Landings—History as a Story—Tangibles and Intangibles—
Tear of the Clouds—The Hudson as a Fiord—The Sailors' Reaches—
Topography—Creeks and Kills—The Palisades—The Highlands—The
Mountains—The Four Great Periods—Historic Figures—Mythical Figures
and Legends of the River—The Hudson's Many Names.

ERE is the story of the Hudson. It is the story of that great river which scarcely escapes obscurity over the first half of its winding half-wild course away from its sources in the northern mountain tarns, but which, when it stands directly south toward the sea, seems to find its destiny, for it advances over this second half of its length to the accompaniment of rare and varied natural splendors, punctuated by important cities, embellished by man in ostentatious mood, until it finally gives itself to its other mother, the sea, at the feet of the greatest metropolis of our hemisphere.

This is not the story of the whole Hudson, nor obviously is it the Hudson's whole story; but only of so much of the river and its history as is most significant, and so most diverting.

The story of the river's natural aspects is written along its banks in a language without words. The diversity of its water stretches, its tumbling banks sweeping up to miniature mountains, the changing lights of sunshine and cloud-shadow, the inexplicable variety of color in calm or storm, on field or forest or peak, all unroll a scroll written in that wordless language which is obvious to every eye. They give themselves direct, without benefit or need of interpreter. They convey the diversions of pleasure or awe with undeviating, inescapable directness.

Diversion and history, however, are not always so intimately associated. That may be, however, because of some neglect of the sense of the word and some lack of perspective in making the intangible tangible, in selecting the threads and their dyes and weaving them into the pattern of the tapestry. History like Nature may be thrilling. It has, too, the advantage of Nature in that it may be amusing, even comic; characteristics which Nature manages generally to escape.

The word "history" is often thought of as representing something austere and didactic, as a grouping of sapless facts, an arrangement of uninspiring dates. History need not be that, indeed it should not be that. Though we derive the word literally from the Latin *historia,* the Italians make a better job of adopting the same word into their language. They have come to call it *storia.* Our word "story," from the same source, has somehow become attached to fiction only. But an arrangement of facts may be made into a story, too.

History told as a story has the added allure that it is not a fabrication, that all its wonderful elements are based on reality, on great or romantic figures who lived, on deeds that were actually done, or flashes of humor and touches of human nature that depend on our universal kinship for their diversion. Hence, though the words history and story may not have identical significance, it is our privilege to humbug ourselves, if need be, with the pretense that here we have clipped the wings of history and that this shall be rather the story of the great river.

The Hudson of our interest is the navigable Hudson. Our race first came to this part of its shore; and over a subsequent period of more than three hundred years, here etched a record of peculiar significance in those three hundred years of American drama. Scenically, historically and humanistically, in its tangibles and intangibles, its cumulative interest is scarcely exceeded, if indeed, it is even matched, by any other of our rivers.

The tangibles of the Hudson are all one sees in sailing the length of its waters. Its intangibles are all the great or amusing characters who have passed or paused on its shores; all the significant events which have happened here; all the alluring myths attaching to it.

From source to sea the Hudson has a length of three hundred miles. Over each of two exact halves of this length, it exhibits curiously contrasting characters. It bubbles into being somewhere in the wild heights of the Adirondacks. Several little lakes send out their waters to make the flow where it is first called Hudson. But any one who knows that one of these little mirrors up against the sky bears the delicately suggestive name of Lake Tear of the Clouds will probably feel that no other name could so charmingly account for the beginning of a river, and so will care to look no further.

For the first one hundred and fifty miles of its course the river is a wild impetuous stream. It foams over rocky barriers, it plunges over waterfalls, and it accepts into its erratic channel a few lesser streams before it reaches the cities of Troy and Albany and becomes its other self. As if exhausted by its own erratic activity it here suddenly subdues its restlessness and becomes calm and serene and expansive as it moves on with majestic reticence over the other one hundred and fifty miles to the Atlantic.

The reason for this metamorphosis is none the less interesting because it is simple. The northern half of its course carries it down from great elevations to a level which is a fraction less than only six feet higher than the point, another one hundred and fifty miles beyond, where it surrenders its identity to the ocean. The whole of that latter relatively level course is actually less river than sea. This navigable Hudson is actually a fiord, with a bed of rock along its entire length, a bed which, with the exception of a few islands, is lower than the contiguous bed of the ocean. The flow from its mountain sources is met and stayed by the insweeping tides. The Indians naïvely but graphically referred to it as "the stream that flowed both ways." Its "sweet" waters hurled down from the mountains lose their sweetness and become first brackish and then salt. This arm of the sea admits ocean-going vessels of a certain draft over its entire length. Actually for this half of its length, where it is not so much a river as a deep fiord, it searches its way inland, sometimes past precipices, sometimes between yielding hills, sometimes in the shadows of mountains.

The tides are not quite equal to the titanic task of turning back the accumulation of the fresh water here with a single sweep. The effect of tide, as it sweeps in from the sea, is felt as far north as Albany. But it requires three tides effectively to stem the current. There are in effect three different though inter-dependent tides along this one hundred and fifty miles of fiord.

Science has discovered a third Hudson, the continuation of these two. Its bed reaches southeast, through a submerged valley over the continental shelf which is a part of the floor of the ocean itself. This is believed to be the channel of an earlier Hudson which flowed there when the land stood two or three thousand feet higher than it does in this age, while the inner gorges of the river above the present city of New York were being excavated. The submerged waters of that third

Hudson, if they may be imagined to have movement, end abruptly at the edge of the shelf where the ocean's floor drops a thousand feet, and so precipitate a silent, invisible waterfall which is more than five times the height of Niagara itself.

On the map the thin thread of the navigable Hudson makes a line due north and south. It would seem as if from the deck of a steamer midstream off the flank of New York City only the curvature of the earth, or perhaps eventual atmospheric opacity, would prevent one looking up this undeviating stretch of water to the towers of Albany and Troy. Actually the river bends little. But this little is enough, accented by the occasional overlapping of high rocky points, to close the river off into many sections, hill-cupped water stretches, like lovely lakes, some of them more than a little reminiscent of Lucerne or Como or Maggiore. To one advancing up the surface of the river only one of these lakes is visible at a time, unless one climbs the higher flanking mountains from which in places there appears to be a series of two or three or four contiguous but detached lakes.

In earlier days, before steam had driven sails off the river, the skipper made from point to point along what were called "reaches." De Laet, writing as early as 1625, indicated these reaches by some of the names that survived. Later they were listed as being fourteen in all between New York and Albany. The first extended along the wall of the Palisades. Then successively on the way up-river they were named the Tappan Zee, Haverstraw Bay, Seylmaker's Reach, Hoge's, Vorsen "which included the treacherous transit of the Highlands," Fisher's Reach to Esopus, Claverack, Bacerack, Playsier, Vaste and Hunter's. This accounts for only twelve. But as it carries up only to Kinderhook neighborhood, the two unnamed reaches presumably account for the difficult narrows between the islands over the remaining twenty-five other miles to the head of navigation. But the fallibility of list and of conjecture is blasted by their failure to take account of Martelaer's Reach under Crow's Nest Mountain in the Highlands; or Lange Rak, or Long Reach, from Wappinger Creek northward to Crum Elbow Point, one of the most frequently remarked of all of them.

Unlike that other great tidal river of the Atlantic littoral, the Potomac, with its own tidal inlets, bays, "creeks" and "rivers," the Hudson marches north between its lofty banks without an opening deep enough to let the tide in more than a mile or two. Along tidewater Potomac a so-called creek is really a tidal inlet. A small fresh-water tributary is called a run. Along tidewater Hudson, where there are no such tidal inlets to preempt the name creek, the term is applied to the smaller fresh-water tributaries, as elsewhere in fresh-water country. The word, however, yielding to the impress of the early period when the streams were christened, more often appears in its near-Dutch guise as a Kill. The pure Dutch word is *Kil*. Sometimes custom has taken no account of the meaning of Kill and so has committed the amusing tautology of twice determining the character of the stream with the two words of identical meaning; as in the instances of Peekskill Creek, Fishkill Creek, Fall Kill Creek and Catskill Creek.

Of these tributaries the principal ones from south to north are, on the east side: Saw Mill River, Pocantico River, Croton River, Peekskill Creek, Fishkill Creek, Wappinger Creek, Fall Kill Creek, Casper Creek, Crum Elbow Creek, Landsman Kill, Stony Creek, Roeliff Jansen Kill, Kinderhook or Stockport Creek, Moordener Creek and Wyants Kill; and on the west side: Popolopen Creek, Moodna Creek, Quassaic Creek, Rondout

River, Esopus Creek, Catskill Creek, Hans Vosen Kill, Corlear
Kill, Murderers Creek, Coxsackie Creek, Coeymans Creek,
Baker Creek, Vloman Kill and Norman Kill.

The reason that the Hudson has no deep inlets along the entire course of its tide is interrelated with the reason for its
width and its depth. It is in fact not broad for a tidal river of
its length. And it is extraordinarily deep for a river of its
width. Along many miles above its mouth it is capable of re-
ceiving ships of the greatest draft as yet built. It does not
attain its greatest depth until more than fifty miles above its
mouth when the bed of the river is two hundred and sixteen
feet below its surface. Its channel narrows and shallows as it
advances northward, but, with some assistance from the
dredgers, it receives ocean-going vessels of a certain draft even
at the docks of Albany.

Between Manhattan Island and Westchester on the east and
the Palisades on the west it maintains an average width of one
mile. Above that it widens to an average of two and a half
miles in Tappan Sea and to over three miles in Haverstraw Bay
before it is momentarily narrowest at several points in the Highlands. Above Poughkeepsie it is rarely so wide as three-quarters
of a mile. Its narrowest span in the Highlands is matched
again at the head of its navigable waters.

The interrelated reason for the absence of inlets, for the
river's limited width and for its great depth, is found in the topography of the land along its shores. From one end to the other
these banks are high, sometimes precipitous, sometimes steeply
rolling, sometimes rising in mountains to a sky-line over sixteen
hundred feet above the water.

One of the most distinguished features of the river is the
character and diversity of its natural scenery. It is nearly

always beautiful. Frequently it is quite ravishing in its combi-
nation of land and water. At times it approaches sublimity in
the assemblage of mountains whose bleak high shoulders and
seemingly lofty peaks present aspects of awesome grandeur.

These hills and mountains are the continuation of, although
on account of their lesser summits they might be accounted an
interruption in, the whole chain of mountains which parallels the
Atlantic coast. They approach the Hudson from the west in a
single range, reaching it in two detached groups of mountains.
Through one of them the river forces its passage in the district
called the Highlands. The other is the much loftier agglomeration called the Catskill Mountains which approaches within eight
miles of the west shore of the river where its tides begin to
wane. The continuation of this chain beyond the eastern shore
of the river soon builds into the Berkshire and then into the
Green Mountains of Vermont and the White Mountains of
New Hampshire.

The shores of tidal Hudson are not extensively devoted to
agriculture. In places they are too steep, and nearly everywhere rock is too near the surface for profitable cultivation. As
the range of the hilly shores is north and south, it is in the
hinterland just over the flanking crests, in valleys between them
and other ranges, that man has for the most part found sufficient
and productive soil. Where creeks have made their way through
the hilly shore, and found a way to bring their waters to the
great river, man has put landings, and about some of them
towns and cities have grown up, market towns for the farmers
of the hinterland, exporting depots for their manufactured
needs. The principal cities here are New York City and its
interdependent cities across the river from it on the New Jersey
shore, Yonkers, Newburgh, Poughkeepsie, Kingston, Hudson,

Albany and Troy. Every one of them has found in the river its reason of being and development. In addition to these cities there are villages every few miles. And where there are no cities, towns or villages, man has preempted the shore for extensive estates, elaborately embellished and studded with pretentious homes.

Transportation on the Hudson has always been one of the most significant of its tangible features. It has, since its discovery, grown unceasingly as a highway. There were two earlier centuries when its surface was alive with sails. Steam supplanted them in a measure with steamboats, which survive in numbers, in spite of all other forms of motor competition. What a procession the ships present as they sail down the three centuries, the *Half Moon* leading the sequence of high-pooped Dutch traders; the yachts of the patroons; the awesome pirate craft that entered, too; the swift English frigates; Fulton's *Clermont;* Stevens's *Phœnix,* first to steam across the Atlantic; the leisurely social fleets of canal-boats; the myriad ferry-boats, the leviathans, the dreadnoughts. They all plowed these waters, they all anchored here. In the rock near the water's edge on both shores are chiseled the pathways of the railroads. Higher up, and nearly always farther back from the water, often not even in sight of it, are the newer avenues of the motor traffic. No other American waterway bears an equal traffic of passengers and freight. The valley of no other river approaches the Hudson in the volume of its traffic. It is one of the greatest commercial and pleasure highways of equal length on this, and perhaps on any other, continent.

The Hudson is no less rich and alluring in intangibles. Its chronicle is bound up inseparably with all our national life. Of the permanent settlements made in the territory which later was to be known as the thirteen original states of our Republic, the third was made on this river in 1624. But when the *Half Moon* sailed up to the head of its navigable waters, Jamestown was the only permanent settlement in that same territory. The *Mayflower's* voyage was still eleven years in the future. The Potomac would have to wait nearly a quarter of a century for the coming of the *Ark* and the *Dove*.

Individuality was given to the settlements and developments made on the Hudson because they were made by the Dutch, in contrast with the English in Virginia, Massachusetts, Maryland and elsewhere. In no other pioneer neighborhood of the thirteen colonies was there such a motley of nationals as here, an early suggestion of the dominant characteristic of the metropolis which rose at the river's mouth, and scarcely less of the internationalistic tone of the population of the Republic as a whole.

Dutch political control lasted only a few years more than half a century. Nevertheless, it will be found that although the English took New Netherland over politically, Dutch character, Dutch customs and other Dutch influences had become so strongly embedded here that they were not wholly superseded by any other nationalistic influence, and their impress is in some phases recognizable even to-day.

After the half-century of Dutch control, and a whole century of English control, the Revolutionary period brought some of its most critical events and some of its clearest defined characters to the river. Washington himself was often here, both in the earlier stages of the war when the struggle of the two contending armies centered on the Hudson, and later when he spent nearly two years on its shores between the surrender at Yorktown and the Treaty of Paris, holding his army together against eventualities and later demobilizing it. Meanwhile, in his retreat in the Highlands Benedict Arnold was discovered at his treason, and more gallant Major André, for his part in the affair, paid with his life just round the upper end of the Palisades.

The names of the great characters of the river include by association, if not by birth, a large percentage of all who have contributed to the military, political and cultural phases of our national life. Perhaps more intimately identified as sons of the river were the Van Rensselaers, the Van Cortlandts, the Beekmans, the Schuylers, the Livingstons, the Clintons, Alexander Hamilton, Martin Van Buren and Washington Irving. But equally a part of its story are the piratical operations of Captain Kidd and Fulton's successful application of steam to water navigation; and in the shadow of the Palisades, Aaron Burr fired the bullet which snuffed the life out of his own great political career as surely as it snuffed the life out of the body of Alexander Hamilton.

The mention of Washington Irving reminds that one of the most unique features of the Hudson is that almost alone of all American rivers is it endowed with its own lore, its own mythology. It is a river of mystery as well as of history. There are tales and fictitious characters, associated with the river, which have become so vivid to the American consciousness that they seem as real as the facts and personages of its real story. Who thinks of the Catskills without thinking of Rip Van Winkle? Who hears the thunder-peals reverberating across the water from mountain to mountain and does not recall that the men of Hudson's ghostly crew are again at their game of ninepins? The mere mention of Sleepy Hollow envisions Ichabod Crane in flight before the Headless Horseman. Just so we think of the burghers of New Amsterdam as Knickerbockers, though the name Knickerbocker existed only rarely and some-what obscurely except in Irving's roguish fancy. There is a spice of irony in the fact that the descendants of the Dutch re-pudiated Irving's Knickerbocker when it appeared, yet their own descendants have since accepted the claim of being "one of the old Knickerbocker families" as a kind of title of aristocracy.

Myths, too, account for the names of hills, creeks, points and other natural formations; a tale is, as it were, in every stone; a book, as it were, in every running brook. Indeed, a legend is given to explain the birth and presence of the river itself. It recites that Amasis, one of the Magi, found his way to this side of the great ocean. He refused to join the natives in their sun worship. Instead, on the summit of High Tor, one of the lesser peaks of the Hudson, he erected an altar for his own rite. This so enraged the Indians that they rose up against him and stormed his mountain, and would have de-stroyed him as well as his altar if it had not been for a miracle. An earthquake cleft the mountains and swallowed his enemies, thus opening the channel through which the Hudson flows.

How comes the Hudson to this unique heritage of myth, ghosts, goblins and other lore? It is not at first easy "to recon-cile the reputation of the Dutch as a phlegmatic and unimagina-tive people with the fact that they and their children endowed the Hudson with more glamour, more of the supernatural and of elfin lores than haunts any other American waterway." But Maud Wilder Goodwin offered a suggestive consideration when she asked:

"Does the explanation perhaps lie in the fact that the Dutch colonists, coming from a small country situated on a level plain where the landscape was open as far as the eye could see, and left no room for mystery, were suddenly transplanted to a region shut in between overhanging cliffs where lightning flashed and thunder rolled from mountain wall to mountain wall, where thick forests obscured the view, and strange aboriginal savages hid in the underbrush? Was it not the sense of wonder springing from this change in their accustomed surroundings that peopled the dim depths of the *hinterland* with shapes of elf and goblin, of demons and superhuman presences?"

The Hudson had many names before its present name became generally accepted. The Indians had many names for it, often many names concurrently along different sectors of it. The French sent Verrazzano to the coasts of the western Atlantic in 1524, and he called it the "Grande Riviere" and "The River of the Steep Hills." The very next year Gomez, a Spanish explorer, "discovered" it and called it the San Antonio, and other Spaniards, writing of the river soon after him, referred to it as Rio de Gomez or Guamas. The name Norumbega is believed to attach to it from maps of about 1569. Hudson himself, in 1609, called it "the Great River" and the Manhattes, after the Indians he found here. But the next year the Dutch, for whom Hudson's expedition had been undertaken, named their new river officially the Prince Maurice, or the Mauritius, after their Stadtholder, Prince Maurice of Orange. But custom prevailed over the officials, and the traders, who came here during many years following, called it indiscriminately the "Groote Rivier, Manhattan Rivier, Nassau River, Noordt Rivier, Montaigne River and Mauritz Rivier." It was casually referred to by its present name, at least as "Hudson's River," in a Relation, soon after 1621. But it was not until the English established political control over the territory contiguous to the river that they officially named it Hudson after the Englishman who had discovered it for the Dutch. But the old Dutch name "Noordt Rivier," or, in English, North River, continues to attach to it to-day, or to at least that stretch of its waters on the west side of Manhattan Island.

Many call the Hudson the North River who do not know the reason of the name. This reason is found in the fact that the colony of New Netherland extended from eastward of the present Hudson River southwest to the Delaware, and the traders during its early years referred to these two waterways respectively as the North River and the South River, the north and the south boundary of their province.

When it is said that this is not to be the story of the entire length of the Hudson from the metropolis of New York City at its mouth to its source in the distant skyward little lake in the Adirondacks, but only of that portion of it which is most significant, reference is made specifically to its navigable reach from its mouth on New York Bay up to its northernmost tidal land just above the port of Albany.

This is just half of its entire length. The upper half of the whole river, on toward its mountain source, is a wild stream which bids no welcome to navigation. It yields to the bridle of civilization in places, where its waters are harnessed to generate power and mill-towns have sprung up. History has touched it at times, though somewhat sparingly. But history follows colonization. The early colonization clung to navigable waterways. Hence, the more far-reaching phase of the Hudson's history attaches to its navigable waters, to the broad southern half of its whole length. Here the explorers came and no farther. Here the first settlers came and built their waterside landings, where landings have ever since welcomed men and ships. Here are the greater cities, linked by stretches of the more luxurious human habitations.

The story of this navigable Hudson, followed from landing to landing, reveals phases which are not only of the first importance in our national history, but which have an individuality unmatched elsewhere because of the Dutch who came, remained and left such an indelible impression as did no other non-English people throughout the thirteen original colonies; because of the lore attaching to it; because of the scenes of our Revolutionary War drama enacted here; and because of the unmatched development along its shores during the last century.

The story begins with the explorers.

CHAPTER II

DISCOVERERS AND EXPLORERS

Verrazzano, the Florentine, for France—Estevan Gomez, the Portuguese, for Spain—Henry Hudson, the Englishman, for Holland—Hudson's Voyages in the *Half Moon*, in Search of the Northwest Passage—The *Half Moon* Sails into the Great River—Journal of Robert Juet, of Limehouse—The *Half Moon* Reaches the Head of Tides—Hudson's Sailors Seek beyond in Small Boats—Success in Failure—Contacts with the Indians—Courtesy, Hospitality and Treachery—Hudson Sails the *Half Moon* out to Sea—His Great Adventure's End.

HE Hudson River is inseparably and properly associated with the explorer whose name it bears. This association is so intimate that the assumption is general that Henry Hudson was the first white man to look upon its waters.

Hudson was, indeed, the first explorer whose voyage here was chronicled, with dates and details. He was the first explorer whom we are privileged to follow day by day, from point to point, along the river's whole navigable length. And it was his memorable exploit that, more immediately than any other, opened the river to European settlement and civilization.

Actually, however, Hudson's entrance on the scene as the discoverer of the river was anticipated by others. The northern Europeans are known to have crossed the Atlantic many times previously. They left scant chronicles, however, to acquaint us with how far west they penetrated. One other at least may have discovered the length of the navigable river, and we know definitely that several others came at least to its mouth and probably entered. Such voyages stretch back behind Hudson for more than a century to the river's slow emergence into our history. The thought of these pioneers of the uncharted watery wastes recalls the apostrophe of Purchas in *His Pilgrimes:*

"How shall I admire your heroicke courage, ye marine worthies, beyond all names of worthness!, that neyther dread so long eyether presence or absence of the sunne; nor those foggy mysts, tempestuous winds, cold blasts, snowes and hayle in the ayre; nor the unequall seas, which might amaze the hearer and awate the beholder, where the Tritons and Neptune's selfe would quake with chilling feare."

Searching back among the somewhat nebulous accounts of the voyages of these "marine worthies," we find that the possible discoverer of the river may have been John Cabot; that the probable discoverer was the Italian, Giovanni da Verrazzano; that it was visited by the pilot Estevan Gomez; by some French traders; and after them by some traders from the Netherlands before the beginning of the seventeenth century.

The details of Cabot's penetration westward in 1498 are veiled in doubt. There is no record which says definitely what, if any discoveries, he made along the last stretch of this voyage. There has been a plausible effort to demonstrate that he followed the western shores of the Atlantic as far as Florida. In that case he was the first European known to have been within reach of a short turn into the mouth of the river we know as the Hudson. But the evidence of Cabot's having sailed so far west is not so satisfactory as to lead beyond the limit of possibility.

After a quarter of a century history becomes more definite. Verrazzano, a Florentine mariner, in 1524, undertook a voyage of exploration for King Francis I of France. Having crossed the Atlantic to a point near Florida, he sailed up the entire coast, and recrossed to France over a northern course. We have his report on this exploit in a letter to his royal patron, and there are confirmatory maps. The letter is comparatively brief, but it is definite. It probably anticipated a fuller report which may have been made and has so far eluded research. In the following paragraph, taken in connection with the other context, Verrazzano reveals definitely that he came to the mouth of the Hudson:

"At the end of a hundred leagues we found a very agreeable situation located within two small prominent hills, in the midst of which flowed to the sea a very great river, which was deep within the mouth; and from the sea to the hills of that [place] with the rising of the tides, which we found eight feet, any laden ship might have passed. On account of being anchored off the coast in good shelter, we did not wish to adventure in without knowledge of the entrances. We were with the small boat, entering the said river to the land, which we found much populated. The people, almost like the others, clothed with the feathers of birds of various colors, came toward us joyfully, uttering very great exclamations of admiration, showing us where we could land with the boat more safely. We entered said river, within the land, about half a league, where we saw it made a very beautiful lake with a circuit of about three leagues; Through which they [the Indians] went, going from one and another part of the number of XXX of their little barges, with innumerable people, who passed from one shore and the other in order to see us. In an instant, as is wont to happen in navigation *a gale of* unfavorable wind blowing in from the sea, we were forced to return to the ship, leaving the said land with much regret because of its commodiousness and beauty, thinking it was not without some properties of value, all of its hills showing indications of minerals. The anchor raised," he sailed toward the east.

The object of Verrazzano's voyage was to find a passage westward to Cathay. Why did he not search his way between "two small prominent hills" and up the "very great river"? It may have been his preconceived notion that the westward passage would be through broader waters, and so to some other was left the distinction of being the first white man to sail the Hudson.

This man may have been Estevan Gomez, a Portuguese mariner in the service of Spain, who came here the year next after Verrazzano, in 1525. He had previously made several voyages to the West Indies and had accompanied Magellan to the Straits. After his voyage here the river was known to the Spaniards as, variously, Rio San Antonio, Rio de Gomez and Rio de Guamas; and according to Ribero, 1527, the stretch of coast between the subsequently known states of Rhode Island and Maryland was charted as Estevan Gomez's Land ("Tiera de Esteva Gomez"). But at this time it is not known that Gomez left any account of his voyage and so, although he knew of the river, it may not be said of him, more than of Verrazzano, that he actually sailed its length.

That the French followed the Spanish and traded with the Indians along the river is known from the testimony of the Dutch themselves, who, in a petition supported by a richly annotated map, stated in 1614 that the French had been the discoverers of the river. They need not have been ignorant of the exploits of Verrazzano and Gomez, and so probably it was meant that the French were the first Europeans to have ascended the river in order to trade there. However conclusive of a stark fact such testimony may be, it nevertheless brings the early story of the river up to Hudson himself for the first person known by name to have navigated the river and for the first known description of it.

If we lack chronicles of sixteenth-century navigation on the river, we do not lack maps made in the middle of this century, which trace its course at least as far as the junction with the Mohawk. One such map is that of Gastaldi, made in Venice in 1556, and another is that of the more familiar Mercator, made at Duisburg in 1569.

Henry Hudson is known to have made only four voyages, all in search of a new passage to India. The first was made in 1607, when he reached Greenland and Iceland before turning back; the second, in 1608, when he sailed in the same direction and reached Nova Zembla, when he was turned back by ice; the third, in 1609, which carried him to the Atlantic coast of North America, into the river which half a century later was to be given his name; and the fourth, in 1610-11, when he tried a more northerly route and reached the great bay which bears his name, and, with eight companions, was there put into a small boat and set adrift, never to be seen or heard of again.

Each of these voyages was made under English auspices except that of 1609, when his patron was the Dutch East India Company of the Netherlands. The name of the company indicates how little the effect of the voyage was anticipated by its purpose. The people of the Netherlands, impoverished by long wars with Spain, like their commercial rivals in England, looked to the fabled wealth of the East Indies to recoup their coffers. When Hudson set out from Amsterdam in the *Half Moon* (*De Holve Maene*) on April 4 (new style), 1609, he hoped to find for his Dutch patrons what he had failed to find for his compatriots, the much-sought north or westerly passage to the East Indies. In the light solely of its purpose, therefore, Hudson's voyage of 1609 was a failure, for the passage was not found. It is in the light of its effect on the advance of civilization on this side of the Atlantic Hudson's third voyage appears as one of the most significant events of our early history.

The *Half Moon* was a small vessel, "a yacht" of eighty

HENRY HUDSON'S SHIP, THE HALF MOON
As Reproduced for the Hudson-Fulton Celebration

t' Fort nieuw Amsterdam op de Manhatans

THE MOUTH OF THE HUDSON RIVER IN 1626

tons burden. Her length is estimated to have been fifty-eight feet and six inches, her greatest breadth of beam sixteen feet, two and a half inches. Her draft was calculated at seven feet. She had a bowsprit bearing a spritsail; a foremast, bearing a square foresail, above it a foretopmast bearing a foretopsail; a mainmast bearing a mainsail, above it a maintopmast bearing a maintopsail; a mizzenmast bearing a lateen-rigged mizzensail; and a complement of bonnets to supplement the area of foresail and mainsail. The interior arrangement took account of a hold, a 'tween-deck, an upper-deck and a poop-deck above the captain's cabin.

The crew numbered between eighteen and twenty men, partly Dutch and partly English. Of these the names of two only are known. One of them was a seaman by the name of John Colman; the other was Robert Juet, of Limehouse, who wrote the surviving narrative of the voyage, Hudson's own journal having come to us only at second hand in quotations made by Van Merteren (1614) and De Laet (1625). As a boy by the name of John Hudson is known to have accompanied Henry Hudson on each of his three other voyages, it is believed that he, too, was one of the crew of the *Half Moon*. This boy is supposed to have been the master's son.

When the *Half Moon* stood out from Amsterdam its destination was the Arctic. But after four weeks Hudson was discouraged by the abundance of ice he met and proposed to the crew that they turn south and west and seek a northwest passage through a river on the western Atlantic coast, at about latitude forty degrees, of which he had been advised by some letters and maps sent him from Virginia by his friend, Captain John Smith. The crew concurred, and, on May fourteenth, the *Half Moon* began its memorable voyage westward. After eight weeks at sea, they sighted land, probably near Cape Sable, Nova Scotia; six days later, on July eighteenth, they anchored in a harbor on the Maine coast, encountered two French shallops and installed a new foremast; on August sixth they made Cape Cod, and steered off to the southwest. They kept this course to a point about one hundred miles south of Chesapeake Bay, when they turned north, entered Delaware Bay briefly on August twenty-eighth, then stood north again, and on September third entered what is now known as New York Bay and came to anchor on its south side just inside Sandy Hook. Juet, in his journal of the voyage, recounts how, during the subsequent nine days, they reconnoitered the bay, traded with the Indians and slowly made their way up the narrows and across what is now New York harbor.

On the twelfth of the month the pilot of the great little ship "turned into the River two leagues and Anchored," at a point estimated to have been opposite the present One Hundredth Street, Manhattan.

There was fair weather next morning, the thirteenth, and in spite of a northerly wind, they advantaged themselves of the flood-tide and moved "foure miles" farther up-river. "The tide being done we anchored," which would have carried them to the protection of the point now known as Fort Washington. They used the afternoon flood to carry them "two and a half leagues," when they anchored for the night, and "had an high point of Land, which shewed out to vs, bearing North by East five leagues off vs." They would have been under the hills of Yonkers with Hook Mountain rising seven hundred and thirty feet above the water near Nyack.

Next day with a fair wind they sailed through Tappan Sea and Haverstraw Bay, "and came to a Streight betweene two

Points," now Stony Point and Verplanck's Point; whence the course lay "North-East by North," into Peekskill Bay beyond which they found "the Riuer is a mile broad: there is very high land on both sides. Then wee went up North-West, a league and a halfe deepe water," so they passed Anthony's Nose; "Then North-East by North fiue miles," where West Point intercepted their course. So they turned "then North-west by North two leagues, and anchored. The land grew very high and mountainous." They had navigated the passage through the Highlands and were at rest somewhere under the flanks of Storm King or Breakneck Ridge.

On the fifteenth a "wind at South" carried them onward another "twentie leagues, passing by high Mountains," coming at night "to other Mountaines, which lie from the Riuers side." This would have found them near the sites of the very city now named after the ship's master, and the mountains distant from the river are recognized as the Catskills, about five miles to the west.

The next day, the sixteenth of September, they lay at anchor, taking on fresh water, until evening, when they "went up two leagues higher, and had shoald water: so wee anchored till day." Thereafter they ran into continual difficulties by reason of the narrow channels between the islands, where they grounded several times and were obliged to await the friendly ministrations of the flood-tide.

Somewhere in the narrows of the river, probably within sight of the heights where now rises the city of Albany, the *Half Moon* lay at anchor for seven days, while the master's mate and members of the crew went in a small boat farther up the river in search of broader deeper water. But they found it not, and on September twenty-third Hudson weighed anchor, began to retrace his way down-river and arrived at its mouth on October second.

In Juet's chronicle of this trip there is no word of frustration or of their disappointment. Yet to Hudson and his men the shoals and shallows near the head of the navigable river must have brought a saddening disillusionment and a blasting of their hopes of finding the coveted passage here.

Throughout the trip up-river a spirited drama must have been enacted in the navigator's mind. He hoped he was on the verge of the great discovery which for so many years had been the ambition of European monarchs and mariners. Was this deep hill-bound fiord to prove to be the strait connecting the two oceans? At the gate of the Highlands the heights of the mountains doubled, the depth of the water increased, its salty tang held, the tides were still with him. The changing course blocked the outlook for more than a few miles ahead. This heroic setting might well have appeared to him to be the portal of the Pacific.

Only another ten miles beyond he must have sensed the frustrating fact of his mistake. The mountains fell away, the tides weakened, the waters became shallower, the salt in them began to disappear under the influence of the waters of springs and melted snows, and before him the ribbon of river stretched on between rolling banks across a valley which bent mistily below the horizon. He realized a continent and not an ocean confronted him. Yet he pressed forward on the forlorn hope, unwilling to turn back until Nature barred his way and he was assured that the only contact with the sea was in the direction from which he had come.

The thought furthest from Hudson's mind, as he submerged his disappointment, was that his voyage here would immortalize him for having shown the most practical pathway into this new continent which was then engaging the avid efforts of the European nations; a pathway which was to prove the broadest and most frequented, by road and rail and water, into the heart of the new Western World, and be acknowledged as one of the most potent reasons for the birth and progress of the greatest metropolis of the Western Hemisphere.

This is not, however, to imply that he was lacking in appreciation of his discovery. Both he and Juet, who reflects him, reveal themselves reticent chroniclers. Yet Juet declared, "This is a very good Land to fall with, and a pleasant Land to see," in one place, and in another, "The Land is very pleasant and high, and bold to fall withal." Hudson found the river "as fine a river as can be found," and the land "as pleasant a land as one need tread upon. The land is the finest for cultivation that I ever in my life set foot upon."

His contact with the natives was full of surprises and courtesies, not unmixed with hostilities and at least two tragedies. The appearance of Hudson's ship evidently created a sensation among the natives here. Its like had not been seen in their lifetime. Their traditions may not have spanned the fourscore and ten years back to the winged craft of Verrazzano and Gomez. As the *Half Moon* advanced word passed like magic along the shore. The natives came in droves to see the new marvel which moved without oar or paddle, with sails bellying before the wind. They came to trade grain and fruit and pelts for strange new tools and baubles; or, if they could not trade, then to steal them, for Hudson and his men found the Indians "exceedingly adroit in carrying away whatever they took a fancy to."

It was while the *Half Moon* was anchored in the lower bay

that the Indians first came out to it. "This day," wrote Juet on the third day at anchor, "the people of the Country came aboord of vs, seeming very glad of our comming, and brought greene Tabacco, and gaue vs of it for Kniues and Beads. They goe in Deere skins loose, well dressed. They haue yellow Copper. They desire Cloathes, and are very ciuill. They haue great store of Maiz and Indian Wheate, whereof they make good Bread. The Countrey is full of great tall Oakes."

The next day the seamen took courage and ventured ashore among the natives, "and saw great store of Men, Women and Children, who gaue them Tabacco at their comming on Land. So they went vp into the Woods, and saw great store of very goodly Oakes, and some Currents. For one of them came aboord and brought some dryed, and gaue me some, which were sweet and good. This day many of the people came aboord, some in Mantles of Feathers, and some in Skinnes of diuers sorts of good Furres. Some of the women also came to vs with Hempe. They had red Copper Tabacco pipes, and other things of Copper they did weare about their neckes. At night they went on Land againe, so wee rode very quiet, but durst not trust them." This final note of apprehension was not unjustified for, next day, as a small-boat party was returning to ship, the Indians set upon them and sent an arrow through Colman's neck, to his death.

At their first anchorage in the river proper, on September twelfth, "there came eight and twenty Canoes full of men, women and children to betray vs : but we saw their intent, and suffered none of them to come aboard of vs. At twelue of the clocke they departed. They brought with them Oysters and Beanes, whereof wee bought some. They haue great Tabacco pipes of yellow Copper, and Pots of Earth to dresse their meate in."

Off Fort Washington more natives came and sold the seamen good oysters "which we bought for trifles," but no one was allowed aboard.

There is no record of any further adventures with the Indians until, as they came within sight of the Catskill Mountains, "our two Sauages," whom they had made prisoners far down-river, "got out of a Port and swam away. After we were vnder sail they called to vs in Scorne."

While at anchor near the present city of Hudson, the master himself went ashore without other escort than a native, and his confidence was met by the amenities of the Indians. Hudson's own words were:

"I sailed to the shore, in one of their canoes, with an old man, who was the chief of a tribe, consisting of forty men and seventeen women; these I saw there in a house well constructed of oak bark, and circular in shape, with the appearance of having a vaulted ceiling. It contained a great quantity of maize and beans of the last year's growth, and there lay near the house for the purpose of drying enough to load three ships, besides what was growing in the fields. On our coming into the house, two mats were spread out to sit upon, and immediately some food was served in well made red wooden bowls; two men were also despatched at once with bows and arrows in quest of game, who soon after brought in a pair of pigeons which they had shot. They likewise killed at once a fat dog, and skinned it in great haste, with shells which they get out of the water. They supposed that I would remain with them for the night, but I returned after a short time on board the ship. The land is the finest for cultivation that I ever in my life set foot upon, and it also abounds in trees of every description. The natives are a very good people; for, when they saw that I would not remain, they supposed that I was afraid of their bows, and taking the arrows, they broke them in pieces, and threw them into the fire. . . ."

At their highest anchorage, near the present city of Albany, they found the natives very friendly, bringing tobacco, grapes,

"Pompions," bearskins and other skins, which they exchanged for beads, knives and hatchets.

On the third day there:

"Our Master and his Mate determined to trie some of the chiefe men of the Countrey, whether they had any treacherie in them. So they tooke them downe into the Cabbin, and gaue them so much Wine and Aqua vitae, that they were all merrie: and one of them had his wife with him, which sate so modestly, as any of our Countrey women would doe in a strange place. In the end one of them was drunke, which had been aboord of our ship all the time that we had beene there: and that was strange to them; for they could not tell how to take it. The Canoes and folke went all on shoare: but some of them came againe, and brought stropes of Beades: some had sixe, seuen, eight, nine, ten; and gaue him. So he slept all night quietly."

The very next day "in the morning our Masters Mate and foure more of the companie went vp with our Boat to sound the Riuer higher vp. The people of the Countrey came not aboord till noone: but when they came, and saw the Sáuages well, they were glad. So at three of the clocke in the after-noone they came aboord, and brought Tabacco, and more Beades, and gaue them to our Master and made an Oration, and shewed him all the Countrey round about. Then they sent one of their companie on land, who presently returned, and brought a great Platter full of Venison, dressed by themselues; and they caused him to eate with them: then they made him reuerence, and departed all saue the old man that lay aboord. This night at ten of the clocke, our Boate returned in a showre of raine from sounding of the Riuer; and found it to bee at an end for shipping to goe in. For they had beene vp eight or nine leagues, and found but seuen foot water, and vnconstant soundings."

On the return trip down-river Hudson and his men had several friendly visits from the natives. When, however, they had passed through the Highlands they had two adventures of a less reassuring kind. On October first the *Half Moon* was anchored in what appears to have been Haverstraw Bay, and Juet recounts:

"The people of the Mountaynes came aboord vs. wondring at our ship and weapons. We bought some small skinnes of them for Trifles. This afternoone, one Canoe kept hanging vnder our sterne with one man in it, which we could not keepe from thence, who got vp by our Rudder to the Cabin window, and stole out my Pillow, and two Shirts, and two Bandleeres. Our Masters Mate shot at him, and strooke him on the brest, and killed him. Whereupon all the rest gled away, some in their canoes, and so leapt out of them into the water. We manned our Boate, and got our things againe. When one of them that swamme got hold of our Boat, thinking to ouerthrow. it. But our Cooke tooke a Sword, and cut off one of his hands, and he was drowned."

This, however, was a trifle compared to the events of the day next following, which in effect amounted to the severest brush the mariners had with the Indians on the river. The ship was anchored somewhere near the Palisades when, as Juet recorded:

"came one of the Sausages that swamme away from vs at our going vp the Riuer with many other, thinking to betray vs. But wee perceiued their intent, and suffered none of them to enter our ship. Whereupon two Canoes full of men, with their Bowes and Arrowes shot at vs after our sterne: in recompense whereof we discharged sixe Muskets, and killed two or three of them. Then aboue an hundred of them came to a point of Land to shoot at vs. There I shot a Falcon at them, and killed two of them: whereupon the rest fled into the Woods. Yet they manned off another Canoe with nine or ten men, which came to meet vs. So I shot at it also a Falcon, and shot it through, and killed one of them. Then our men with their Muskets, killed three or foure more of them. So they went their way. . . ."

That night, October second, the *Half Moon* rode at anchor in the lee of the rock now known as Stevens Point, Hoboken. Foul weather held the ship at its mooring there all the next day. But on the fourth day of the month weather and wind

43

were both fair, and the crew weighed anchor. "By twelue of the clocke," wrote Juet, "we were cleere of all the inlet. Then we took in our Boat, and set our Mayne-sayle and sprit-sayle, and our top-sayles, and steered away East South-east, and South-east by East off into the mayne sea." The brave little yacht once more breasted the Atlantic. Hudson's adventure here was ended.

CHAPTER III

The Dutch Period

Their High Mightinesses—Fur Trading—The Dutch West India Company—
Rivier Mauritius, Groote Rivier and Noordt Rivier—Colonization Begins to
Come—Patroons and Patroonships—Playing the Fur Market—A Dutch
Girl's Speculations—New Amsterdam and Beverwyck—Babel on the River—
Cellar Houses of the Settlers—Dutch Houses—Furnishings—Dutch Life
and Manners—Food and Drink—Dutch Dress—Religious Life and Cus-
toms—Dutch Christenings, Weddings and Funerals—Feasts and Sports—
Education—Communications—"By the Skipper, Whom God Conduct."

HE Netherlanders were deliberate to take organized advantage of the territory and opportunity
presented by Hudson's "discovery." Individual
adventures began almost immediately. A small
group of Amsterdam merchants sent a ship out to the "Groote
Rivier" the next year after Hudson's return, 1610, to trade
with the Indians, by which is meant that they came for fur,
for which they exchanged baubles and implements. The object
of that voyage keyed the Dutch attitude toward their river during much of the period of their political control of it.

The ships found the southern tip of Manhattan Island a
natural situation for a post. There they anchored. Thence
parties left in smaller boats to go up-river to gather in the pelts
of beaver, otter and, in a lesser degree, of other wild creatures
of the new world.

Almost coincidentally with the establishment of a trading-
post on Manhattan Island, Captain Christiaensen and a few
trappers and traders, in sailing up the river, established trading

45

connections at two points: one where now stands the city of Kingston, and the other where now stands the city of Albany. At the latter place they built a stone house, surrounded it by a protective stockade, fortified it with cannon, garrisoned it with a few Dutch soldiers and named it Fort Nassau. This was in the winter of 1613-14. But within the next ten years the site of the fort was twice changed.

Their High Mightinesses of the States General of Holland granted, in 1614, to Dutch merchants, under the name of the United Netherlands Company, a charter specially privileging them to trade on the western coast of the Atlantic Ocean between "Virginia and New France," actually between the fortieth and forty-fifth parallels, roughly between Cape May and Nova Scotia, for three years. There were only private trading enterprises here again after the expiration of this charter and until the formation of the Dutch West India Company, which was chartered in 1621, and until the erection of the territory into a province, called New Netherland, in 1623. The management of the new Company was assigned to the Chamber of Amsterdam, and their local administrator, called a director, actually governor of the province, was seated at the fort on the south tip of Manhattan Island. The operations of the Dutch vessels on this side of the Atlantic extended from the South River (now called the Delaware) to the eastern end of Long Island Sound, and the members of the Company looked upon all the intervening territory as their province of New Netherland. But the local seat of the government of it, and its principal trade and development, attached to the waters of the "great river" which they forthwith named the Mauritius.

Colonization on the river had lagged during the first twelve years after the appearance and disappearance of the *Half Moon* there. They were years of trade only; barter with the Indians; the exchange of beads, cloth, liquor and implements for fur. A few gardens were planted and a few fields were cultivated at each end of the river; but such agricultural enterprises were undertaken only as a necessary support for the traders' local agents and for the provisioning of the traders' ships. As the possibility of the fur trade was better appreciated the first efforts at settlement were made. That, however, was not until 1624, when the first director, Cornelius Jacobsen May, arrived in the ship *New Netherland,* with thirty families of colonists. Only a small number of these, however, settled along the North or Mauritius River. The complaint was constant that agriculture did not keep pace with, that is, did not adequately support, commerce.

Settlements in New England, and even along the Saint Lawrence, increased much faster than those of New Netherland. The administrators of the United Netherlands Company were nevertheless diligent in their efforts to secure colonists. The soil was richer and the climate more ingratiating in their preserves than in those of the English and French farther east and north. The reason colonists came slowly lay in something more subtle. It was not in the soil or the sun, but in the hearts of the people.

American colonization has been based on necessity, sometimes economic, sometimes social. The Puritans, who came to New England, and the Catholics, who founded Maryland, left home and founded new homes in the wilderness to escape religious persecution and to worship with freedom and in peace. The Germans of the Palatinate fled from economic destruction. The Huguenots were exiles, driven out of their homes and out of their country. But the Netherlands at the beginning of the seventeenth century presented no such difficulties for its people. There was neither war, economic depression nor religious persecution. The Dutch found their country a good place to dwell. They might go abroad to trade, to profit themselves, but they came home to spend and to dwell. A high historic significance attaches to this and to the fact that, even in that first shipload of colonists only a part were Dutch. Through the period of the half-century of Dutch political control on the river, this parallel prevailed. The population was polyglot. And in this it was more prophetic of twentieth-century America than was any other of the colonies here; and its tiny island capital was from the first suggestive of what it is to-day, a town of many tongues.

As the great fur trade grew, the necessity of supporting it, at bases at each end of and at intervening points along the river, drew in agriculturists. For reasons already explained it was difficult to draw settlers out of Holland. As the advantages of the soil, the climate and transportation became better known, however, it was easier to entice families across the ocean. To promote settlement in New Netherland the company's council, "The Assembly of the XIX," in 1629, granted a charter of "Freedom and Exemptions," and in 1640 they granted an extension of the freedom and exemptions of that charter; and the result was to make conditions and opportunities for settlement on the river more attractive. But among the real enticements to come must be counted the spread of the news that religious freedom was enjoyed here. That is what drew Huguenots from France, Walloons from the Low Country, non-conformists from England, Scotch Presbyterians, Quakers and Jews. Moreover, there was an influx of other English from Massachusetts and Virginia because of the limited religious freedom in these two colonies.

In spite of other elements the Dutch exercised political, trade
and major land control during the first fifty years of settlement
on the river. It was definitely a Dutch period here. The Dutch
who came established and reflected here the traits of character
which have held them for centuries in their low corner of
Europe—courageous, enterprising, intelligent, self-confident,
lovers of liberty, haters of tyranny, aggressive, domineering,
greedy, inquisitive, cultured, and one of the most indomitable
national units in spite of the influence and attacks of other
such units larger and apparently more powerful. And it is
significant of this enduring quality of Dutch character that,
long after Dutch political control ceased in New Netherland
and the balance of population had turned against the preponderance of the Dutch in it, the river country felt their influence and
counted it one of the most enduring and sustaining qualities.

This Dutch period engages a particular interest not only
because of the character of the people along the river, their
mode of land tenure, of domestic, social and religious life, but,
further, because it was the only colony of its character in the
territory which later comprised the thirteen original states.
The English who controlled the adjacent territory, east and
south, during that same period, brought the pattern of their
laws, their civic units, and their domestic and social life with
them from England.

Under its charter the West India Company had virtual political as well as trade sovereignty in the new colony. It was
privileged to enact laws, to administer justice, to make treaties,
and as already noted, to appoint the governor or director and
other officials. There were four conspicuous directors during
the forty years of the Dutch West India Company's control.
They were Pieter Minuit, a just and honorable man; Wouter

van Twiller, epitomized by Irving as "the doubter"; William Kieft, who made up in energy what he lacked in tact; and Peter Stuyvesant, who stood firm on his two legs, albeit one of them was of wood, a masterful paternal despot.

It was in an effort to bring permanent settlers on to the land and to promote agriculture, that the Company, in the year 1629, granted its significant Charter of Privileges and Exemptions. Under it any member of the Company might purchase from the Indians and possess himself of a tract of unoccupied land, elsewhere than on Manhattan Island, extending sixteen miles along one side of the river, or eight miles on both sides, and "so far into the country," that is to say, east or west, "as the situation of the Occupyers will permit," provided he plant on it a colony of fifty persons. The charter allowed others than members to take up as much unoccupied land as they were able to improve. Such colonists as were so introduced were for ten years free from the payment of customs, taxes, excise or other contributions.

The most extensive and successful such sub-colony on the river was Rensselaerwyck, founded by Kiliaen Van Rensselaer, a pearl merchant of Amsterdam. He took more than full account of his privileges and bought a tract extending twenty-four miles north and south on each bank of the river at the head of its navigable waters, and forty-eight miles east and west. The cities of Albany and Troy later rose at the heart of this principality.

The founder of such a "colony" within the colony was styled a patroon. He in his turn was practically sovereign on his own land. He was empowered "to administer civil and criminal justice, in person, or by deputy, within his colonie, to appoint local officers and magistrates; to erect courts . . . ; to keep a gallows, if such were required, for the execution of male-factors, subject, however, to the restriction that if such gallows happened, by any accident to fall, pending an execution, a new one could not be erected, unless for the purpose of hanging another criminal." The hangman, or *Scherprecter,* was a recognized official on a patroonship, and among the accounts left by one of them appears this item: "For so much coming to him for executing the late Wolf Nysen, fl. 38."

But a patroon was not without his limitations. He might traffic, but not in furs. This was reserved as a perquisite of the Company. And furs were the gold of this Klondike. They were to the Hudson what was tobacco to Virginia and Maryland. A good annual shipping home by the Company was thirty-six thousand skins. The beaver skins after they were sent from the river across to Holland were forwarded thence to Russia to be tanned and then exported to other European countries. As values in those other colonies were reckoned in tobacco, here they were recorded in pelts. They were not only the chief wealth of the region, they were its principal money as well, although wampum and seawan were used in exchange; "tokens, stamped by the church and redeemable at certain times, were received instead of money;" and some florins and stivers of Dutch coinage found their way across the ocean to the river. Moreover, the looms of Holland were too hungry to permit the use of these machines in her colony. So, neither, might the patroon allow the weaving of linen, woolen or cotton cloth on his lands.

In common with every other colony along this coast the Dutch had to contend with the Indians. On the whole, they got along well enough together. If the natives seem to have been paid little for their land—in beads, cloth, blankets, implements, firearms and liquor—neither party to the bargain pre-visioned the present price of the same real estate. Human nature being what it is, there were misunderstandings, injustices and massacres. In 1643 the bouweries, as the Dutch called their farms, on both sides of the lower river were raided, dwellings, storehouses and barns were burned; cattle were slaughtered; the colonists were massacred. The catastrophe would have discouraged hearts less stout. As late as 1658 Governor Stuyvesant was advising the colonists on Esopus Creek to insure their safety by concentrating in villages and there to fortify themselves. To the warlike menace of the Indians must be added the threat of the French to descend from Lake Champlain and the upper river, and of the English from New England. These were apprehensions of the Dutch along the river which were not shared by the English on the Chesapeake.

Though furs were the principal medium of exchange, they were not, in a primitive society, such as at that time obtained on the Hudson, the only means of barter. In contact with the Indians some wampum and seawan were used. But in buying the furs from the trappers, both Dutch and Indian, coin was of no account. They wanted goods. Hence it was that ships from Holland came to the mouth of the river, anchored and disembarked cargoes of cloths, clothings, implements, blankets, liquor glasses of all sizes, candles, liquors, cattle, and a variety of baubles at the Company's warehouse in New Amsterdam. The river traders then came in their *vlie booten,* or flyboats, deposited their cargoes of pelts on account, and took in pay, in larger part at least, from the importations in the warehouses. With this stock stowed in the hold of his little vessel, the fly-man spread his sail and tacked up the reaches. He would tie up at one landing after another and expose his imported wares, until the last of them had been bartered for the furs which he took back down-river for his credit with the Company and eventual transshipment to Holland.

The possibilities of profit in the fur trade on the Netherlands' new American river provoked an interest in the Low Countries that was shared by all classes. Investments, which amounted in effect to mere gambling, made on borrowed capital, were not made in money as such. Not the cash itself but all manner of chattels were sent "out" to be exchanged for the precious furs.

The patroon occupied a privileged position on the river, of which his family and connections at home were quick to take advantage. The correspondence of Jeremias Van Rensselaer, patroon of Rensselaerwyck, covering the period between 1651 and 1664, furnishes repeated instances of consignments of goods from home, many articles in which were to be exchanged for beaver skins. Possibly one such instance will suffice to give an idea of the character and variety of the chattels sent out in the holds of the stout Dutch sailing ships. The following list is from an invoice sent to the patroon in the ship *de Otter* by his brother, Johan Van Rensselaer, in 1659:

"For the account of myself, Jan. Baptist van Rensselaer
  2 half-pieces of gray cloth, each 15 yards long
  1 piece of serge, marked VR No. 11
  2 half-pieces of fine linen
  6 pieces of bombazine; 5 white and 1 colored, Nos. 13-18
  10 packages of cord, Nos. 1-10
  1 package containing 2 lbs. of silk, No. 2
  1 gross large gold and silver buttons
  10 gross small buttons
  3 spools of cord (*treckoort*)
  3 bundles of braid (*lidtskoordt*)
  7 pieces of ribbon; 3 black, 2 red and 2 blue

1 black hat for my boy, Theunis, of which I make him a present
1 silver clasp (*haeck*) for Mr Jacob, which I promised him
1 black serge suit of clothes for Jan Bastiaenss.

"For the account of Jeremias van Rensselaer
  1 black cloth suit of clothes with a black mantle
  6 shirts
  1 pair of black silk stockings and 1 pair of gray sayette ditto
  1 black hat with a gold braid
  1 piece of armozine ribbon
  24 yards of black figured ribbon and 24 yards of colored ditto
  some black and white buttons
  1 horse blanket

"For the account of Teunis Dirckss
  3 pieces of linen, marked TD
  1 silver under-girdle (*onder riem*)
  4 yards of red cloth and 4 yards of fine linen
  1 silver needle for his daughter, of which I make her a present
  1 gray hat for his son [in payment] for the mudde of wheat

"For the account of Volckert Janss
  1 piece of serge
  1 brocade (*kaffa*) waist
  gros-grain (*Tours*), with the band, for an apron
  English damask for an apron
  1 pair of blue silk stockings
  1 pair of white woman's-stockings
  1 pair of gray boy's-stockings
  3 pairs of children's stockings
  2 pieces of lace
  several papers with spices
  5 packs of cord for the Indian trade (*hansjoos koordt*), containing 50 pieces
  1 silver signet

"For the account of Jan Thomass
  Cloth for a suit, with the lining and what belongs to it, tied up in canvas

1 piece of 24 yards of colored silk
1 silver spoon which I owed him

"With the aforesaid chest there was shipped in the said ship a
    small case VR No. 3, containing as above, for my
    account,
9 pieces of linen, Nos. 2, 3, 4, 5, 6, 7, 8, 11, 12
Also 1 piece ditto, No. 19, with red earth (*met roodt aerdt*)
Also 3 pieces of linen for Volckert Janssn VID
Also 1 piece of linen for Teunis Dirckse TD
Also 2 pieces of linen for Jan Thomasz IT

"Also shipped for the account of Jeremias van Rensselaer in a
    case,
No. 2 VR, all the rope harness (*touwerck*) ordered by him
1 saddle, 1 bit, 2 headstalls, 1 curb bit
1 blanket, 1 pair of hair lines, 6 leather halters
1 mirror, 12 grain bags, and 5 whips, one for you, one for
    Curler, one for Jan Bastiaense, one for Volckert and
    one for Jan Thomassen's Jack and Joy
1 half-worn saddle for Jan Bastiaenss and a bit with a head-
    stall for Gysberdt op de Bergh's son [in payment] for
    the deer"

But the most engaging of the speculations revealed by this
correspondence was that of Talckien, a serving maid in the Van
Rensselaer family in the Netherlands. "Talckien sends here-
with, from the little she has and out of what she has now
and then scraped together and saved out of her mouth," wrote
the patroon's mother, in April, 1657, "in a small box . . . 6
silver spoons, which cost fl. 30. Do your best to send shortly
something in return for them." The patroon wrote his mother
in June the same year: "The silver spoons of Taltie may bring
a beaver apiece and I have offered to let them go for fl. 60 the
half dozen, about which I am still negotiating. The silk stockings have been sold for fl. 20." A letter of the following August
shows the conclusion of the trade to have been, in terms of beaver

skins, "5 ditto and one half-beaver for Talletien for her spoons and 2½ ditto for the silk stockings." Having so soon doubled her money, Talckien plunged straight back "into the market," for, the next year, in August, we find the patroon acknowledging the receipt of forty-six florins' worth of "Holland, for shirts," twenty-three florins' worth of buttons and clasps and sixteen florins' worth of shoes for her account. She seems on her second plunge to have shared the common fate of other investors, then and since. Indeed, there is more than a suspicion that "Taltie" was importunate; probably she was making the Van Rensselaers regretful that they had let her come into the fur trade. There is a familiar ring to these lines in a letter, written two years later to the patroon:

"The goods sent to you by brother Nicolaes belong to our servant girl. Please see to it that she gets her returns at the first opportunity. That rascal has made the maid believe a good deal, so that she has borrowed some money for that purpose on which interest must be paid."

Here are other references in these letters to such speculations:

". . . In the case there is also a piece of Kersey which your sisters are sending to you to trade it for them. They bought it from Mr. Libert at 36 stivers a yard, but it is worth more. See that you get cash payment in beavers for it, for it is not paid for and they would like to pay with the skins sent in return. . . .
". . . At the first opportunity inquire and let me know some time whether you could trade with profit 2 or 3 beds. . . . They would have new ticks and feathers from my large bed and they would be about 2 yards wide and long in proportion. You must inquire sometime how many beavers you could get for them. . . .
". . . With my confrater, Nicholaes Noppe, I am sending a fine double barrelled gun and a small gun of 2 feet, which has a drawn barrel. They are fine to shoot with. You might try

to sell these to our best advantage and to send us beavers or other goods for them."

And in a letter in August, 1658, the patroon's brother, Richart, writing from Amsterdam, says: "I wish to remind you that when you were here you always said that when you would be on the other side you would send us some beavers to lay a new stone floor in the entrance hall."

The fine forests on the river hills soon suggested trade in lumber and ship-building. Both enterprises flourished. Even as early as 1631 a ship more than twenty-five times the tonnage of the *Half Moon* was built at Manhattan, and it had a contemporary fame as one of the largest ships afloat. Though it was a merchant ship it carried thirty guns for defense against pirates, the common practise at that time. When such ships had few or no guns, then false portholes were painted from stern to stern to bluff any pirates who did not come aboard to investigate the ruse!

As the Dutch were fur traders first it was natural that the earlier social units were towns and villages about the landings. It was trade, plus the need of self-protection which gave towns and villages precedence over plantations on the river. Up to the end of the Dutch Company's control of the river, however, the only towns there were New Amsterdam (later New York), Beverwyck (later Albany), and Rondout (later Kingston). Other communities were villages. The farms or bouweries at first clustered about these protective units. As the Indian receded and the white population increased, the farmers became more independent and took up land farther from the settlements.

It was only in the last decade of the Dutch régime that settlers came in encouraging numbers. At that time the Company gave them free passage for themselves, their wives and children, "provided that whenever they wish to return here they shall pay double fare."

"The farmer, being conveyed with his family over sea to New Netherland, was [according to Secretary Van Tienhoven's Information of 1650] granted by the Company for the term of six years a Bouwery, which was partly cleared, and a good part of which was fit for the plough.

"The Company furnished the farmer a house, barn, farming implements and tools, together with four horses, four cows, sheep and pigs in proportion, the usufruct and enjoyment of which the husbandman should have during the six years, and on the expiration thereof return the number of cattle he received. The entire increase remained with the farmer. The farmer was bound to pay yearly one hundred guilders [forty dollars] and eighty pounds of butter rent for the cleared land and bouwery.

"The risk of the Cattle dying is shared in common and after the expiration of the contract, the Company receives, if the Cattle live, the number the husbandman first received, and the increase which is over, is divided half and half, by which means many people have obtained stock and even to this day, the Company have still considerable cattle among the Colonists, who make use on the above conditions of the horses in cultivating the farm; the cows serve for the increase of the stock and for the support of their families."

A nice care was taken in the shipment of live stock from Holland. Nicholaes Van Wessenaer gives us an account of how, on one voyage at least, they were stowed and crated. Each animal had his attendant whose reward depended on delivering his charge alive on this side. Each animal had his stall aboard ship, and the floor of it was covered with "three feet of sand." This sand was taken into account as ballast for the ship. In the hold were stowed three hundred tons of fresh water for the beasts' use at sea.

The conventional farm crops were cultivated: corn, oats and wheat. But the general dependence on beer encouraged the cultivation of hops as well. When, in 1652, the high export duty was taken off tobacco, the planters went in heavily for the production of this plant, stimulated, no doubt, by the fact that their neighbors in Maryland and Virginia to the south were making their fortunes off the weed. Whereupon the Company's director required planters to plant as much land to corn, peas or grain as they did to tobacco, in order to prevent "the apprehended scarcity of Bread." Manure was seldom used as fertilizer. Such fertilizer as was used included the rotted oyster shells found in great banks along the river, left there by generations of Indians.

It may have been true, as Kieft told Father Jogues, in 1644, that there were men of eighteen different languages on the island of Manhattan and its environs, but he probably included among them the sailors ashore from the transient ships of many flags. The Dutch far outnumbered the total of all the other nationalities on the river, although among the colonists here were Swedes, Norwegians, French, English, Germans, Scotch and Irish.

This takes no account of the black population. There were negro slaves on the river from the beginning of its settlement. The Company ships captured them or traded for them in the West Indies and brought them in. But the colonists seem not to have requested them or wanted them. Agriculture in which they might have aided did not flourish early on the river, and the black was neither a trader nor a mechanic. Such as there were, were used on the Company's own bouweries or as house servants for the officials. Indian slavery was not encouraged.

In giving information and advice to prospective colonists, as late as 1650, Van Tienhoven stressed town-sites first:

"Before beginning to build, it will above all things be necessary to select a well located spot, either on some river or bay, suitable for the settlement of a village or hamlet. This is previously properly surveyed and divided into lots, with good streets according to the situation of the place. This hamlet can be fenced all round with high palisades or long boards and closed with gates, which is advantageous in case of attack by the natives who heretofore used to exhibit their insolence in new plantations. Outside the village or hamlet other land must be laid out which can in general be fenced and prepared at the most trifling expense."

Van Tienhoven gives us this picture of the "cellar houses" of the settlers during their first years here:

"Those who have no means to build farm houses at first according to their wishes, dig a square pit in the ground, cellar fashion, 6 or 7 feet deep, as long and as broad as they think proper, case the earth inside with wood all round the wall, and line the wood with the bark of trees or something else to prevent the caving in of the earth; floor this cellar with plank and wainscot it overhead for a ceiling, raise a roof of spars clear up and cover the spars with bark or green sods, so that they can live dry and warm in these houses with their entire families for two, three and four years, it being understood that partitions are run through those cellars which are adapted to the size of the family."

After two or three years, with his fields cleared, his crops rotating and his cattle multiplying, the farmer raised himself a real house, sometimes over the cellar house. The Dutchman built as he remembered his houses at home in the Low Countries. He found stone abundant and easy to work. Available clay made brick buildings equally popular, especially in the towns. The houses were small at first and expanded with the growing prosperity and the family of the colonist.

The walls of the stone houses were often two feet or more

*From the Manors and Historic Homes of the Hudson Valley, by Harold D. Eberlein,
Published by J. B. Lippincott Company*

VAN CORTLANDT MANOR HOUSE
At the Junction of the Croton and Hudson Rivers

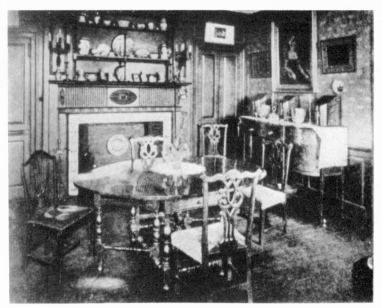

*From the Manors and Historic Homes of the Hudson Valley, by Harold D. Eberlein,
Published by J. B. Lippincott Company*

THE DINING ROOM OF THE VAN CORTLANDT MANOR HOUSE

OLD DUTCH CHURCH, TARRYTOWN

thick, held rigidly together with mortar of ground oyster shells. As such a house rarely rose to a full second story, and as the ceilings were made low so that the rooms might easily be heated, such wall thickness could scarcely have been required to insure its standing up and supporting great weight. The reason of it may have been the traditional conservative disposition of the Dutchman, and, equally, the idea of defense against the Indians. Indeed, defense showed itself also in the custom of building the walls with loopholes, through which slender openings, with doors and windows barred, the colonist thrust his musket to snipe the enemy.

The Dutch farmhouses were built without any apparent esthetic impulse whatever. The low walls, the high sweeping roof, and the little windows placed at random, gave a solid, snug and sometimes quaint effect, however. In a neighborhood which enjoys periods of stern winter cold it is surprising that there was so rarely an entry hall to cut off the wind at the outside door. The houses grew a room at a time, under pressure of one need or another, more often without account of agreeable proportions, of balanced window openings, or of any patterned relation of the new room to the senior portion of the house.

The town houses of New Amsterdam and of Beverwyck were of more considered pattern. They reflected, as remembered by the builders, the town houses of the old country. They were built of holland brick, not brick from Holland, for the name of the brick reflected the convention of its size and not the place of its manufacture. Generally they were of a yellowish tint. Such houses were narrow, built without space between them and the walls of contiguous houses. They rose to two and three stories with attic chambers under the steep roof. The gable ends faced the street and were made quaintly decorative by ascending on each side by a succession of steps—so-called "crow steps"—supposed to have been so constructed to enable the sweeps easily to reach the chimneys. Another distinctive feature of the façade of the Dutch town house was the metal decorations at the ends of the anchoring irons. Sometimes these took the form of enormous iron figures dating the year of the building, sometimes large iron letters proclaimed the initials of the proprietor, or of the owner and his wife. At the top of the roof perched "a fierce little weather-cock to let the family into the important secret which way the wind blew." It is said that even the prosperous burgher sometimes cannily kept his house down to a modest story and a half to escape the tax which mounted with the mounting stories. Were it town house or country house the outer doors were almost inevitably divided horizontally in half; permitting air and light to enter through the open upper half, while the closed lower half kept the children inside and the pigs and cows and wilder life outside.

When the interior of the triangular story under the eaves was finished off into bedrooms, the only light was admitted to them by small windows in the wall-ends. And when more pretention prevailed, and the dormer-windows were introduced, those on the Dutch house were given individuality by their own roofs which were flat instead of peaked, and beginning flat at or near the ridge-pole line, continued flat as they extended down in one unbroken sweep to their blunt termination over the window itself. This fashion survives in many of the oldest houses along the river. Such dormers may be observed in the Senate House at Kingston, the Teller house at Beacon (Fishkill Landing), the Bevier house at New Paltz, and elsewhere.

All the houses built by Dutch colonists do not date to this earlier and definitely Dutch period of the colony. Examples of more ordered and ornate houses, still characteristic of the Dutch builders, were erected after the beginning of English political control by later comers from the Low Countries or by prospering descendants of the early colonists, and they will be referred to in the next chapter.

The interiors of the first houses were dark, confused in pattern, austere and solid in construction. They were, moreover, characterized by rooms which in excess of one or two were small, by floors of planks each often fifteen inches wide, by built-in cupboards, and ingenious economy in utilizing crannies. It has been said that "a Dutchman's house is like his breeches, capable of holding anything he can cram into them."

The items of that list of goods sent out by Johan Van Rensselaer, to be exchanged for beavers, indicate what furnishings might have been found in the Dutch colonist's house of about 1660. A good standard of domestic life developed soon after the passing of the hardships and primitive devices of the first years of settlement on the river. The Netherlander in the old country lived as luxuriously in his house as any other contemporary people, and the assumption is fair that examples of such accustomed furnishings followed the adventurers into the new world. This was especially true of the richer burghers of New Amsterdam and Beverwyck, and of the patroons on both shores of the river intervening.

They drank out of glass as well as pewter and silver, but they ate off of pewter and silver rather than china which was less in evidence at the time, and, in the case of Oloff Van Cortlandt at least, ate off of mahogany even before the English superseded oak with furniture of that wood. The chief objects in silver used by the Dutch settlers were, according to C. Louise Avery, "baptismal basins, beakers, cups, tankards, porringers, wine tumblers, bowls and teapots," which were "generally simple, massive, and imposing, splendidly proportioned and beautifully executed." But characteristic, too, were the "bite and stir" sugar boxes, partitioned in the middle, on one side loaf sugar to be nibbled with the tea, on the other soft sugar to be stirred in it; and the *ooma,* or sifter, for the cinnamon and sugar to be sprinkled over cakes and toast and waffles. Some of the other more significant features in the furnishing, of the house of a patroon at least, are found in these excerpts from the Van Rensselaer correspondence between 1657 and 1662:

". . . Send me . . . two brass candlesticks, each for two candles, and which slide up and down, according to the new style, and half a dozen knives, a pen knife, some paper and pens. . . .

". . . I leave it to your discretion what I ought to get for the use which you have had of my table cloths, napkins, pots and kettles and whatever else I left you at my departure. The blue curtains with the valence and the hearth rug belong to me, as also the rush-bottom chairs. . . .

". . . Please to send the following things, namely, a bedstead with curtains and its appurtenances and a hanging for the mantle piece, 6 yards long, for last summer when the General was up here, he would have liked to stay at my house, but I had no accommodation. Furthermore, 8 Spanish chairs for the gentlemen, to be used when we hold council, for at the present we use only pine benches; a large mirror, the width of which, with the frame, should be about one ell. . . .

". . . I had much trouble [in Amsterdam, Netherlands] in procuring the small table plates [that is, probably plates of delft or other earthenware], as not many are being made, for the people now all use pewter, so that I could not get any better ones."

And we know from this lively incident in a letter of Jacob Sandersz Glen that the colonists had pool tables:

"Know also that [An]dries Herpertsz and Seger Cornelissen had words together and started to fight. Seger dealt Andries Herpertsz some blows with the *cue* of the *pool-table* (*trock tafel*), whereupon Andries ran after him with a knife and stabbed said Seger Cornelissen in his left side, below the short ribs. After having stabbed him, Andries dealt him five blows on the head, so that they claim that his scull is cracked. This happened on Friday, being the 24th of June, and on Sunday, the 26th ditto, he died. Andries Herpertsz has retired to the [other] side," that is, of the river.

And when they sat down to table, what kind of food and drink did they find in the trenchers and tankards? The Dutch were lusty trenchermen. They loved to eat rugged food and lots of it. In addition to the more obvious natural yield of mill, pasture, garden, orchard and dairy, they made pies and puddings, milk cheeses, pickles and preserves, sausage, scrapple and headcheeses; they had oysters, perch, sturgeon, bass, smelt, shad, pike, alewives, carp, eels, and tomcod out of the river; and birds, deer and other wild creatures out of the forests. In the cellars were cool butter in firkins, pickled pork and salt fish and sauerkraut by the barrel; stone jars of pickles, kegs of soused pigs' feet, and reserves of winter apples, potatoes, turnips, pumpkins and carrots by the bin.

Against one wall of such a teeming cellar was apt to be a row of barrels full of cider vinegar and ale, supported by jugs of rum and gin, and pipes of wine. These liquors did not always reach the table in their simpler form but found their way into punches, sangarees and other devious concoctions which were sipped about the table or fireside, while the men pulled clouds of smoke out of their gay porcelain pipes with pendulous stems, to the accompaniment, it seems probable, of solid intervals of ponderous Dutch silence.

The drinking bouts did not, however, necessarily end in silence. Cornelius DeVries, writing of events on the river in 1636, furnishes accounts of two social occasions in New Amsterdam town when the guzzlers stirred up unanticipated consequences.

"The 25th of June, I went with the commander and minister, to Pavonia, over from the fort, in the colony of Michael Pauw, where the person who was in command there for Michael Pauw, was named Cornelis van Vorst. He had arrived, with a small English bark, from the Northern English, bringing with him from thence good Bordeaux wines; and as the commander was fond of tasting good wines, he went over there. Whilst we were there, it so happened that there were some words between the commander and minister and Cornelis van Vorst, in relation to a murder that had been committed there; but they separated afterwards good friends, when Cornelis van Vorst, wishing to give the commander a parting salute, fired a pederero which stood upon a palisade before his house, when a spark flew upon the house, which was thatched with rushes, and in half an hour it was entirely consumed."

"The 8th of August, the gunner of the fort gave a parting feast, and had a tent erected on one bastion of the fort, where a table and benches were set and many people bidden. When the banquet was at its highest, the trumpeter began to blow, as to which some words were passed; when the keeper of the store, Heyndrick Hudden, and the keeper of the merchandise, Corelaer, railed at the trumpeter, who gave each of them a *santer quanter,* whereupon they ran home, and brought out a sword, and wished to have revenge upon the trumpeter. They went to the house of the commander and used much foolish language, one calling out, 'I am the same man who took the life of Count Floris.' But when they had slept upon it, their soldiership was all over, and they rather feared the trumpeter than sought him; and thus the matter passed over."

Similarly, out of old letters, bit by bit, we are able to visualize the dress of the colonists of three hundred years ago. The women multiplied their petticoats under a full skirt, gathered at the waist and made of cloth or silk or satin, as were their buttons of base or precious metal, according to social position. They wore their sleeves tight and elbow-high, a white kerchief folded to a triangle to dress their shoulders, and on their heads a linen cap held back before each ear by an ornate metal button whose pattern often suggested the neighborhood in Holland whence they came. The men, too, made themselves broad below the waist in billowing knee-breeches. The farmer wore a coat-shirt of cotton or wool called a *hemdrok,* over it a larger cloth *paltrok* for warmth, a steeple-hat, and wooden shoes for work-days and leather shoes for Sundays. The patroon and rich burgher class wore broadcloth and velvet, a flowing cape, as many buttons as possible, silver buckles on shoe and knee and hat, with a feather sweeping over the hat's broad brim.

So much for the general, but here from old letters are a few particulars of articles ordered or sent from the Netherlands:

". . . winter under stockings . . .
". . . 4 fine hat bands . . .
". . . Silk stockings . . .
". . . sayette stockings . . .
". . . Armozine ribbon . . .
". . . of these shirts the sleeves must be somewhat finer than the body and somewhat wider than they are usually made, for I am to wear them daily as half-shirts for the sake of coolness, for in summer one always goes about here with open sleeves. . . .
". . . Have a black cloak and suit made for me. My cloak was stolen this summer, from my chest, out of the house, and from the gray cloak I had clothes made, so that I have no cloak. Have the coat made with a little skirt, according to the fashion. . . .
". . . the suit should have slashed sleeves. . . .
". . . 2 pair of gray shoes, 1 pair of Spanish leather boots, 1 pair of short sayette stockings, and a serge cloth suit, but

somewhat stylish, with half a dozen bands, among which I should like to have at least two with lace, and so much red cloth and silver braid as are necessary to make a waistcoat.

". . . The things ordered by my wife, to wit, the golden head-dress with a pair of pendants, I had expected by these ships.

". . . A silver-plated rapier with baldric and a hat with plume, to be presented to Rutger Hendrixsz van Soest in his capacity as officer and *Schout*. . . ."

". . . also 4 black hats with silver bands . . ."

". . . I send you here with the *Panssert* . . . ," armor, which Van Laer says, may mean either a cuirass or a coat of mail, but probably the former.

While it is true that religious freedom attracted settlers to New Netherland, the Dutch Reformed was the state church, and other sects were merely tolerated. This sufferance was tightened somewhat, toward the end of the Dutch régime, on the coming of Dominie Megapolensis, who was something of a heresy hunter. This policy drove the nonconformists to holding services in private houses. Actual persecution raised its shameful head, however, only in the treatment of the Quakers.

As there were few dominies and each seems to have been a man of strong character, each was something of a power. They disciplined the life of the colonists, and before high officials they often showed a bravery that was somewhat more than spunk; as when Dominie Bogardus called Governor van Twiller "a child of Satan" and threatened to "preach him such a sermon next Sunday as will make him shake in his shoes." He thundered from his pulpit at Director Kieft, too, whereupon Kieft posted soldiers at the church door and ordered them to drown the dominie's invective with a deafening roll of drum. When this failed, the director ordered the roaring of the big guns of the fort to reenforce the rattle of the drums. But the dominie would not be silenced.

Some quaint customs adorned religious life. Whether or not there was a church-bell to call the people to service, the practical Dutch took no chances, and we can believe that other towns and villages maintained the Rondout custom for the old sexton to go from door to door rapping with his ivory-headed cane and calling out "Church time! Church time!" When the dominie began his sermon the *vooringer* inverted the hour-glass to time his talk. The pulpit generally rose to a commanding height above the congregation, so high, indeed, that when the clerk wished to pass a notice to the dominie there, he put the paper in the split end of a bamboo pole, and so was able to reach it up to his highness. Contributions were taken up after the sermon and it was naturally a moment of some shut-eye. But attached to the money-bag at the end of the reaching-rod there was a bell to jangle the sleeper to consciousness, and doubtless to self-consciousness. At communion the members always stood at the table to receive the sacrament.

The early church buildings were small, smaller than some of the houses, and generally they were rectangular. But the patroon of Rensselaerwyck, in writing to his commissary, Arendt Van Corlear, ordered an octagonal structure:

"I again commend you to the building of the church; . . . It ought not to be a very complicated matter, the shape being mostly like an eight-cornered mill; it cannot cost a great deal either as it is small, its greatest width on the outside measuring but 48 feet. . . . It is my definite intention that this church be put opposite Castle Island . . . south of the farm of Gerrit de reux . . . near or on the bank of the river."

The means used in getting building funds was sometimes

devious. When New Amsterdam was in need of a respectable church, in 1642, Director Kieft saw to the subscription. De-Vries, historian of the incident, led off with a gift of one hundred guilders, but his followers were few. So, when Dominie Bogardus's stepdaughter was married a few days later, Kieft saw and took his opportunity. Wine flowed freely at the wedding breakfast, and advantaging himself of the consequent effect of the cheer, Kieft passed a pledge-paper and got it covered with generous subscriptions. . Later, and too late, the sobered burghers realized their commitments.

It seems to have been the custom to accompany all occasions of piety with punch; not only weddings, but christenings and funerals as well. The babe was brought to the *doop-becken,* the dipping bowl, about a week after its birth. The mother's mother carried the babe in the procession to the church, and there the father's mother presented it for baptism. The company was invited to rejoice afterward at the home of the proud parents. In the early days along the river such a party was simple if not too solemn. The men came at noon and sat over gin and bitters while they blew smoke from their massive pipe-bowls. The *vrows* came in afterward to nibble *muisjes,* literally mice, actually rusks spread with aniseed, which they washed down with egg-nog. At a later period such simplicity gave way to caudle parties, when the appetizing brew of raisins, lemons and spiced wines was served in silver bowls hung about with spoons with which the guests helped fill up a pledging cup. Sometimes there were presents for the baby and its parents. At a later convenient time the young mother was "churched."

A funeral was a medley equally of grief and junketing. Each arrival at the house of the deceased was met with a glass of rum. After the service and the journey to the grave, the family and friends returned to the house to discuss the deceased, or perhaps any other late gossip, in the midst of wreaths of tobacco smoke, to the accompaniment of more potations from the flowing bowl.

In addition to such diversion as there was in church-going, christenings, weddings and funerals—and there were even then many of that type of character that finds deep social satisfaction in a funeral—their other amusements were simple. In contrast with Puritan New England, religious holidays were here celebrated socially as well as piously. New Year's Day was given to the exchange of calls. Next after came a holiday called *Pinkster,* in the seventh week after Easter, when the orchards and gardens and woods were in bloom. Early in the morning the children gathered flowering boughs, sprinkled them with water and so hung them over the doors of late sleepers, that when the latter got up and opened their doors the branch would drench them. The *Kermis* was a kind of fair, with booths for goods and goodies, and it went on from week to week with dances and processions and general merrymaking. Saint Nicholas, or Santa Claus, did not visit the Dutch boys and girls at Christmas. He came at the time of his own feast day, the sixth of December. On the eve of that day the children spread a white sheet on the floor and about it sang verses, of which a popular one was—

> "Saint Nicholas, good holy man,
> Put your best tabard on,
> And ride away from Amsterdam
> From Amsterdam to Spain"—

with promises that if he would serve them, they would serve

him always. The songs kept up until the door opened and a shower of goodies landed on the sheet, and the good saint himself appeared, attended by Knech Ruprecht, his servant, a black man. Black Ruprecht carried a sack into which he threatened to put all the bad children, and a bundle of switches with which he threatened; while the good Saint Nicholas, meantime, from his pack, distributed presents.

In addition to foot-races, horse-races, bob-sledding and cock-fighting, the general summer sport on the river was sailing, in winter it was sleighing and skating. When the luxury of metal runners was not obtainable for the skates, domestic ingenuity fashioned them out of ox-bone. The sleigh-races took place on the river which, above the Highlands, frequently froze over solid from shore to shore, and so made a matchless course. In Van Rensselaer letters sent back to Amsterdam, we find:

". . . The winter set in here so late that many thought that we would not have any, but on the 5th of January, although in the afternoon it was still raining, it began to freeze during the night, so that in the morning the river was frozen over, which is quite remarkable, as it did not look that way. It then froze for 14 days in succession as hard as within the memory of Christians it has ever done, so that with the sleigh one could use the river everywhere, without danger for the racers, in which [sport of racing] we now indulge [a great deal]. . . .

". . . As to news, I have not much to write, except that it has been a severe winter, so that we could have all the racing with the sleigh we wanted. But I have been again in trouble, for my sleigh turned over with me on the river, or was upset by another sleigh, so that I severely hurt my left hand, from which I suffered much pain, but now it is again nearly all right. . . .

". . . Last winter we passed the time reasonably well in racing on the river with the little sleigh."

No place else than in these letters have I seen reference to the sport of falconry on the river, but Jan Baptist wrote: "My falcon came over in good shape. He is still keen and alert and is king of all New Netherland. He now dares to take a chance against one twice his size, but he soon gives up."

Of games, bowling seems to have been the most popular. To this day, when thunder rumbles down the river, reverberating sharply between the mountains, it is remarked that the spirits of Henry Hudson's crew of Dutch sailors are bowling on the summits. Pins and balls and men have long since disappeared from New York, but the Bowling Green survives to remind that here the burghers once played their favorite game. A *tick-tack bort* was a kind of backgammon board, and on it the game was played with pegs as well as men. It was popular all along the river, but in 1656 the playing of it was prohibited in New Amsterdam during the hours of divine service. Another game was *Trock*, played either indoors on a table or out-of-doors on a board. The mode of playing was to cast "little bowles at a board with 13 holes in it."

The practise of medicine was in a primitive state. Doctors as such seem to have been scarce. Pieter Barentsen, Commander of the post at Fort Orange in 1626, was also designated as *Kranck-besoecker* (comforter of the sick), a somewhat common title then. There was also, on the river, a dominie, "versed in the art of Physick," who not only dealt out drugs but prescribed them too. But in 1652 the Chirurgeons of New Amsterdam petitioned that "none but they be allowed to shave" and that "Ship Barbers shall not be allowed to dress any wounds or administer any potions on shore."

Though the devotion of the New Netherlander to his religion was constant and often touching, he did not, early at least, evince anything like the same regard for education, in spite of the devotion of the Netherlander in Europe to learning and culture. The first schoolmaster to reach the river, Adam Roelantsen, did not arrive until 1633; nor did his coming advance the cause of learning. He was "as precious a scoundrel as ever was set to teach the young," and it was accounted among "the most creditable items of his scandlous career" that he eked out his income by taking in washing and conducting a bleachery. Nevertheless, under hardships which would have discouraged less hardy spirits, the young educators carried on, teaching their classes where they could—in some cases in their own rooms, in others in the church when there was one available—during long hours from early morning until after dark, and they were required to supplement their meager pay, as was Roelantsen, by doing odd jobs, as bell-ringer, sexton, and general-aide to the dominie. It was not until 1658 that an attempt was made to found an academy. Up to that time, the New Netherland lads of the more fortunate class were sent into New England in order to learn the classics. In summing up a scholarly account of Dutch education in New Netherland, Kilpatrick says:

"During the Dutch régime, the West India Company supplied salaries for the New Amsterdam schools—both parochial and Latin—and assisted some of the villages in supporting their schoolmasters. In no true sense, however, was there a central colonial system in the management of school affairs. Control was in the hands of the local magistracy and consistory, except that in New Amsterdam a third factor was the director general. As in Holland, so in New Netherland, tuition charges were universal, save for 'the poor and needy.' The expression 'free school' was nowhere found among the American Dutch. Girls attended the school on the same footing as boys, but sat apart and recited in different classes. Evening schools seem to have been the rule throughout Dutch America. Dame schools were very seldom found.   The curriculum of the elementary school was exactly transferred from Holland.   The parish school taught always two of the three R's but offered the third only where commerce made reckoning necessary.   A little modern history was taught in Holland and possibly at places in America. The religious part of the curriculum was much stressed."

From the beginning the river was the great highway for travel.   The hills and mountains at its water's edge retarded road development until the end of the Dutch régime.   Small boats, however, sped about from landing to landing whether for business or pleasure.   The accepted length of time for a trip with fair winds from New Amsterdam to Beverwyck was five days, which was extended to seven days if the winds were adverse.

Postage cost nothing because there was not yet a postal system.   Letters went by the private favor of travelers or ships-captains.   Packages went by the same private favor.   Sometimes a ship-captain took his fee in kind, as when one of the colonists shipped several tubs of little sassafras trees from the forests along the Mauritius to friends in Holland, and the captain of the conveyancer took one tub for their transit and his care of them.

The oversea voyage took varying time according to direction. Usually a ship on the eastern voyage between the two Amsterdams, new and old, took about five or six weeks.   The same voyage westward took twice the time.   That made letters particularly precious, rare and frequently long.   As there were no newspapers the letters sometimes were journals in themselves. Here, for instance, is a brief history of the state of Europe set out in a single page of a letter from Jeremias Van Rensselaer at Rensselaerwyck to his father-in-law, Oloff Stevensen Van Cortlandt, at New Amsterdam, in 1673:

"The news brought here from the Maquas country by the papist, Bruas, is that 7 ships have arrived in Canada and that the eighth is expected; that in England there is freedom of religion and that the Duke of York is entirely on the side of the Catholics; that the Turck has made great progress in Poland and Transylvania and in some other places, yes, that they must yearly pay him a tribute of one hundred and fifty thousand rixdollars; that Hungary has revolted against the emperor and that the empress has died; and that Maestricht, after a siege of eleven days, was taken by the French on the first of July. He says also that freedom of conscience would be the end of the war. What he said of Amsterdam we could not well understand, except here and there a word, but the letter has been sent to our governor, van Kollve, and you will be able to understand the contents better there, as here we have no one who can read and understand French thoroughly."

The letter-writers usually added a pious prayer after the address, thus:

"By the ship De Bever, which God protect."

"By the ship De Gelderse Blom. May God preserve her!"

"Pr skipper Cornelis de Beer van Lansmeer, whom God preserve."

"By a friend whom God preserve."

"By the ship De Vergulde Bever, which God conduct."

"By the skipper, whom God conduct."

Though the river country was scenically unlike anything in the colonists' home country, they were natively Dutch and in character, language and customs they produced a replica of their Netherlands life here. But the Dutch West India Company and its colonists on De Groote Rivier did not enjoy their slice of the new world without question. Thrust in between English colonies, which flanked them solidly on the east and to the south, they were from the first an irritation to British homogeneity on this coast and an object of cupidity on the part of the British monarch. Less than fifty-five years after Henry Hudson brought the flag of the Netherlands here, it was lowered. The English seized the colony in 1664, the river became an English river, and the English flag and political control were established. New Netherland as such ceased to be. But the Dutch remained, other Dutch came, they carried on in their own way, eventually sunk into the minority, but left a deep ineradicable mark here on the life that came after them.

CHAPTER IV

THE ENGLISH ERA

Bases of English Claims to the Hudson—Dutch and English Connections—
New Flag, Names, Language and Administration—The Hudson River
Receives Its Name—New Netherland Becomes New York—New Amsterdam
Becomes New York City—Beverwyck Becomes Albany—First Provincial
Assembly—Creation of the Counties—Erection of the Manors—Relations
with the Indians—Pirates on the Hudson—Captain Kidd—Slavery- Uprisings
of the Blacks—Skulls for Bird Nests—House Furnishings—Church of Eng-
land—Literary Personages—English Influences on Social Life—Theatrical
Entertainments—A Hint to Dominie Freylinghausen.

HE English fleet of five vessels anchored in the
Narrows at the end of August, 1664, when their
commander, Colonel Richard Nicolls, made formal
demand upon the Governor of New Netherland to
surrender the province at once to the King of Great Britain.
The Company had so little foreseen the contingency, and had
otherwise been so indifferent or so niggardly in providing ade-
quate defense, that the citizenry forced Governor Stuyvesant to
surrender against his blustering will on September eighth.

Whereupon the Dutch officials hauled down their flag and, led
by Stuyvesant, sailed back to Holland. The English landed
at the Battery, and raised their flag in token of possession.
It was the realization of a claim which the English had made,
even if they had not maintained it, from the first years of the
Dutch possession. They immediately began to make changes
which put a wholly new complexion on life on the river.

There was a momentary interruption of the English régime

here when, on August 9, 1673, the Dutch fleet retook their former province. But, only six months later, the Treaty of Westminster was signed and it handed the province back again to the English.

The story of the English governors of New York is not an edifying one. With three or four exceptions they were lacking in the sincerity, honesty and integrity which would have obviated the constant brawls with people and assembly in which they involved themselves. It is a significant fact that all the royal appointees who were poor when they took office managed to leave office rich, with only three exceptions: Lord Bellamont, Robert Hunter and William Burnet.

The English claim to the territory which the Dutch called New Netherland was based on discovery by Cabot, Smith and other Englishmen, and on the assertion of dominion to the coast of North America from Cape Fear River on the south to the Bay of Fundy on the north, as set out, in 1606, by King James in the charter of Virginia. The English sought, moreover, to advantage themselves of the part Henry Hudson had played by assuming the doctrine that territory discovered came under the dominion of the monarch of the discoverer and not of his employer. The Dutch contention was that they had found no Englishmen when they came to the Great River, and cited Queen Elizabeth's doctrine that discovery followed by neglect was not enough, that discovery must be followed by occupation.

Whatever the merits of their claims the English had not failed to assert them often. When Nicolls raised his flag over New Amsterdam in 1664 it was not the first time that the English flag had flown on that precise spot. The English Governor of the Plymouth Colony sent a ship to Manhattan in 1619 to protest the Dutch trading in the river; the English ambassador to The Hague complained to the States General, in 1621, that Dutchmen were trespassing on English territory at "Hudson's River"; and a few years later Governor Bradford of Plymouth asserted this English claim to Director Minuit of New Netherland, but acrimony seems to have had no part in that particular discussion for, though Bradford conceded that Charles I "graciously" gave the Dutch permission to trade in this slice of "English territory," Minuit with his letter declining to accede, sent Bradford "two Holland cheeses, with a runlet of sugar, to sweeten its flavour."

Two years after the English protest of 1619 against the Dutch trading in the river, the British ship *William* anchored before Fort Amsterdam, on a trading expedition under Jacob Elkens, a Dutchman, who had been kicked out of the Dutch West India Company's service. Director van Twiller challenged his right to trade in a river belonging to the Dutch. Elkens protested that the river belonged to England by right of discovery by Hudson who was an Englishman. Van Twiller's reply was to raise the blue, white and orange flag and to fire a salute in honor of his monarch, the Prince of Orange. Elkens's retort was to raise the English flag over his ship and fire a salute in honor of King Charles. Whereupon Elkens departed—up-river! Van Twiller consoled himself by rolling out a cask of wine and calling upon his fellow-Dutchmen to drink to their Prince. Having conquered whatever doubt he had, he then sent an expedition up-river after Elkens. They found him collecting beaver skins near Fort Orange, seized his cargo, and forced him to leave the river. But another English protest against Dutch occupation had been made.

The change from Dutch to English dominion worked little hardship on the colonists. The two nations were not entirely foreign to each other. There had already been a large admixture of Dutch blood in England by migration before the beginning of the seventeenth century. It is reasonable to suppose that the English who supplanted the Dutch in political control in America were, in considerable numbers, children and grandchildren of the Dutch immigrants into England under Elizabeth. The union of the two nations even had been suggested to Elizabeth by the Dutch in 1584; and the English had on their part suggested it to the Dutch in 1651. The very English king who was to rule over the Dutch on the river before the end of the century was William, Prince of the great Dutch house of Orange. But in the year 1651 the English parliament passed the Navigation Act, and the two nations, which had so long fought shoulder to shoulder against common foes, came to naval blows against each other. Their second war in 1664 gave the English their occasion forcibly to assert sovereignty over the Dutch territorial wedge in their American coast.

The most significant political effect of the change was the accomplishment of the territorial solidarity of the English colonies on the American coast, a unification which simplified their military and civil and commercial jurisdiction; but, too, unsuspectedly at the time, unified all the colonists there, making possible a united front of Revolution a century later, and establishing the territorial unit which was to be the unit of the new republic.

The symbol of the change on the river was the new flag which now floated there. Where the change actually touched the Dutch colonists was in the required adjustments to new place names; to new weights, measures and coins; to a new civil organization and administration, made slowly and with due consideration for Dutch habituation to old forms; and to the strange new language which set Heeren and Vrouwen a pate-cracking task, for all were required to use English in commercial documents and in all official intercourse.

"Now it seems that it has pleased the Lord to ordain that we must learn English," wrote Van Rensselaer to his mother. "The worst of it all is that we have already for nearly four years been under this jurisdiction and that as yet I have learned so little. The reason is that one has no liking for it."

Mrs. Grant, in her Memoirs, writing of Albany, in 1760, nearly one hundred years later, guardedly admitted that there, even then, "the English language began to be more generally understood."

The arbitrary new place names were at first so few that they could be counted on the fingers of one hand, but the change erased, nevertheless, the most significant and best-known names. The colony of New Netherland became the colony of New York, named after James, Duke of Albany and York. After him, too, the name of New Amsterdam was changed to New York and that of Beverwyck to Albany. Rondout became King's Town, or Kingston. The river itself, already known by so many other names, was now given that by which the English had long referred to it. In honor of the "discoverer" of 1609, it was thereafter to be known as the Hudson River.

Otherwise the old names of the lesser localities were allowed to linger on, so that to-day we speak, as did the Dutch who named them, of Hoboken and Harlem, of Spuyten Duyvil and Peekskill, of Kinderhook, Catskill, Watervliet, Yonkers and Fishkill. Other souvenirs of the receding Dutch days which survive on the river are the frequent recurrence of the prefix *van* in surnames, and, in place names, of the words "beck" for *beek* and "hook" for *hoek*. Other such Dutch survivals, among many, are Verplanck's Point, Dunderberg, Paarda Hook, Dans-kammer and Van Wyck Ridge. But, apart from the single instance of its appearance in Amsterdam, the word *dam,* so popular in the Netherlands, does not appear on the Hudson. The reason is that in the hilly country here there were no dykes or dams as oversea in the old Low Country of canals.

The people on the river were without any representative assembly throughout the Dutch régime. There had, however, long been among the Dutch popular sentiment for "taxation only by consent." But they were emboldened to demand it forcibly only when, on the founding of Pennsylvania and the release of New Jersey to young George Carteret, the people of both those colonies were conceded popular assemblies. Governor Dongan came with the grant of a New York assembly in 1683. It sat in New York, and the Hudson Valley was represented by delegates from Albany, Rensselaerwyck, Esopus and New York. But it got on to no sound and permanent basis until the accession of William of Orange to the English throne. The beginning of real constitutional government in New York dates from 1691.

The Assembly had, however, in its very first week, passed an act creating political divisions to be known as "Shires or Counties." Such divisions of the river's tidewater valley were called New York, Westchester, Dutchess, Albany, Orange and Ulster. With increasing population, the area of these counties was eventually found too vast for convenient and economic administration. In 1786, nearly thirty miles was cut off the south side of that part of Albany County on the east side of the river, and of it Columbia County was established. In 1791, all that so remained of Albany County on the east side of the river was allocated to a new county called Rensselaer. In 1798, twenty-two miles cut off the south side of Orange was erected into Rockland County. In 1800, what remained of Albany County on the west side of the river was dismembered and twenty-seven miles of its shore-line to the south went into the new county called Greene. Finally, in 1812, the south eight miles of Dutchess' river shore was taken from it and became the western boundary of a new county called Putnam. Meantime, in 1682, the territory west of the entire stretch of the New Jersey shore of the river became Bergen County. So, by 1812, the counties on both shores of the tidal river were established as they have since been maintained.

Under the new régime the English manorial system was established here. There were never, however, more than four permanent manors on the Hudson. Rensselaerwyck was the first and largest of them. As a long-established land unit, it was taken over intact from patroonship to manor, soon after the change of provincial administration. Robert Livingston, first of his family to come to the river, was granted lands abutting on the river for ten miles, about thirty miles south of Albany, and extending eastward to the Connecticut line, with the status of manor, in 1686. This holding comprised one hundred and sixty thousand acres. Frederic Philipse began accumulating land between Spuyten Duyvil and the Croton River in 1672 and he had obtained control of a land unit whose western boundary extended about twenty-two miles along the river, when it was erected into a manor in the year 1693. Van Cortlandt Manor, erected in 1697, completes the list of manors on the Hudson. Its first lord was Stephanus Van Cortlandt, uniquely the only first lord of a Hudson manor who was born on the river. The Hudson River frontage of his estate extended from Croton River to a point north of Anthony's Nose, a distance of over

From the Original, Painted and Engraved by W. J. Bennet About 1831

WEST POINT AND THE HIGHLANDS OF THE HUDSON IN THE OLD SAILING DAYS

The Upper Highlands of the Hudson as Seen from West Point

ten miles. One other manor was granted on the Hudson; it was that of Fox Hall, just above the Esopus, and was patented in 1672. It was not comparable in area with the other four great manors here, however. Moreover, it was never confirmed and it lapsed soon after the death of its first lord, Captain Thomas Chambers, who died childless.

These manors were granted under an act, passed in 1660, which provided: "that all tenures hereafter to be created by the King's Majesty, his heirs or successors, upon any gifts or grants of any manors, lands, tenements, or hereditaments, of any estate of inheritance at the common law, shall be free and common soccage only, and not be knight service or in capite." In plainer words no feudal rights or privileges were granted in New York manors, which were in fact modern freehold manors, not feudal.

The lord of a manor held title to his land by purchase from preceding owners. The other rights and privileges conveyed by his manorial charter he held from his sovereign by the payment of an annual rental. Such a rental was always nominal. The annual rental for Philipsborough Manor was four pounds, twelve shillings, to be paid "yearly and every year, on the feast day of the Annunciation of the Blessed Virgin Mary, at our fort at New York unto us, our heirs and successors." The annual rental of the neighboring Fordham Manor as prescribed in the royal charter was "twenty bushels of good peas, upon the first day of March, when it shall be demanded."

The lord of the manor might sell portions of his land outright, and the purchasers were known as freeholders. They thus secured a title in fee, but they still owed a political allegiance to the lord of the manor. He might rent his land, and tenants of such lands were known as copy-holders. Such tenants usually came to the manor house twice a year to pay their rent, sometimes in cash and sometimes in produce. This gathering was generally made a gala occasion whereat the landlord entertained with a barbecue "and plentiful draughts of 'Sopus ale.' "

With the royal charter for a manor there generally passed "the advowson and right of patronage of all and every church" thereon; the right of sending a representative to the Provincial Assembly; and the right of holding courts-leet and -baron on the manor, and the perquisites included in their fees and fines. The manor was held together by the law of primogeniture, sometimes qualified by small bequests to younger children.

The title "Lord of the Manor" was freely and properly applied to the landlord of such a domain, as, similarly, we use the word landlord. But he was not privileged to the use of the title "Lord" before his surname. It has never been so used in England nor in the Province of New York except as a bit of ignorant ostentation.

Under the English régime there were marked gains in population. This was less on account of the influence of this political and commercial régime than because the ground had been broken, the crudest and heaviest pioneer work had been done, the advantages of the river country had become known in many European countries, and, moreover, because the increasing domestic birth rate made a contribution which left the colony not wholly dependent on immigration for its increase in population. In 1664 the total population of New Netherland was ten thousand persons, of whom one thousand six hundred dwelt in New Amsterdam. In 1756, the population of the Province of New York was ninety-six thousand seven hundred and sixty-five, of whom seventy thousand nine hundred and fifty dwelt in counties along tidewater Hudson. It is at first surprising, in analyzing the figures for this latter year, to find that Albany was the most populous county, and that New York ranked fourth. But it must be borne in mind that Albany County had a comparatively vast area whereas New York County was limited to Manhattan Island. It is not less surprising to find that included in the total population of ninety-six thousand seven hundred and sixty-five there were thirteen thousand five hundred and forty-two blacks.

Indians were not counted in these figures, but they lived among the whites on the river, even as far south as Yonkers, as late as the year 1755. Mrs. Grant gives us this sketch of the Indian contacts with the white residents on the shore of the river just above Albany, about 1763:

"They generally built a slight wigwam under shelter of the orchard fence on the shadiest side; and never were neighbors more harmless, peaceable and obliging; I might truly add, industrious: for in one way or other they were constantly occupied. The women and their children employed themselves in many ingenious handicrafts, which, since the introduction of European arts and manufactures, have greatly declined. Baking trays, wooden dishes, ladles and spoons, shovels and rakes, brooms of a peculiar manufacture, made by splitting a birch block into slender but tough filaments; baskets of all kinds and sizes, made of similar filaments, enriched with the most beautiful colors, which they alone knew how to extract from vegetable substances, and incorporate with the wood. They made also of the birch bark (which is here so strong and tenacious, that cradles and canoes are made of it), many receptacles for holding fruit and other things curiously adorned with embroidery, not inelegant, done with the sinews of deer, and leggions and moomesans, a very comfortable and highly ornamented substitute for shoes and stockings, then universally used in winter among the men of our own people. They had also a beautiful manufacture of deer skin, softened to the consistence of the finest chamois leather, and embroidered with beads of wampum, formed like bugles; these, with great art and industry, they formed out of shells, which had the appearance of fine white porcelain, veined with purple. This embroidery showed both skill and taste, and was among themselves highly valued. They had belts, large embroidered garters, and many other ornaments, formed, first of sinews, divided to the size of coarse thread, and afterwards, when they obtained worsted thread from us, of that material, formed in a manner which I could never comprehend. It was neither knitted nor wrought in the manner of net, nor yet woven; but the texture was formed more like an officer's sash than anything I can compare it to. While the women and children were thus employed, the men sometimes assisted them in the more laborious part of their business, but oftener occupied themselves in fishing on the rivers, and drying or preserving, by means of smoke, in sheds erected for the purpose, sturgeon and large eels, which they caught in great quantities, and of an extraordinary size, for winter provision.

"Boys on the verge of manhood, and ambitious to be admitted into the hunting parties of the ensuing winter, exercised themselves in trying to improve their skill in archery, by shooting birds, squirrels, and racoons. These petty huntings helped to support the little colony in the neighborhood, which however, derived its principal subsistence from an exchange of their manufactures with the neighboring family for milk, bread, and other articles of food.

"The summer residence of these ingenious artisans promoted a great intimacy between the females of the vicinity and the Indian women, whose sagacity and comprehension of mind were beyond belief.

"It is a singular circumstance, that though they saw the negroes in every respectable family not only treated with humanity, but cherished with parental kindness, they always regarded them with contempt and dislike, as an inferior race, and would have no communication with them. It was necessary then that all conversations should be held, and all business transacted with these females, by the mistress of the family. In the infancy of the settlement the Indian language was familiar to the more intelligent inhabitants, who found it very useful, and were, no doubt, pleased with its nervous and emphatic idiom, and its lofty and sonorous cadence."

In spite of the change of political control the Dutch continued to cross the ocean and settle on the Hudson in at least as large numbers under the English as they had under their own people. And they came in greater numbers as farmers, as the Indian became less of a menace with the increase of population, and as there was increasing knowledge and appreciation of the fertility of the lovely valleys which follow the little tributaries of the great river in behind the hills which hold fast to its very shore.

The English naturally came in increasing numbers. Religious persecutions and the ravages of war drove into exile several thousand Germans of the lower Palatinate on the Rhine, many of them coming from the town of Neuberg, and they came to the Hudson and settled above the Highlands on both sides; but principally on Livingston Manor and on lands on a part of which is now the city of Newburgh. Similarly, the persecutions of the Huguenots drove one-seventh of the population of France beyond the borders of that kingdom, and the Hudson received its share as is witnessed by such ancient New York names as Bayard, De Lancey, Desbrosses and Jay. The Province of New York had, indeed, a much higher percentage of non-English population than any other of the thirteen colonies.

Trade was the life of the river, agriculture holding a conspicuous but supplementary position. It thrived especially at each extremity of the tidewater reaches. At the southern end of the river, trade received its impetus from its international contacts. At Albany it received its stimulus from contact at first with the Indians of the vast hinterland and later with the settlers pushing westward into the Mohawk Valley.

Piracy played no inconspicuous part in commerce here. The early days of the English régime on the river were the heyday of piracy on the high seas, especially of the looting of the rich argosies of both the Dutch and the English East India Companies in the Indian Ocean. A freebooter, having gorged his vessel's hold with such treasure, would often make a course for the mouth of the Hudson, produce "some Dog's eared letter-of-marque and swear he had taken all this Oriental stuff from Frenchmen as a lawful privateer." Or he would steer for Madagascar, await a merchant vessel from New York, exchange "gold pieces, gems, and Eastern shawls," for rum, firearms or whatever useful was found. When the merchant vessel returned to the Hudson no questions were asked as to where or how its master had accumulated its precious cargo. The risks in such traffic were great, but the profits were greater.

The pirate captains, from all accounts, were indeed somewhat distinguished figures in old New York Town. On one occasion there were nine pirate ships in its harbor at one time. Captain William Tew was the honored guest of the royal governor, and rode at his side in his "coach and six," a resplendent rascal, and he dressed it colorfully, right down to the knitted girdle from which hung a dagger, its hilt blazing with jewels. Coates, another such pirate, loaded the governor with gifts and even gave him his ship to be sold for eight thousand pounds.

But the pirates did not stop at the little city at the mouth of the river. They boldly pressed up-river; for, according to the Albany Records of 1696, "pirates in great numbers infest the Hudson River at its mouth and waylay vessels on their way to Albany, speeding out from covers and from behind islands and again returning to the rocky shores, or ascending the mountains along the river to conceal their plunder."

At the height of this freebootery, the Earl of Bellamont was appointed royal governor of the Province of New York. His first instructions were to break up the piracy on the Hudson. Before he left London a stock company was formed for that purpose. Along with the king and many other men of title one of the shareholders was Robert Livingston, first lord of Livingston Manor on the Hudson. A galley called *Adventure,* carrying thirty-six guns, was secured for their purpose, and it may have been at Livingston's own suggestion that the command of it was entrusted to a sea captain, a resident of the city of New York, at that moment in London. This man had a pleasant and proper house on Liberty Street, he had some fortune, and he not only wrote "Captain" before his name, but "gentleman" after it. His name was William Kidd.

In 1697 he sailed the *Adventure* out of New York harbor for Madagascar, in search of pirates, and nothing was heard of him during the ensuing two years. The ironic fact was that the pirate-catcher had himself turned pirate! His own story was that the voyage having failed by reason of his failure to encounter any other pirates, provisions being exhausted and the crew mutinous, he had been forced in self-defense to turn outlaw. Such is the genesis of the redoubtable Captain Kidd. He eventually boldly sailed back home to protest his innocence. He was arrested in Boston, was sent thence to London for trial on a trumped-up charge of having murdered one of his seamen, and eventually, and unjustly some thought, was found guilty. Immediately thereafter he was tried and found guilty of piracy, and was hanged.

The curious fact has been noted that though Captain Kidd became noted as a criminal of incredible depravity, he would, had he died a few years earlier, have been remembered as one of New York's most successful and respected citizens.

More attention was given by the English, than had been given by the Dutch, to the transmission of communications. The eighteenth century was old, however, before the swift sloops on the river were abandoned as the swiftest conveyances for letters and packages; except during a brief winter period when ice prevented them. But those earlier letters transmitted by the courtesy of the carriers, "whom God preserve," in the early Dutch days, were now supplanted, in part at least, by road-riders. There was a post between New York and Albany, carried by white postmen in the summer when the roads were passable; but in winter it was carried, at least as early as 1672, "by the Indian Post." There is a hint that the red men made the transit on foot, for, in a notice of 1730, we read that the New York postmaster will receive applications of "whoever inclines to perform the foot-post to Albany this winter." One letter so dispatched from Albany on January 11, 1673, arrived in New York after nine days, on January twentieth. A tri-weekly post also sprang up, between the two towns at either end of tidewater Hudson, which was ridden on the west side of the river. But in winter all mail schedules were casual. Even after 1730 we find the New York postmaster making a collection of mail, over a period of several weeks, which was noted as "the first post to Albany this winter."

Irrelevant as they may seem here, I can not dismiss the fact of the Indian mail-carriers without two items from one of the letters carried by them, the content of which gave us at least one documentary proof of their existence and of the actual number of days required for brief transit between Albany and New York. The chatty letter is from J. O. Clarke, "ffrom ye Secretary's Office in ffort James," to "Captain Sylvester Salisbury, Governor of Fort Albany."

"For our City news," wrote Clarke, "let us satisfy, that t'other day, we had like to have lost our Hang-man, Ben Johnson, for hee, being taken in Divers thefts and Robbings, convicted and found guilty, scaped his neck through want of an-

other Hang-man to truss him up, soe, that all the punishment
that hee received for his 3 years Roguery . . . was only thirty-
nine stripes at the Whipping Post, loss of an Ear and Banish-
ment.

". . . Another Disaster about 12 days since befell a young
man in this Town, by name one Mr. Wright, a one-eyed man,
a Muff-maker by trade, who drinking hard upon Rum one evening with some ffriends, begann a health of a whole half-pint
at a Draught, which hee had noe sooner done but down he fell
and never rose more . . . by which we may see, that though there
is but one way of coming into this world, yet there is a thousand
ways of going out of it."

Class distinction was marked during the eighteenth century;
a few aristocrats at the top on a sharp aloof pinnacle; a gaping
hiatus; and then a broad foundation of middle and lower classes.
The aristocrats, in the rarified atmosphere of the heights, were
the families of the lords of the manors, of the greater business
men and of the bankers. A few traders and bankers were extensive landholders, but they were planters only incidentally.
The professional classes developed slowly. Far below these
aristocrats, in the absence of a well-developed middle class, were
the small tradesmen, artificers and artizans, and farmers of
whom the lesser portion owned small acreages and the larger
portion rented from the lords of the manors and other landlords. There was a comparatively small group of indentured
white servants, some of them convicts, some of them kidnaped
and sold into servitude, and some of them redemptioners who
worked their way to freedom. But there were far fewer of
these on the Hudson than on the Chesapeake.

Under the Dutch régime it has been seen how the introduction
of the negro slave, as attempted by the Company, did not thrive,
even though it may have been only because the slow development
of agriculture did not furnish any need of them. There was a

marked increase of blacks under the English. When in 1756 there was one black man for every nine white men in the entire province, there were in New York Town two thousand four hundred and forty-four slaves in a total population of eleven thousand seven hundred and twenty-three, that is, one black to every four whites. The land was tended by tenant farmers. There was little need there for slaves. The greater number of the blacks stayed in the towns because there they were employed as cooks, valets, porters, chairmen, coachmen, footmen and gardeners. Children were consigned to the care of negro nurses less frequently here than in the South. In fact negro slavery was never the economic necessity on the Hudson that it was in the southern colonies.

The blacks in general seem to have been well treated. Dissatisfied slaves were allowed to seek new masters and negotiate their own sale, the proceeds going, of course, into the pocket of the prior master. In the families of gentle folk the slaves seem to have been treated with the same consideration as in families of similar status in the South. Based on her intimacy with the Schuylers and families in and about Albany, Mrs. Grant found "Even the dark aspect of slavery was softened into a smile. . . . A great deal of that tranquillity and comfort, to call it by no higher name, which distinguished this society from all others, was owing to the relation between master and servant being better understood here than in any other place. . . . I think I have never seen people so happy in servitude as the domestics of the Albanians."

An amusing, if not quite similar, situation is reflected in an anecdote told of an old slave at Clermont, a little way downriver from Albany, on Livingston Manor. It was said that "Mrs. Livingston once offered freedom to a slave woman of ungovernable temper on condition that she would leave Clermont and never return. The reply to this offer was an indignant refusal: 'I was born on this place and have as good a right to live here as you have. I do not want to be free.' "

This relation was far different at the mouth of the river. In New York the slaves were not regarded without fear by their masters. Even as early in this régime as the year 1684, an ordinance declared that not more than four negroes might meet at any time or in any place except in their master's service. They might not go armed with gun, club, sword or stone under penalty of ten lashes at the whipping post. No negro could go about the streets at night without a lighted lantern. Eventually there were two alleged "insurrections."

In 1712 a group of about forty negroes attempted a massacre of the whites. It was a futilely mad plot. But nine whites were killed and many wounded; for which, six negroes having done away with themselves, twenty-one were put to death, one was broken on the wheel, a few were burned, but the majority were hanged.

In 1741 the negroes were accused of attempting to burn the town, for which fourteen were burned at the stake, eighteen were hanged and seventy-one were transported. The penalties for the so-called insurrection of 1741 were believed to have been so unjust that they seem to have produced a revulsion of feeling in favor of the blacks. At any rate, within ten years they were admitted to the franchise, and thereafter there was no concerted disturbance.

Petitions to the governors from up-river masters reveal the fact that negro slaves, in running away, sometimes hid among the Indians, with whom even they sometimes intermarried. A natural sympathy may have been engendered between the two races by the fact that Indians, too, were sometimes held in slavery by the whites. Catharine Van Cortlandt Philipse, widow of the first lord of Philipsborough Manor, in her will, dated 1730, directed "that Matty and Sarah, my Indians or muster slaves, shall be manumitted and set at full freedom." Even earlier, in 1705, Elizabeth Legget of Westchester, made a deed of gift, to her daughter, of "my two negro children, born of the body of Hannah, my negro woman, of the issue of the body of Robin, my Indian slave." There are also, recorded in Westchester, bills of sales of Indian squaws, but for what purpose is not indicated.

The English influence on architecture made itself felt here before the middle of the century. Dutch patterns had established themselves, especially in the towns. The country houses, however, were of hardly any school whatever except that they reproduced the northwestern European farmhouses of the same time, and these, in their stark simplicity, were very like in all countries of that area. New York and Albany were quite distinctly Dutch, however, and it took a long time to make them over.

When Madame Sarah Knight, of Boston, rode horseback over to New York in 1704 she left a brief sketch of that town, and the Dutch of it comes out in the way the houses of glazed brick were "of divers Coullers and laid in checkers" and in the way the *vrouwen* kept the insides "very white scour'd." Set out in her Journal, it read:

"The Buildings are Brick Generaly, very stately and high though not altogether like ours in Boston. The Bricks in some of the Houses are of divers Coullers and laid in Checkers, being glazed, look very agreable. The inside of them is neat to admiration; the wooden work, for only the walls are plastered,

and the Sumers and Gist are planed and kept very white
scour'd as so is all the partitions made of Bords."

Nearly fifteen years later Per Kalm, the Swedish botanist,
testified, in a book of his travels in America, that, even after
nearly a century of English rule, Albany still had a strong Dutch
surface:

"The houses in this town are very neat, and partly built with
stones covered with shingles of the White Pine. Some are slated
with tiles from Holland, because the clay of this neighborhood
is not reckoned fit for tiles. Most of the houses are built in the
old way, with the gable-end towards the street; the gable-end of
brick and all the other walls of planks. The gutters on the roofs
reach almost to the middle of the street. This preserves the walls
from being damaged by the rain, but it is extremely disagreeable
in rainy weather for the people in the streets, there being hardly
any means of avoiding the water from the gutters.
"The street doors are generally in the middle of the houses
and on both sides are seats, on which, during fair weather the
people spend almost the whole day, especially on those which are
in the shadow of the houses. In the evening these seats are
covered with people of both sexes, but this is rather troublesome, as those who pass by are obliged to greet everybody
unless they will shock the politeness of the inhabitants of this
town. The streets are broad and some of them are paved; in
some parts they are lined with trees. The long streets are almost
parallel to the river, and the others intersect them at right
angles."

Had he looked carefully he might have observed vanes in the
figures of lions, horses, geese and sloops at the tops of the
houses; at the bottom, cellar-window shutters with loop-holes;
and that the brick houses were ornamented with dates and other
patterns in wrought iron, or picked out with glazed black brick.
One wonders the significance of the "two black brick-hearts"
which were still so embedded in the wall of the governor's
house that Chandler observed them there in 1755.

So far as we know, all the important houses on the Hudson built in the eighteenth century were either frankly English or showed marked English influence. It was inevitably true of the official buildings erected by the English Government at the little capital or elsewhere. It was natural too, if not inevitable, in the cases of the English families, such as the Clintons and the Beverley Robinsons, of Ellison, and even of the Scot, Livingston. But it is true, equally, of the Dutch families who built Philipse's manor house in Yonkers, the Schuyler house in Albany, the Van Cortlandt house in Van Cortlandt Park, and in certain superficial interior features of the Van Cortlandt manor house itself. Such eighteenth-century homes on the Hudson in many ways resembled the great houses of Virginia and Maryland, which were frankly imitatively English in origin. Even the impressive old Mill House of Gomez the Jew, at Marlboro, was laid in "Liverpool bond," alternating courses of all headers and all flanks.

A characteristic noted in some of the stone houses of the Hudson, irrespective of the date of their origin, is the ornamental brick frame about doors and windows. It appeared early, and usually in the houses of men who wanted a better job than that usually furnished by farm-hands or ordinary masons. The reason for thus varying stone work with brick trim was that it made for easier and better construction and less stone-cutting at door- and window-jambs and at portholes, and permitted of window arches to take the weight of the stone off the timber window-frames. Moreover, it made for a decided varying in color, taking away the usual utilitarian effect of most of the stone farmhouse types.

With what gardens the colonials may have surrounded their houses the chroniclers leave us much in doubt. Flower gardens are not always well distinguished from kitchen or vegetable gardens, or yards, or lawns. But, surely, none of the embellishment elsewhere, however beautiful, was more curious than that which Mrs. Grant found about Mrs. Schuyler's house, the Flats, near Watervliet:

"Now let not the genius that presides over pleasure-grounds, nor any of his elegant votaries, revolt with disgust while I mention the unseemly ornaments which were exhibited on the stakes to which the deals of these same fences were bound. Truly they consisted of the skeleton heads of horses and cattle in as great numbers as could be procured, stuck upon the above said poles. This was not mere ornament either, but a most hospitable arrangement for the accommodation of the small familiar birds before described. The jaws are fixed on the pole and the skull uppermost. The wren, on seeing a skull thus placed, never fails to enter by the orifice, which is too small to admit the hand of an infant, lines the pericranium with small twigs and horse hair, and there lays her eggs in full security. It is very amusing to see the little creature carelessly go out and in at this little aperture, though you should be standing immediately beside it. Not satisfied with providing these singular asylums for their feathered friends, the negroes never fail to make a small round hole in the crown of every old hat they can lay their hands on, and nail it to the end of the kitchen, for the same purpose. You often see in such a one, at once, thirty or forty of these odd little domicils, with the inhabitants busily going out and in."

So, too, in their furnishings, the river houses became, before the Revolution, more English than Dutch. Transocean commerce with the river was carried on in English bottoms, and they filled the shops in New York and Albany with English goods. Commercial contacts with the Netherlands weakened until they almost ceased. The Dutch furniture and furnishings in evidence here when the century had attained threescore and ten years were in the main heirlooms, souvenirs of a vanishing era.

Instead of reading of detached instances of a book or two being brought in at a time, as earlier; now Philip Schuyler went to London, in 1710, and having "conversed with Addison, Marlborough and Godolphin," came back with a whole library which included "all the works then published of that constellation of wits which distinguished the last female reign"; and we are conscious of a new era when we note these works of English "wits" coming to share shelf-room with stodgy Dutch classics. Wills and letters begin to reveal, too, the appearances of portraits on the walls, and the "pencil that limned" was in nearly every instance in the hand of an English artist.

But the furnishings of many of the homes, especially in New York, are credibly believed to have varied the purity or simple mixture of Dutch and English patterns with rugs from Anatolia or Daghestan, tables of carved teakwood, vases and other vessels of hammered brass and silver, Bagdad portières, and fans of ivory or sandalwood; for these were brought in by the pirates and were offered as presents to big-wigs or were as boldly displayed for sale in the shops here as in the bazaars of Teheran or Bagdad.

The Church of England became the established church, "the church of state." The governor and his staff made a ceremony of his appearance at the Anglican services held in the fort by the chaplain, the only Anglican clergyman in the province in 1664. The same condition obtained at least as late as 1687, from Governor Dongan's report of the following conditions in that year:

"New York has first a Chaplain belonging to the Fort, of the Church of England; Secondly, a Dutch Calvinist, Thirdly, a French Calvinist, Fourthly, a Dutch Lutheran. . . . Here bee not many of the Church of England; few Roman Catholicks; abundance of quakers preachers men & Women especially; Singing

Quakers, Ranting Quakers; Sabbatarians; Antisabbatarians; Some Anabaptists some Independents; some Jews; in short of all sorts of opinions there are some. ... The great church which serves both the English & the Dutch is within the Fort which is found to bee very inconvenient."

But there was little interference in fact with the other churches. They were too firmly entrenched, and so continued too powerful numerically, especially the Dutch Reformed, which was the rich and powerful church and at least as fashionable as the Anglican all through the eighteenth century. The English were ever a practical people. There was set up in New York and along the Hudson no such "establishment" as obtained from the first in Virginia and which was set up in Maryland after the accession of William and Mary to the English throne. The growth of the English Church along the Hudson was normal and solid, if somewhat slow.

The Dutch clung as tenaciously to their schools as to their church and their language. Their schools were actually parochial schools. Outside of New York they became in some sense public schools, but in that town the English and the Dutch showed little disposition to cooperate, and public education, therefore, did not flourish there during the century of English control. It is symptomatic that the idea of establishing a university was under consideration for more than fifty years before it was carried into effect when King's College opened, July 17, 1754, in the schoolhouse belonging to Trinity Church, New York, with a class of eight students. After the independence of the colonies had been won, King's College became Columbia University.

Above the horizon, behind which the Dutch period disappeared, remain the names of two writers, poets both, and residents of New Amsterdam. They were Jacob Steendam and Nicasius DeSille. Another poet, Dominie Selyns, lived to see Captain Kidd sail away to Madagascar after a third of a century of English influence here, but the legacy of rhymes he left were all in Dutch. The Hudson developed its first real literary figure in Cadwallader Colden, who, though he was born in Scotland, spent his middle life in New York and his later years farther up-river at Coldenham. He is less conspicuous than others of his own period who were less able than he, possibly because he was a loyalist. He was a man of extraordinary range of culture, philosopher, scientist and historian. He corresponded with Benjamin Franklin, Linnæus, Doctor Samuel Johnson and other leading intellectuals on both sides of the Atlantic, and he wrote *The Cause of Gravitation, The History of the Five Nations,* and numerous treatises on botany, medicine, mathematics, physics, and mental and moral philosophy. Buffon, in 1778, asked Jefferson to replace his own lost copy of Colden's *Principles of Action in Matter.* Colden was born in 1688 and died in 1776. In his eighty-third year he was appointed lieutenant-governor of the colony which he continued to rule vigorously until his eighty-seventh year, save for brief interregnums of several governors. A contemporary of Colden's later years was William Smith, born in New York, whose historian he became. He and Colden might be imagined to have been congenial, but Colden having been critical of Smith's history, and human nature being what it is, and probably always has been, the two were not friends. In this period, too, were born here Philip Freneau and Eliza Schuyler, whose distinction in two words were, respectively, that Freneau was "the poet of the Revolution," and Eliza Schuyler Bleecker was "the first poetess of New York." The colonial canvas was not crowded with literary figures.

With the introduction of governors with such names as Francis Lovelace, Richard Ingoldsby, the Earl of Bellamont and the Earl of Dunmore, whatever may have been their private morals and their capacity for government, one is scarcely surprised that life in the colony took on a twinkle and that the whole social picture brightened as English manners and customs leavened at least, if they did not wholly overlay, those of the Dutch.

New York became an English provincial capital, and to it and Albany were added the gaiety and stir of becoming garrison towns, with governor and staff in the colorful costumes of eighteenth-century London, and officers and men not less colorful in their crimson tunics.

The reaction, indeed, produced a kind of Anglomania. Its effect at the head of tidewater was thus reflected in the good Scot rigidity of Mrs. Grant's account:

"A sect arose among the young people, who seemed resolved to assume a lighter style of dress and manners, and to borrow their taste in those respects from their new friends. This bade fair soon to undo all the good pastor's labors. The evil was daily growing; and what, alas, could Domine Freylinghausen do but preach! This he did earnestly, and even angrily, but in vain. Many were exasperated but none reclaimed. The good domine, however, had those who shared his sorrows and resentments; the elder and wiser heads of families, indeed a great majority of the primitive inhabitants, were steadfast against innovation. The colonel of the regiment, who was a man of fashion and family, and possessed talents for both good and evil purposes, was young and gay; and being lodged in the house of a very wealthy citizen, who had before, in some degree, affected the newer modes of living, so captivated him with his good breeding and affability, that he was ready to humor any scheme of diversion which the colonel and his associates proposed. Under the auspices of this gallant commander, balls began to be concerted, and a degree of flutter and frivolity to take place, which was as far from elegance as it was from the honest artless cheerfulness of the meetings usual among them. The good domine more and more alarmed, not content with preaching, now began to prophesy; but like Cassandra, or to speak as justly, though less poetically, like his whole fraternity, was doomed always to deliver true predictions to those who never heeded them."

This contemporary picture of life at the island capital seems somewhat long drawn, though it is written by a foreign writer:

"The first society of New York associate together in a style of elegance and splendor little inferior to Europeans. Their houses are furnished with everything that is useful, agreeable, or ornamental; and many of them are fitted up in the tasteful magnificence of modern luxury. Many have elegant equipages. The dress of the gentlemen is plain, elegant, and fashionable, and corresponds in every respect with the English costume. The ladies in general seem more partial to the light, various, and dashing drapery of the Parisian belles, than to the elegant and becoming attire of our London beauties, who improve upon the French fashions. The winter is passed in a round of entertainments and amusements. The servants are mostly negroes or mulattoes; some free and others slaves. Marriages are conducted in the most splendid style, and form a most important part of the winter's entertainments. For three days after the marriage ceremony the newly married couple see company in great state. It is a sort of levee. Sometimes the night concludes with a concert and ball."

The governor and his lady keyed their entertainment to the London mode, and the colonials did their best, which often was good, to emulate those standards; though they were roused to resentment when Governor Cornbury gave a public impersonation of his cousin, Queen Anne, petticoats and all, and when, once too often, his avaricious wife asked for objects which she admired in other people's houses. Gaiety was more in key. Even at little Kingston Sir Francis Lovelace "spent an evening of great hilarity." At Dongan's invitation large house-parties assembled at the hunting lodge he used on Van Cortlandt Manor. And there were individual colonials who "cut a figure," as did Philip Livingston, who lived "with courtly magnificence" in the three "princely establishments" which he supported in New York, Albany and on his manor. Mrs. Lamb describes him as having been "dashing and gay; he had a winning way with women, and went about breaking hearts promiscuously."

With the English came, too, the theater. A license to act plays was given by the acting governor to one Richard Hunter about 1700, but it is not known that the eight hundred and eighteen families of all classes in New York Town furnished practical encouragement sufficient for Hunter to act on his license. However, the fact that there was a theater of sort in New York in 1732 is attested by this bit of correspondence from New York, dated December eleventh of that year and printed in the *New England and Boston Gazette:*

"On the 6th instant, the *New Theatre* in the building of the Hon. Rip Van Dam, Esq., was opened with the comedy of *The Recruiting Officer,* the part of Worthy acted by the ingenious Mr. Thos. Heady, Barber and Peruque maker to his Honor."

In 1769 the old John Street Theater entered upon its honorable career as the first permanent home of drama in New York, and it closed in 1774 on the Congress's recommendation to close all places of amusement. Other places of diversion grew up, among them two which opened in 1765: Ranlagh Gardens "For breakfasting, as well as the evening entertainment of Ladies and Gentlemen. . . . As an addition thereto, a compleat band of Musick . . . to perform every Monday and Thursday evenings"; and Vauxhall, advertised as "one of the pleasantest rural

Retreats near this City" and "situated on Greenwich Street, overlooking the Hudson River."

In Albany the drama had made its bow about the same time, on an amateur plane. "A private theater" was fitted up in a barn and the officers of the garrison, assisted by "some of the more estimable" young people of the town, gave a performance of *The Beaux Stratagem*. Although "great and loud was the outcry produced by it," the "converts to the new fashion" were so numerous that *The Recruiting Officer* was announced for another night. Up to this time Dominie Freylinghausen had been the local arbiter of morals. Yet, early on a Monday morning, after the dominie's Sunday tirade against the new form of deviltry, according to Mrs. Grant:

"Some unknown person left within his door a club, a pair of old shoes, a crust of black bread, and a dollar. The worthy pastor was puzzled to think what this could mean; but had it too soon explained to him. It was an emblematic message, to signify the desire entertained of his departure. The stick was to push him away, the shoes to wear on the road, and the bread and money a provision for his journey."

The good pastor took the hint to heart and sailed away on the first ship bound out of the river for Holland, announcing, however, that he would return in a short time. Far from that being in his mind, he seems to have planned another journey, for while his ship was at sea he disappeared and was never seen again.

With this sobering note and the recollection that the Congress had ordered the closing of all places of amusement, we close the brief story of the English period, and pass on to the days of the Revolutionary War when, the people's representatives having declared their colony to be free and independent, the English required them to bear arms for seven years to make it so.

CHAPTER V

THE REVOLUTION ON THE HUDSON

The River the Key of Britain's Entire War Plan—General Washington on the Hudson—Loyalists and Patriots—British Capture New York—Battle of the Tappan Sea—British Take Manhattan Island—First American Submarine—British Devastate the Shores of the Hudson—The Significance of the British Defeat at Saratoga—Defenses at West Point—Titanic Chain Stretched across the River to Block the British—"Mad" Anthony Wayne's Capture of Stony Point—*Aaron Burr's Wooing*—Treason of Benedict Arnold—Capture of Major André—Washington and the Continental Army at New Windsor and Newburgh—The Commander-in-Chief Refuses a Crown—Military Fêtes—Britain's First Salute to the Young Republic—Washington Repossesses New York City and Bids Farewell to His Officers.

HE Revolutionary War brought an unaccustomed activity to the landings along tidewater Hudson, and to the towns and detached homes behind them. No other equal area in any of the other thirteen original states saw so much of the Revolutionary Army and its great commander or of the British forces and their commanders.

The British seized New York City early, and held it for the entire seven years between the beginning of hostilities and the day that they reembarked and sailed back across the Atlantic. From the first they made it their fixed policy to seize the Hudson and to hold it as a wedge to divide the Revolutionary forces of New England and of the South, and to prevent such dismembered forces from communicating, much less cooperating, with each other. This forced Washington to hold the river at all costs to prevent that objective, and he, on his part, during the latter half of the war, kept as many of his army as possible on the Hudson so as to be able quickly to use it in the defense of the states to the east or to the south of it.

The major and most colorful events in the war, of which tidewater Hudson was the scene, were the British attack on New York and its seizure in 1776; the flight of Washington and his army, after the battle of White Plains, across the river and to the south; the British naval expedition up the river in 1777; the return of Washington and his army to the Hudson in 1778, when he crossed to its eastern shore again; the capture of Stony Point by "Mad" Anthony Wayne in 1779; the treason of Benedict Arnold and the execution of Major André in 1780; and Washington's frequent sojourns on the banks of the river, including his residence at Newburgh, which was for the longest continuous period of his adult life that he spent in any one place without frequent returns to Mount Vernon.

The patriot party along the Hudson had from the first a strong opposition from those who professed loyalty to the Crown. The loyalists in and about New York City were supported in their expediency or conviction by the British control there throughout the war. Flick in his study of loyalism in New York says of the character of that group:

"In character the loyalists have been judged too harshly on the one hand, and too leniently on the other. Most American historians have characterized them as unprincipled royal office-holders, scheming political trimmers, a few aristocratic landlords and merchants, who were fearful of losing their wealth and indifferent to the rights of man, together with their dependents, and the preachers and teachers of the Anglican church. Not a few English historians take this same view. These writers look upon them as a negative force in the revolutionary movement without any positive program and as unqualified supporters of England's conduct. The loyalists themselves and their apologists, on the contrary, have asserted that their ranks included all the best, the wealthiest, the most educated and those of highest social rank in the colony. Both of these views are partly right, but mostly wrong. Among the loyalists were all grades of worth and unworthiness, as among the Whigs."

In the composition of this group or party he cites: Royal officials, "led by self-interest, official bias, fidelity to oaths, and conviction of duty"; large landed proprietors, "at heart and by habit they were true aristocrats and denunciators of the democratic movement"; professional classes—lawyers, physicians, teachers and ministers, "some from a sense of duty, others because of a distrust of the success of the Revolution, a few through a hope of reward, and many on account of alliance with royal officials and the aristocracy"; conservative farmers in Winchester and Albany Counties, because "happy and prosperous under the old régime"; colonial politicians, "who neither cared for nor even saw any principle involved in the contest. They changed sides with the greatest ease as victory, and with it the hope of reward, passed from the English to the American side, or the reverse"; conservative masses, prompted by "loyalty, religion, interest or influence . . . they formed a large part of the loyalist soldiers and sailors, carried out the will of their leaders and made loyalism an efficient force in coping with the revolution." It was so, indeed, that the party was composed at the beginning of the war, but, later, others among them besides the colonial politicians "saw a light," as the British forces were gradually squeezed until finally they held only the cities of New York, Philadelphia and Charleston.

With this sort of opposition among the loyalists or Tories, the patriot party, or Whigs, composed in part of members of nearly all of those same classes, had a stiff fight to get support for their cause. The loyalists were in control of the Assembly.

There was no unanimous backing for the Continental Congress. In this situation the patriots called a Provincial Convention which met in New York City in April, 1775, and took over the functions of the Provincial Assembly and government, ignoring the governor and council. The further crystallization of the Revolutionary movement, as given impetus by events elsewhere, showed itself here by the issue of Paine's *Common Sense,* written and printed in New York; by the thwarted plot of British Governor Tryon to kill General Washington, and the hanging of Hickey, Tryon's principal tool, in the presence of twenty thousand people; and by the events following the proclamation of the Declaration of Independence. This Document was read by one of Washington's aides in the General's presence to a brigade of the Continental Army drawn up in a hollow square on the common in the vicinity of present City Hall Park. In the evening a crowd of soldiers and citizens went to Bowling Green and pulled down the statue of King George III. It was made of lead, which was converted into bullets for the use of the Continental soldiers.

The military activities of the British made their plan of campaign apparent soon thereafter. As the Hudson was the key to their whole scheme to crush the Revolution, they proposed to capture New York City and Albany and establish British posts along the river between these two communities. General Howe was to seize the city at the mouth of the river and move up its waters to fortify it as far as Albany, which another army was to descend on from the north, and capture.

The British regulars and their Hessian mercenaries had assembled in New York harbor by the middle of summer, 1776. There were thirty thousand such troops at the disposal of General Howe. Washington had anticipated the plan and had there or thereabout ready for the defense of the city an army of about twenty-seven thousand men, mostly militia, and a fourth of them were ill. Most of the American troops were on Manhattan Island. Other troops were concentrated for the defense of Brooklyn, of Powles' Hook where Jersey City later rose, and of King's Bridge across Spuyten Duyvil. The hulks of vessels were sunk between Governor's Island and the Battery, and chevaux-de-frise also were set there to prevent the passage of the East River.

Meantime defenses along the Hudson were prepared to check the advance of British war-ships up the river. Fort Washington on the east bank and Fort Lee on the west bank were established at points now practically at either end of the George Washington Bridge. Some of the other principal defenses were at Stony Point, Verplanck's Point, Fort Independence near the north lip of the mouth of Peekskill, Fort Clinton on the south and Fort Montgomery on the north sides of Popolopen Creek, Fort Arnold, Fort Putnam, Constitution Island and West Point; and fire-rafts which had been constructed at Poughkeepsie were floated down-river and anchored in a line between Anthony's Nose and Bear Mountain; all of which reflects the American intention to stop an advance up the river at the Highlands, if at all.

Howe's first offensive was to send his Majesty's war-ships *Rose* and *Phœnix* later in July up the Hudson to keep open communication with that British Army which he expected to effect a union with him from the north. These ships reached Tappan Zee without difficulty, but in Haverstraw Bay their efforts to land or to advance were foiled by militia which followed their advance on each shore, and by five American ships which sailed up the Tappan Zee on August third, the *Lady Washington,*

Spitfire, the *Shark,* the *Whiting* and the *Crown.* The American ships were the smaller, but they were well armed. An engagement took place immediately and lasted an hour and a half. Though there were many dead and wounded on each side, the result was not decisive. The Americans withdrew and, in spite of their fear of meeting British reenforcing ships, they sailed down-river to Spuyten Duyvil in safety. Two weeks later the two British ships dropped down-river and joined their fleet in the harbor. This battle of Tappan Zee was the only naval engagement in the Hudson, or for that matter elsewhere in northern waters, during the war.

Howe concentrated his first land attack on Long Island. The battle, fought on August twenty-seventh, was stubbornly but vainly contested by the Americans. Washington withdrew his troops to New York City. Howe next surrounded Manhattan Island with the fleet at his disposal. Washington scented the inevitable and withdrew from New York and established his headquarters at the deserted home of Robert Morris on Harlem Heights. Morris was a loyalist and had fled to the home of Beverley Robinson on the shore of the Hudson in the Highlands. After the war his house became the home of a celebrated character, Madame Jumel, widow of Aaron Burr, and has ever since been known as the Jumel Mansion. The British marched into New York and remained in possession of that city until the end of the war.

On his way north Washington stopped one day at the home of Robert Murray on Murray Hill, situated between the present Fourth and Fifth Avenues, Thirty-Sixth and Fortieth Streets; and one day at Mott's Tavern, near the present One-Hundred-and-Forty-Third Street and Eighth Avenue. At the Murray home Washington called a council of his officers and it was decided to send a spy into the British camp to report on their plans. Captain Nathan Hale was chosen for the service and here, and on this occasion, he received instructions for the expedition which cost him his life.

In the course of the next month Howe received reenforcement from ten thousand additional Hessians. He divided his army, concentrating part on Manhattan Island below Harlem, and sending another part into Westchester County to attack the Americans from the rear. The latter division was engaged with the Americans on October twenty-eighth when the battle of White Plains was begun. The Americans retreated from their position, and Washington put his main army safely across the Hudson, and encamped them between Fort Lee and Hackensack. Fort Washington was then the only point on Manhattan Island remaining in the hands of the Americans. It fell before the attack of the enemy on November sixteenth, two thousand American soldiers were made prisoners, and the British had accomplished the undisputed control of Manhattan Island. Writing to General Charles Lee, five days later, Washington said:

"Yesterday morning the Enemy landed a large Body of troops below Dobb's Ferry, and advanced very rapidly to the Fort called by Your Name. I immediately went over, and, as the Fort was not tenable on this side, and we were in a narrow neck of land, the passes out of which the enemy were attempting to seize, I directed the troops to move over to the west side of the Hackensack River."

Washington now went into winter quarters at Morristown. The British were in possession of the mouth of the Hudson, and there were no further military activities on the river for nearly a year.

In the midst of related but minor activities on the river meantime, we catch a glimpse of a curious contrivance for destruction in the pages of General Heath's Memoirs, published in 1798. Some American ships, among them the sloop *Turtle,* were sailing down-river on October ninth, when the *Turtle* was sunk by the enemy. The significance of this detached incident is that the sloop had on board, according to General Heath:

". . . the Machine invented by, and under the direction of, a Mr. Bushnell, intended to blow up the British ships. This machine was worked under water. It conveyed a magazine of powder, which was to be fixed under the keel of the ship, then freed from the machine, and left with clock-work going, which was to produce fire when the machine had got out of the way."

This David Bushnell was the inventor of the first American submarine, used against the English at the mouth of the Hudson.

Military activities in this first year of the war were not the only excitement provided by it on the river. While Washington moved his army about, the Assembly, or Convention, naturally had not remained stationary in New York. It became, indeed, a peripatetic body. As Howe came into New York, it moved out, and kept moving up the river, with brief sittings in Harlem, Kingsbridge, White Plains, Tarrytown, Fishkill, Poughkeepsie, and finally in Kingston.

The respite from active warfare during the winter and spring of 1776-77 gave the state of New York an opportunity to set its government in order. The Constitutional Convention met at Kingston and adopted the Constitution of the State of New York, practically as drafted by John Jay, later the first Chief

Justice of the Supreme Court of the United States. At the first election thereafter, in the May following, General George Clinton was elected governor and Pierre Van Cortlandt, lieutenant-governor; both Hudson River men. Clinton was elected vice-president of the United States in 1804 and again in 1808. The newly elected Legislature met this same spring at Kingston and elected Walter Livingston, another Hudson River man, to be its speaker.

The British made their supreme effort to divide the colonies and quickly to end the war, by seizing and fortifying the Hudson, in October, 1777. The Americans concentrated their effort to arrest this movement in the narrows of the Highlands near West Point. General Israel Putnam was in command of the area with headquarters at Peekskill. In addition to a chief dependence on the resistance of Forts Clinton, Montgomery and Constitution, however, a chain and boom was stretched across the river from Anthony's Nose to Bear Mountain, where it was in the defensive range of Fort Montgomery.

Burgoyne was well along on his march south past Lake Champlain to the capture of Albany, when, on October fourth, Sir Henry Clinton, with about four thousand men, embarked at New York City on two frigates, five or six square-rigged vessels and about forty flatboats and sailed up-river. He made feint landings at Tarrytown and Peekskill which were intended to deceive Putnam, and did. But when Governor George Clinton heard that the British were advancing up the river he at once came from Kingston with all available forces to the defense of the forts in the Highlands. He was too late. On the morning of the sixth, under cover of a heavy fog, Clinton had landed two thousand of his troops near Stony Point, and they were marched over the tangled defiles of Dunderberg to

Forts Clinton and Montgomery, twelve miles away. Meantime British ships broke the chain and boom stretched across the river, and advanced. In spite of a gallant defense by the Americans, the British captured both forts and so attained their immediate objective. At this moment, however, the British Commander received word that Burgoyne had been defeated at Saratoga. The capture of the Highlands was thus robbed of its significance.

The enemy were bent, however, on laying waste the Hudson Valley while the opportunity presented itself. With the river open before them, the British Commander sent northward, in the words of Lossing, "a flying squadron of light frigates, under Sir James Wallace, bearing three thousand six hundred men, under the command of General Vaughan, which sailed up the river. They were instructed to scatter desolation in their track, and well did they perform their mission. Every vessel upon the river was burned or otherwise destroyed; the houses of known Whigs, such as Henry Livingston, at Poughkeepsie, were fired upon from the ships; and small parties, landing from the vessels, desolated neighborhoods with fire and sword. They penetrated as far northward as Kingston, where they landed on the 13th of October. The frigates were anchored a little above the present landing on Kingston Point, and a portion of the invaders debarked in the cove north of the steam-boat wharf. Another division, in small boats, proceeded to the mouth of Esopus (now Rondout) Creek, and landed at a place a little northeast of Rondout village, called Ponkhocken Point. The people at the creek fled, affrighted, to Marbletown, seven miles southwest of Kingston, and their houses were destroyed. The two divisions then marched toward the village, one by the upper road and the other by the Esopus Creek Road. . . . Almost

116

Courtesy of the Gallery of Fine Arts,
Yale Univ.

ALEXANDER HAMILTON

From the Original Portrait by Gilbert Stuart

CHANCELLOR LIVINGSTON

GEORGE CLINTON

From "John Stevens, an American Record"
by Archibald Douglas Turnbull, published
by The Century Co.

JOHN STEVENS

MAJOR ANDRÉ'S PRISON HOUSE, TAPPAN

THE MONUMENT MARKING THE SPOT WHERE MAJOR ANDRÉ
WAS EXECUTED

every house was laid in ashes, and a large quantity of provisions and stores situated there and at the landing was destroyed. . . . The enemy, however, fearing their wanton cruelty would bring the people in mass upon them, hastily retreated after destroying the village. A detachment crossed the river and marched to Rhinebeck Flats, two miles eastward, where they burned several houses; and, after penetrating northward as far as Livingston's Manor, and burning some houses there," they dropped down-river and rejoined the fleet, which then returned to the mouth of the river.

The conquest of the Hudson might well have proved the turning-point of the war in favor of the British had it not been for Burgoyne's defeat at Saratoga. As it was, the events of October, 1777, proved the turning-point of the war in favor of the Americans. Not only were they heartened by the failure of the British plan, but their prestige rose in Europe, and they found that they were a matter of interest to France.

Nevertheless, the British having relinquished the fruits of their success in the Highlands, it was not proposed that another effort there should meet with similar success. West Point was again selected as the position best tenable and the thorough fortification of the river at this point was ordered. Washington was equally solicitous and emphatic that this should be done. The old Fort Clinton at Bear Mountain was abandoned, and a new Fort Clinton was erected at West Point. Other forts near it were Webb, Wyllys and Putnam. In connection with these defenses, the experiment of locking the river with a gate of booms, which had failed at Anthony's Nose, was again under-taken in a more thorough and interesting manner, this time where the river is only three-eighths of a mile wide between Constitution Island and West Point. This time the barrage of booms across the river was secondary to a double strand of great iron chains supported and held in place by a series of transverse booms.

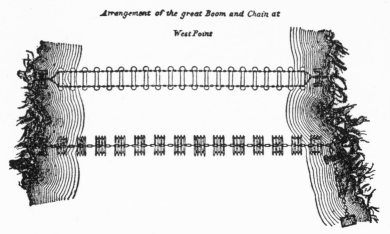

Arrangement of the great Boom and Chain at

West Point

George Clinton wrote General Gates in November, 1777:

"I know of no other method of obstructing the passage of Hudson's River, but by Chevaux-de-frise, Chains, and Booms, well defended by heavy artillery and strong works on the shore. The former is impracticable at any place lower down than where the present are, near this place; and even there, the river is rather too wide to admit of their being properly defended; they may, however, when completed, be a very considerable obstruction. This with a chain or boom, at a part of the river called the West Point, where it is quite narrow, and the wind, owing to the crookedness of the river, very uncertain, with proper works on the shore to defend it, and water-batteries on shore calculated to annoy shipping, would, in my opinion, perfectly obstruct the navigation."

The point, as to catching ships coming up-river at a disadvantage here, was well made as is obvious to any one who knows these waters. The river makes a sharp right-angle turn to the west, around West Point, where the waters in the Highlands are narrowest and the surrounding mountains are apt either to lessen the wind or to render its course inconstant.

The chains were constructed by the Sterling Iron Works in the western corner of Rockland County, about five miles southwest of Sloatsburgh and thirteen miles from the Hudson. The specifications called for "an iron chain of the following dimensions and quality: that is, in length five hundred yards, each link about two feet long, to be made of the best Sterling iron, two inches and one quarter square, or as near thereto as possible, with a swivel to every hundred feet, and a clevis to every thousand feet, in the same manner as the former chain, . . . also . . . twelve tons of anchors."

The links and other forged appurtenances of the chain were transported overland, on roads paralleling the west bank of the river, from the iron-works to New Windsor, a few miles above West Point. Here it was put together in two strands with logs attached to it at short intervals to buoy the chains and hold them parallel, and with the anchors designed to give it stability against the winds and tides and currents. So it was floated down-river to its proposed position where it was finally made fast, the latter part of April. This double chain remained in position, whenever the river was navigable, to the end of the war. Each winter, as the period approached when it was expected that the river would be frozen over, or gutted with broken ice, the chain was drawn, by windlass, up to a safe position on the West Point shore.

There are a number of questionable traditions regarding this celebrated chain. According to one of them Governor Clinton walked across the Hudson on this chain, and the same claim is found in the narrative of others. This, however, is not improbable. Boynton, in his history of West Point, remarked that

such statements "are easily reconciled by substituting the word
Boom for that of Chain. The Boom could readily be converted
into a bridge, and it is not improbable that in its construction
reference was had to this object, as it would afford facilities
for the transport of troops from one side of the river to the
other." Another tradition refers to a treasonable weakening of
the chain by the removal of one of its links, so as to let the
enemy's vessels through. But that, far from having been
proved, is held to have been forbiddingly impractical.

Washington came to the Hudson again that summer. In
mid-June the British withdrew eleven thousand troops from
Philadelphia and began a northward march across New Jersey,
with Washington, emerging from his winter at Valley Forge,
in pursuit. The two armies clashed at Monmouth without
advantage to either side. The British then made a forced night
march, crossed the Hudson and attained security in New York
City.

Washington's forces pushed forward and on July fifteenth
reached Haverstraw on the Hudson. The next day the General
visited West Point to view the new defenses there. He was
greeted with thirteen cannon, the number of the then new
states. Returning to Haverstraw, he saw the transfer of the last
of his soldiers over the river at King's Ferry, whose eastern terminus was on Verplanck's Point, below Peekskill, on the nineteenth. The next day he settled in camp at White Plains. While
there he journeyed up-river to visit the hospital commander at
the Robinson house, opposite West Point, and farther up to
Fishkill, where generally he quartered at the home of Colonel
John Brinckerhoff, or that gentleman's nephew, Colonel Derrick
Brinckerhoff. Washington's fixed headquarters remained at
White Plains until he went into winter quarters at Middlebrook,

New Jersey. The army meantime was deployed in camps extending from that place across the Hudson as far as Danbury, Connecticut. Winter quarters on or near the river were established at Smith's Clove, West Point, Fishkill and Continental Village. Washington anticipated the British Army might move out of New York, but unadvised as to what direction they might take, he disposed his army so as to have troops available to come to the defense of New England as well as of New Jersey and of the Hudson Valley.

Once more this winter, in December, Washington started for the Hudson when he heard that the enemy were again on their way up-river. On the seventh he wrote Governor William Livingston, of New Jersey:

"I have returned to this place [Paramus, west of Haverstraw] from Elisabethtown, upon hearing that the enemy had gone up the North River, in considerable force. Their ships proceeded as far as King's Ferry, but they yesterday fell down again."

Five days later he wrote Joseph Reed:

"Sir Harry's later extra manœuvre up the North River kept me upon the march and countermarch from the 5th till yesterday, when I arrived at these very quarters for the winter, and employed too much of my attention to investigate his designs, to indulge in more agreeable amusements."

Washington spent the entire summer and fall of 1779 watching the possible moves of the British who were concentrated in New York. He moved the army over toward the Hudson and made his headquarters at New Windsor from June twenty-first to July twenty-first, and at West Point thereafter until November twenty-eighth, when he retired to winter quarters at Morristown.

This spring the British had taken Stony Point, on the west shore below Dunderberg, and Fort LaFayette, on Verplanck's Point opposite. King's Ferry, which connected these two points, was of inestimable value to Washington, for the principal road out of New England, available to the Americans, came through Peekskill and terminated at Verplanck's. Its continuation west and south on the opposite side of the river began at Stony Point. The paralleling alternate way across the river was at Fishkill, was cruder and was much longer. Hence, on July ninth, Washington wrote General Anthony Wayne:

"While the enemy are making excursions to distress the country, it has a very disagreeable aspect to remain in a state of inactivity on our part. The reputation of the army, and the good of the service, seem to exact some attempt from it. The importance of Stony Point to the enemy makes it infinitely desirable, that this post could be the object. The works are formidable, but perhaps on a fuller examination they may be found accessible. . . . I beg you to inform yourself all you can, and to give me your opinion of the practicability of an attempt upon this post. If it is undertaken, I should conceive it ought to be done by way of surprise in the night."

He wrote Wayne again on the fourteenth:

"I have reflected on the advantages and disadvantages of delaying the proposed attempt [on Stony Point], and I do not know but the latter preponderate. You will therefore carry it into execution to-morrow night, as you desire, unless some new motive or better information should induce you to think it best to defer it."

Two days later he had it spread on the Order Book:

"The Commander-in-Chief is happy to congratulate the army on the success of our arms under Brig. Gen. Wayne, who last night, with the corps of light infantry, surprised and took the enemy's post at Stony Point, with the whole garrison, cannon and stores, with very inconsiderable loss on our side."

Wayne and his men took Stony Point swiftly and heroically against great odds in what has been called "the most brilliant exploit of the war." It heartened all Americans, civilian as well as military, and it served notice on the British that they had an alert and vigorous foe. The exploit did not open the short route across the river between New England and the South, however, for Washington did not retake Verplanck's Point or feel confident of holding Stony Point. Wayne's was, indeed, a brilliant exploit, but it was crowned with no more than a moral victory.

Another figure, conspicuous in the American story, made his appearance as a military character on the river the previous winter. He was a youth of twenty-two years, who had entered the army as a private two years earlier and now held the rank of lieutenant-colonel. His name was Aaron Burr.

He had command of the outposts stretching east from Tarrytown to the Bynam River, but immediately found that his troops were more interested in loot than in service. The method he was directed in orders to use to occupy the hands of these offenders against patriots and loyalists alike and prevent their running away, was as ingenious as it was amusing:

"Handcuffs will be furnished you as soon as they can be made. If you have a number of prisoners at any time to send up, let them be fastened right and left hands, and the guards cut the strings of their breeches, and there will be no danger of their making their escape, as they will be obliged to hold them up continually with one hand."

Burr's military career was less satisfactory than his romantic experiences while here. He was fretting under Washington's refusal to have him a member of his staff because even then Washington read his character and "mistrusted" him, and he resigned in March, 1779, and took up the law.

Meanwhile he had made the acquaintance of a Mrs. Theodosea Prevost, the widow of a British officer. She lived with her mother about ten miles west of the river at Paramus, in New Jersey. She was ten years older than Burr, but he fell deeply in love with her, crossed the Hudson many times to woo her and finally married her. These crossings were made the subject of Edmund Clarence Stedman's poem, *"Aaron Burr's Wooing":*

"From the commandant's quarters on Westchester height
The blue hills of Ramapo lie in full sight;
On their slope gleam the gables that shield his heart's queen,
But the red-coats are wary—The Hudson's between.
Through the camp runs a jest: 'There's no moon—'twill be dark;
'Tis odds little Aaron will go on a spark!'
And the toast of the troopers is: Pickets, lie low,
And good luck to the colonel and Widow Prevost.'

"Eight miles to the river he gallops his steed,
Lays him bound in a barge, bids the escort make speed,
Loose their swords, sit athwart, though the fleet reach yon shore
Not a word—not a splash of the thick-muffled oar!
Once across, once again in the seat and away—
Five leagues are soon over when love has the say;
And 'Old Put' and his rider a bridle path know
To the Hermitage manor of Madame Prevost."

In the course of the late summer of 1780 the river was the scene of one of the most famous and vital episodes affecting the destiny of the American people. At that time Washington was awaiting the arrival of the second division of the French fleet and one of his contemplated moves was to make a concerted effort to recapture New York City. The British, still held at bay south of the Highlands of the Hudson by the great stronghold at West Point, which they did not cease to covet, were probably not unaware of the coming of the French, or of Washington's hopes. In these circumstances they planned a swift, easy and surprising scheme to capture West Point and control the length of the tidal river, and so divide the American forces and communications, and finish either remnant of their enemy at their own convenience. The failure of this scheme revealed the treason of General Benedict Arnold and culminated in the hanging of Major André.

Arnold was at that time in command of "a corps of invalids" at West Point, and he made his home on the opposite shore in the Beverley Robinson house. General Washington was absent on the Connecticut River, at Hartford, consulting with Count de Rochambeau, Admiral de Ternay and other French officers. The moment for the delivery of West Point seemed propitious, for the British already had entered into an agreement with Arnold, made on his initiative, that, for the sum of fifty thousand dollars in gold and a brigadier-general's commission in the British Army, he would surrender "the Gibraltar of the Hudson."

A meeting between Arnold and Major André, Clinton's adjutant, to arrange the time and final details of the treachery, was effected on the night of September twentieth–twenty-first. André, who had conducted the preliminary correspondence with Arnold, came up the Hudson aboard H.M.S. *Vulture* on September twentieth. After dark, he disembarked on the west shore between Haverstraw and Stony Point, his uniform concealed under an enveloping greatcoat.

Arnold met André on the shore and there they conferred until dawn, when he induced the British officer to accompany him to the house of his friend, Joshua Hett Smith, near by, for the continuation of the conference. Although André was

ignorant of the fact, Smith's house was inside the America
lines. The conference there lasted until nightfall. Arnol
agreed so to weaken the defense of West Point by his disposi
tion of its defenders that it would be unable to resist the Brit
ish attack, and he would make an early and plausible surrende
He signed a pass for André which read: "Permit Mr. Joh
Anderson to pass the guards to the White Plains or below, i
he chooses, he being on public business. B. Arnold, M.G."

Other than this André, when he set out to return to hi
ship, carried no papers except the notes regarding the positio
and defense of West Point and its supporting posts, which h
placed inside his stockings under the soles of his feet. He ex
changed his uniform for a suit of Smith's civilian clothes.

Meantime, however, the *Vulture* had been under fire from
Teller's Point on the opposite shore and had been obliged t
drop some distance down-river. As a result André was oblige
to undertake to get down-river and back within the British line
by a land route. Smith put him across to the eastern shor
of the river where André secured a horse and rode south alon
the Albany Post Road toward Tarrytown.

He was now about to traverse some sixteen miles of what wa
loosely known as "neutral territory." To the point of the sub
sequent episode, it was at least so much so, that it was the pre
of both the so-called Cowboys and Skinners. The former wer
loyalists who preyed upon Westchester County farmers fo
their cattle which they drove down-river into the British line
and sold to their own obvious profit. The Skinners were mem
bers of an equally if not more nefarious band of pretende
patriots who preyed on the same people in the alleged interest o
the American Army farther up-river. André is cited as havin
been nervous in passing through this zone but felt that "Joh

nderson's" pass would see him safely past the Skinners, and is true character would, of course, enable him to pass any owboys.

A little way outside of Tarrytown, as he approached that illage, he passed three young American militiamen; by name, ohn Paulding, David Williams and Isaac Van Wert. Pauld-ig had recently been a prisoner in the British lines where he ad been stripped of his own jacket and given a worn-out British :ooper's scarlet tunic, which inclined André to believe him to e a Cowboy, at least, if not a Britisher.

In his testimony, given later, as to what then transpired on ie morning of that September twenty-third, Paulding said: We saw several persons we were acquainted with, whom we :t pass. Presently one of the young men who were with me, aid, 'There comes a gentleman-like looking man who appears o be well dressed and has boots on, and whom you had better tep out and stop, if you don't know him.' (The party must ave observed André rising the hill out of Sleepy Hollow; vhen first observed, he was walking his horse.) On that, I ;ot up and presented my firelock at the breast of the person nd told him to stand, and then I asked him which way he was ;oing? 'Gentlemen,' said he, 'I hope you belong to our party.' asked him what party. He said 'the lower party.' Upon that, told him I did. Then he said, 'I am a British officer out of the ·ountry on particular business, and I hope you will not detain ne a minute;' and to show that he was a British officer he pulled ut his watch, upon which I told him to dismount. He then .aid, 'My God! I must do anything to get along,' and seemed to nake a kind of laugh of it, and pulled out General Arnold's ·ass, which was to John Anderson to pass all the guards to White Plains and below; upon that he dismounted. Said he,

'Gentlemen, you had best let me go, or you will bring yourselves into trouble; for your stopping me will detain the General's business,' and said he was going to Dobbs Ferry to meet a person there and get intelligence for General Arnold."

But the three Americans were not satisfied. They required "John Anderson" to step into the woods where they searched him and eventually, in his stocking under his soles, they discovered the incriminating papers in the handwriting of both Arnold and André, revealing the details of the defense of West Point and its vulnerability. They did not quite realize the importance of their quarry. But they marched him to North Castle, the nearest military post, twelve miles northeast of Tarrytown, and delivered him to its commander, Colonel Jameson.

André protested to him that he was "John Anderson," an American; showed Arnold's pass; and begged him to get word to General Arnold, his commander, at West Point, that, in spite of the fact that he bore the General's pass, he was detained as a prisoner. Jameson was so ingenuous as to accede to this request.

Washington, accompanied by Knox, LaFayette, and his own aide, Colonel Alexander Hamilton, returning to the Hudson from Hartford on the morning of September twenty-fifth, sent Colonel Hamilton on to Robinson House to tell General and Mrs. Arnold that they would take lunch with them that day and were meantime detained inspecting some fortifications.

Just before the noon hour the courier arrived with the message which Colonel Jameson forwarded from "John Anderson." Arnold understood that he was undone and realized that his life depended on his reaching the protection of the British flag. Mrs. Arnold received the bitter facts from her husband, whereupon he rushed to the river-landing where his six-oared barge was moored, drew his pistols and ordered his men to row with all speed down-river, as he was on "a mission of the greatest urgency for General Washington." He found the *Vulture,* which was his objective, off Teller's Point, and there he received the security of the British Commander and proceeded to New York. He soon afterward went to London where he spent nearly all his remaining days until he died there in 1801.

Meantime, Washington and his party had arrived at Arnold's quarters, at the hour of their appointment for luncheon, to be told the shocking story of the perfidy of one of the Commander's leading officers, only an hour after the traitor's escape.

André and Smith, who also had been apprehended at Fishkill, were brought first to the Robinson house and thence were taken down-river to Tappan, a village behind the north end of the Palisades on the Jersey shore, at the time headquarters of the American Army. There he was imprisoned. Washington had reached Tappan by this time. André was given a military trial on the twenty-ninth by a board of fourteen general officers and was condemned to die by hanging at noon, October second; and was then so executed.

Smith, too, was tried by court martial, which, however, failed to convict him. He was then turned over to the civil authorities, but escaped from jail, made his way to New York in the disguise of a woman, accompanied the British troops to England at the close of the war, but returned to die in New York City in the year 1818.

Washington spent the winter and spring of 1780-81 in headquarters at New Windsor, a few miles south of Newburgh. Here he occupied the William Ellison house, demolished early in the last century, and made frequent visits to West Point,

Fishkill, Peekskill and other near-by points. Later in the summer he moved down to Dobbs Ferry, where he was joined by the French troops from Rhode Island and prepared for an attack on the British in New York. For this he depended on the arrival and cooperation of the French fleet, under De Grasse from the West Indies. But word soon arrived that De Grasse had instead put into the Chesapeake. From that moment the campaign against Cornwallis in Virginia was under way.

He wrote to LaFayette on July thirtieth: "I think we have already effected one part of the plan of the campaign settled at Weatherfield; that is giving a substantial relief to the southern States, by obliging the enemy to recall a considerable part of their force from thence."

During the last days of August the American and French Armies crossed the river at King's Ferry and began the march which terminated at Yorktown. The Commander-in-Chief left the Hudson for the York, full of hope. The culmination of that march was the defeat and surrender of Cornwallis on October nineteenth, and the cessation of hostilities.

Thereafter, Washington held as many as possible of his army together until news arrived in March, 1783, that the treaty between Great Britain and America had been signed at Paris. During this interim he assembled the army in camp on the west bank of the Hudson, in the neighborhood of Newburgh, and made his headquarters there on the banks of the river at the Hasbrouck house from March 31, 1782, until August 18, 1783.

The sojourn at Newburgh covered a period of many amenities. Mrs. Washington spent the whole period with her husband. It was an interval of comparative relaxation for the General who found time to indulge in his favorite diversions of

Courtesy of The American Science and Historic Preservation Society

THE HASBROUCK HOUSE AT NEWBURGH
General Washington's Headquarters

"The Room of Seven Doors and One Window" in Washington's Headquarters at Newburgh

dancing, card-playing and fox-hunting, to make visits to other points on the river, and to receive frequent addresses from a grateful citizenry for his successful conduct and termination of the war. As fishing was never one of his diversions it is to be presumed that he did not go "a-whale-hunting on the Hudson," on the famous midsummer expedition organized by General Von Steuben at his headquarters at Mount Giulian across the river, when the German's "whale" turned out to be an eel.

The first major event after Washington took up his residence at Newburgh was the so-called "offer of a crown." The suggestion that the head of the new state, which a victorious war had assured and which circumstances indicated Washington would be called upon to head, should have the title of king came in a letter from Lewis Nicola, colonel of a corps of invalids. Whether he represented himself merely or a considerable party in the army has since been a matter of controversy. There was no indefiniteness, however, in the terms of Washington's reply to the suggestion:

"With a mixture of great surprise and astonishment I have read with attention the Sentiments you have submitted to my perusal. Be assured, Sir, no occurrence in the course of the war has given me more painful sensations than your information of their being such ideas existing in the Army as you have expressed, and I must view with abhorrence and reprehend with severity. . . . I am much at a loss to conceive what part of my conduct could have given encouragement to an address which to me seems big with the greatest mischiefs that can befall my Country. If I am not deceived in the knowledge of myself, you could not have found a person to whom your schemes were more disagreeable."

More agreeable to the General were two occasions when he went down-river; one in September to Verplanck's Point and

the other the following spring to Dobbs Ferry. The former
trip was made to join the American Army encamped there and
do honor to Rochambeau's French soldiers who had recently
reached the Hudson from Yorktown. He reviewed the French
Army on the twentieth. The next day was made gala in honor
of our allies. One of the French officers wrote of it:

"This day the Americans were under arms. . . . Their
camp was covered with garlands and pyramids, as so many
trophies gratefully raised by the hands of liberty. The army
was drawn up at the head of their camp. Twenty-four battal
ions of the states of New Jersey, Massachusetts, Rhode Island
Connecticut, and New York formed a line of two miles extent
The most exact uniformity, the neat dress of the men, the
glittering of their arms, their martial look, and a kind of mili
tary luxury gave a most magnificent appearance to this assem
blage of citizens armed in defence of their country. . . . A
discharge of cannon was the signal for manœuvering. That
exactness, order and silence which distinguish veteran armies
was here displayed: they changed their front, formed and dis
played columns, with admirable regularity. The day was ter
minated with an entertainment of more than ninety covers
served with true military magnificence in the pretorium of the
consul (for I rather express myself thus than by saying in the
tent of the general). In fact, everything in this army bears a
particular character; and things uncommon ought not to be
described by common expressions. A band of American music
which played during the dinner, added to the gaiety of the
company."

The trip to Dobbs Ferry in the May following was for a
conference with Sir Guy Carleton in relation to the evacuation
of the British troops. Washington was rowed down the Hudson in his barge, attended by a sloop. Sir Guy came up the
river to meet him in a sloop of war. The conferences are said
to have been held at the Van Brugh Livingston house.

Not the least pleasing feature of the occasion were the hon-

rs accorded to the American Commander-in-Chief on the oc-
asion of a dinner on a British war-ship anchored opposite
Dobbs Ferry. When he went aboard, accompanied by Governor
Clinton, he was saluted "with the firing of a number of cannon,"
ut when he left the ship "she fired seventeen guns," in honor
of Washington's exalted military rank. This honor, here on
he Hudson, was of particular significance because "it was the
irst complimentary salute fired by Great Britain in honor of an
officer of the United States and virtually the first salute to the
nation."

The General embarked on July sixteenth and ascended the
river to Albany, and went thence on a visit to Ticonderoga,
Crown Point and other historic places; a journey, as he proudly
wrote McHenry on his return to Newburgh, "of at least seven
hundred and fifty miles, performed in nineteen days."

This sojourn at Newburgh had not been wholly one of relaxation tinctured with trips and celebrations. Anxiety had
continually stalked in the background of Washington's mind.
On one occasion (July 10, 1782) he had written John Laurens:

"Sir Guy Carleton is using every art to soothe and lull our
people into a state of security. Admiral Digby is capturing all
our vessels, and suffocating as fast as possible in prison-ships
all our seamen, who will not enlist into the service of his Britan-
nic Majesty; and Haldimand [Governor-General of Quebec]
with his savage allies, is scalping and burning on the frontiers.
Such is the line of conduct pursued by the different commanders,
and such their politics."

And a little later (September 12, 1782) he had written these
famous lines to McHenry:

"That the King will push the war, as long as the nation will
find men and money, admits not of a doubt in my mind. The

133

whole tenor of his conduct . . . shows the impolicy of relaxation on our part. If we are wise, let us prepare for the worst. There is nothing, which will so soon produce a speedy and honorable peace, as a state of preparation for war; and we must either do this, or lay our account to patch up an inglorious peace, after all the toil, blood, and treasure we have spent."

The last incidents of the Revolutionary War were consummated at the mouth of the Hudson. They were the evacuation of the British troops and loyalist civilians and the triumphal entry of Washington and his army into New York City.

Washington came down from West Point in mid-November, 1783. "On Friday, the 21st of November," said the *Pennsylvania Journal,* "arrived at Haerlem at Day's Tavern [near the corner of the present One-Hundred-and-Twenty-Fifth Street and Eighth Avenue] nine miles from the city of New York, his Excellency General Washington, and his Excellency George Clinton, Esq., Governor of that State." The party remained there over Sunday. On the morning of the twenty-fifth the American troops marched "from Haerlem to the Bowery Lane," according to the same *Journal.* "They remained there [near the present junction of Third Avenue and the Bowery] until about one o'clock, when the British troops left the post in the Bowery, and the American troops marched in and took possession of the city.—After the troops had taken possession of the City the General and Governor made their public entry in the following manner :—Their excellencies the general and governor with their suites on horseback. The lieutenant governor, and the members of the council for the temporary government of the southern district four a-breast.—Major-general Knox, and the officers of the army, eight a-breast.—Citizens on horseback, eight a-breast.—The speaker of the assembly, and citizens, on foot, eight a-breast. . . . The procession proceeded down

Queen [now Pearl Street,] and through the Broad-way to *Cape's* Tavern. The governor gave a public dinner at Fraunces's tavern; at which the commander in chief, and other general officers were present."

Such bald and literal statements but little reflect either the spectacular features or the emotions of the occasion. It was not only the end of a long discouraging war, but the day definitely gave the land into the undisputed possession of Americans.

One other affecting event, related to all that had gone before, took place here in New York on December fourth, when Washington took formal leave of the principal officers of the army at a dinner in Fraunces's Tavern. Having filled his glass with wine, the General rose and bade farewell to his companions in arms with this toast: "With a heart full of love and gratitude I now take leave of you. I most devoutly wish that your later days may be as prosperous and happy as your former ones have been glorious and honorable."

After each officer had come forward and made a personal leave-taking with his Commander-in-Chief, Washington left the room, walked to Whitehall through lines of saluting soldiery, to the accompaniment of cheering crowds, descended into a barge and was carried across the mouth of the Hudson to Powles' Hook; whence he made his way south to Mount Vernon.

CHAPTER VI

DURING THE NINETEENTH CENTURY

Evolution of Transportation—Old Sailing Days—Ferry-Boats—Advent of Steam—Stevens and Fulton—First Passenger Steamboats—The *Phœnix* and the *Clermont*—The Erie Canal Unites the Hudson and the Great Lakes—A Canal-Boat Pageant from Buffalo to New York— Stage-Coaches and Shore Travel—A West Shore Trip to Albany in 1831—Speeding General Winfield Scott from New York to Albany by Sleigh Overnight—Advent of the Steam Railroads on the River's Shore—The Golden Age along the River—Millionaires, Statesmen, Writers and Painters—Nature Prevails over Population.

FTER the Revolutionary War, tidewater Hudson entered upon a wholly new epoch, in which its expansion of population and of activity about the landings, from mouth up to tide's end, increased with slow and measured pace, but led eventually, after ten other decades, into the golden age of life along the river.

The dawn of the post-Revolutionary period found life on the river ambling along at about the same casual gait it had held for a century previous. But leisurely as life appeared in the first decades after the English left, the forces were at work which developed the river's destiny. Pioneering on the river was a thing of the past. This generation of pioneers pushed north and west beyond the tidal waters. As their numbers multiplied, their needs increased. Though this was not the single influence which made the valley of tidewater Hudson what eventually it became, it was the first great such influence of man's making and it was the constant in the ratio of the river's development,

136

for the dependence of those in the hinterland on the sea and its great estuary spurred those on its shores to epic efforts and results.

Nature fixed the first factor in the destiny of the river when, eons before history, in those dimly remote days, when, in process of cosmic adjustments, the mountains opened here as nowhere else along this Atlantic litoral and gave entrance far inland to the waters of the sea. The latest influencing factors were of man's own making. They were the use of the Hudson's course as a part of an inland waterway from the ocean to the western-most reach of the Great Lakes, and practically contemporaneous with it, the development of the use of steam as power and the successful harnessing of it to vehicular transportation.

The Dutch and English periods now gave way to political, geographical, scientific and cultural influences and developments which produced the American period. Now the people along the river held their political destinies entirely in their own hands. Now the impulse to material advancement began to come from the West instead of from the East, from the newly peopled western frontiers instead of from across the eastern sea, from within instead of from without. The scientific inventions which transformed the economy of transportation were made here by American savants. A new life evolved which swept up to in-ordinate heights of nabobbery, but on its way developed a new cultured class in a long list of writers, artists, scientists, edu-cators and other intellectuals.

The evolution of the latest phase of life along the river seems best expressed, and most graphically realized, in the story of transportation on its waters and on its shores. The lives of people appear to take their stride from the velocity of their vehicles. Until well into the nineteenth century movement on the river was paced by sails bellied by the fickle breezes; along the shores, by the strength and speed of horses, so it happened that life was deliberate; its margins of leisure were broad.

There was a peculiar kind of romance and spectacle here in the old sailing days. At the mouth of the river a forest of masts extended along the water-fronts on both shores, rising out of the hulls of ships which habitually beat about the world to every port but principally to England, a voyage they often made in twenty days, scarcely more than a third of the time consumed by their voyage in this direction against gales and Gulf Stream when, indeed, they were not driven to a securer course farther south by way of the West Indies and thence up, with the aid of favoring wind and current. All ships in port did not tie up at docks. A good proportion of the vessels anchored out in the stream, swinging about with the varying tides and making the river seem more thickly sprinkled with ships then than now.

Farther up, in Zuider Zee, it was not uncommon to be able to count one hundred sailing ships in sight at once. Some were schooners, some were sloops, some the brave square-rigged three-, four-, or six-masters from off all of the seven seas. The square-riggers often, by reason of rows of square black port-holes for deck-guns, affected a fierceness which, if they were put to it, they could not sustain, for such "portholes" were only painted on to deceive the pirates on the Spanish Main and in other insecure waters. The Hudson sloops were renowned for the enormous quantity of sail they carried. When they weighed anchor and unfurled their white canvas to the breeze they often moved up-river in little fleets of from six to a dozen sail, as Willis wrote:

". . . all scudding or tacking together, like so many white sea birds on the wing. Up they come, with a dashing breeze, under Anthony's Nose, and the sugar loaf, and giving the rocky toe of West Point a wide berth, all down helm and round into the bay: when—just as the peak of Crow Nest slides its shadow over the mainsail—slap comes the wind aback and the whole fleet is in a flutter. The channel is narrow and serpentine, the wind baffling, and small room to beat: but the craft are worked merrily and well; and dodging about as if to escape some invisible imp of the air they gain point after point till at last they get the Dunderbarrck behind them and fall once more into the regular current of the wind."

The passenger-bearing vessels were those sloops which sailed between New York and Albany. Such a lengthy trip as this entire course was one not lightly to be undertaken. It was a matter of more days than a fast liner takes between this and the European coast to-day. Irving, describing such a trip made by him in 1800, said:

"The constant voyaging in the river craft by the best families of New York and Albany, made the merits of captains and sloops matters of notoriety and discussion in both cities. The captains were mediums of communication between separated friends and families. On the arrival of one of them at either place he had messages to deliver and commissions to execute which took him from house to house. Some of the ladies of the family had, peradventure, made a trip on board of his sloop, and experienced from him that protecting care which is always remembered with gratitude by female passengers. In this way the captains of Albany sloops were personages of more note in the community than captains of European packets or steam ships at the present day."

The skipper of Irving's sloop was of old Dutch stock of Albany, his crew were entirely blacks and, curiously, such a captain gave his orders to the blacks in the Dutch language, which they understood. The length of the trip was more than double the length of its sailing time, for the daylight stops were made at the landings to embark and disembark freight and passengers or to market for milk and eggs and vegetables and for fish newly out of the seines of the fishermen for the ship's mess, and as darkness fell the crew furled the sails and dropped anchor, and the sloop swung idly with the tide until daylight returned, and the course and other carriers in it were again visible.

Even in these days not by any means all of the water vehicles sailed lengthwise of the river. A goodly proportion made a course east and west. These were the ferries plying from shore to shore, a traffic which seemed always to have been a lively feature of this water's life. The Hudson's great width has defied all but the latest and most powerful facilities of the contemporary engineer for bridging it. It not only separated neighbors along shore with commercial and civil interests in common but there it lay, a north and south barrier one hundred and fifty miles long between manufacturing New England and its market, the widening area of western agricultural development.

The first ferries were canoes, then came oared boats, after them the sail-drawn vessels, sometimes called "Periaguas" when they were flat-bottomed and struck their masts. Then in the first days of the nineteenth century the fleet of ferries was joined by a "magnificent vessel," which never had name other than "horse boat," but in one aspect was akin to the catamaran. It consisted of two boats measuring eighty by thirty feet over all with some sort of a connection or platform abeam which supported a water-wheel, the power to turn it being furnished by four horses aboard.

But the doom of horse and sail for the power of watercraft had been in the making for some time at the dawn of the century. The study of steam and its application to water navigation had made definite progress. Scientifically it was alive only in the consciousness of savants. Practically it received its first commercial demonstration and leaped into the public consciousness here on the Hudson in August, 1807, when the *Clermont,* a steamboat designed by Robert Fulton and built under his direction, made its celebrated trip from New York to Albany.

Although Robert Fulton's *Clermont* seems to exist in the popular consciousness vaguely as the first steamboat ever to have been invented, built and operated, this is not the fact, nor is it so assumed by careful chroniclers of Fulton's great achievements. A great invention rarely springs full-fledged from the brain of any one man. Rather, and almost invariably, it is the result of the imagination, study and ingenuity of several individuals, each of whom will have made some contribution to the ultimate result. The invention of the steamboat will always be associated with the genius and initiative of five men: Rumsey on the Potomac, Symington on the Forth and Clyde Canal, Fitch on the Delaware, and John Stevens and Fulton on the Hudson.

Fulton's advantage over the others was not wholly as a marine engineer or ship designer, but also largely in the fact that he had a sound commercial and executive instinct. He beat others in securing backing, and it was also his luck to have as his backer not merely a rich man but one of the most prominent and astute legal minds of his generation. He found his Mæcenas here on the Hudson in the person of Chancellor Robert R. Livingston. This great man had not confined his study to the law but had the vision to foresee the possibilities in various experiments being made in the application of steam to the generation of mechanical power, especially in the propulsion of ships. He was not only united to John Stevens of Hoboken by his marriage to Stevens's sister, but was in negotiation with that great engineer and inventor up to the time that he cast his fortunes with Fulton. Livingston secured from the state of New York a monopoly of rights to operate steamboats on the Hudson, and this, in connection with the contract between these two men, was the determining factor in the public preeminence which Fulton has since been given as a pioneer in the history of steamboats.

The *Clermont* took its name from Chancellor Livingston's country place in the upper reaches of tidal Hudson. It was built at the shipyard of Charles Brown in East River. The engine for it was made in England by Messrs. Boulton and Watt of Birmingham. Fulton, in one of his letters, said, "My first steamboat on the Hudson River was one hundred fifty feet long, eighteen feet wide, drawing two feet of water, bow and stern sixty degrees." It had one deck and two masts. It had parallel sides, a V-shaped bow and a stern which was V-shaped at and below the water-line, but above the water merged into a square overhang. The two side paddle wheels were each fifteen feet in diameter and were uncovered so that, in a breeze, those aboard were apt to be well drenched. The engine had a twenty-four-inch cylinder with a four-foot stroke and developed twenty horse-power. Fat pine wood was used for fuel, and caused the single tall smoke-stack to belch smoke and sparks in such quantity, the one conspicuous by day and the other equally conspicuous by night, that it caused one spectator to refer to the new enigma as "The Devil in a sawmill" and another to describe it as "A monster, moving on the river, defying wind and tide, and breathing flames and smoke."

From the Manors and Historic Homes of the Hudson Valley, by Harold D. Eberlein,
Published by J. B. Lippincott Company

THE BRETT-TELLER HOUSE AT BEACON (FISHKILL LANDING)
Illustrating Hudson River Dormer Windows

ROBERT FULTON'S STEAMBOAT, THE CLERMONT
As Reproduced for the Hudson-Fulton Celebration

From "John Stevens, an American Record" by Archibald Douglas Turnbull, published by The Century Co.

THE FIRST AMERICAN LOCOMOTIVE ON WHEELS

At Colonel John Stevens' Castle Point, Hoboken, New Jersey.

It is not to be imagined that on the occasion of the historic trial trip of this steamboat, the general public had the slightest appreciation either of Fulton's genius or of the momentous work he had accomplished. The *Clermont* was cast loose from her moorings at New York near the old State's Prison, which stood on the square now bounded by Washington, Charles, West Tenth and West Streets, on North River. Fulton had made his preparation for the start "to the accompaniment of jeers and cat-calls." The thousands of people who lined the river shore, to witness the departure of the strange craft "had come to deride 'Fulton's Folly.'"

At one o'clock, on August 17, 1807, the hawser was drawn in, the throttle was opened, the big wheels turned, and "amid the curious hush which immediately fell upon the multitude," the *Clermont* moved out into the stream and headed north. Edgar Mayhew Bacon quotes this interesting but unidentified contemporary account of the crowd's secondary reaction:

"Nothing could exceed the surprise and admiration of all who witnessed the experiment. The minds of the most incredulous were changed in a few minutes. Before the boat had made the progress of a quarter of a mile, the greatest unbeliever must have been converted. The man who, while he looked on the expensive machine, thanked his stars that he had more wisdom than to waste his money on such idle schemes, changed the expression of his features as the boat moved from the wharf and gained her speed; his complacent smile gradually stiffened into an expression of wonder. The jeers of the ignorant, who had neither sense nor feeling enough to suppress their contemptuous ridicule and rude jokes, were silenced for a moment by a vulgar astonishment, which deprived them of the power of utterance, till the triumph of genius extorted from the incredulous multitude which crowded the shores, shouts and acclamations of congratulation and applause."

Fulton himself gave the significant details of the triumphant voyage in these simple lines:

"I left New York on Monday at one o'clock, and arrived at Clermont, the seat of Chancellor Livingston, at one o'clock on Tuesday—time, twenty-four hours: distance, one hundred and ten miles. On Wednesday, I departed from the Chancellor's at nine in the morning, and arrived at Albany at five in the afternoon—distance, forty miles; time, eight hours. The sum is one hundred and fifty miles in thirty-two hours, equal to near five miles an hour.

"On Thursday, at nine o'clock in the morning, I left Albany, and arrived at the Chancellor's at six in the evening: I started from thence at seven, and arrived at New York at four in the afternoon—time, thirty hours; space run through, one hundred and fifty miles; equal to five miles an hour. Throughout my whole way, both going and returning, the wind was ahead; no advantage could be derived from my sails: the whole has, therefore, been performed by the power of the steam-engine."

Sails were to endure however, as probably they will endure as long as there is wind and water and lovers of the magic of flight on these most natural of artificial wings. But after the trip of the *Clermont*, life on the river took on a new aspect, a new acceleration. Soon the variety of craft which are identified with it to-day took their place in increasing numbers on its waters and at its landings, especially the lusty little tug, the bulldog of the river, ready to tackle anything from a lighter to a leviathan; and its sprawling companion, the steam ferry, which seems to walk the waters with the crawl-stroke of a titanic turtle whose feet only are below the surface.

The sailing-masters saw their vessels outspeeded, outdistanced, and frequently outfavored by their old passenger and their old freight patrons. But many of them bravely seized the helms of the new monsters and became steamboat captains in the new era. A race of mighty men they were too, and their names still flourish in gilt and color on the wheel-box of each beam of some of the latest steamboats.

The mounting years have seen steam craft mount in size and in number, accelerate in speed, embellish themselves as no peacock might ambition, and on no other of our rivers have steamboats maintained their prestige so successfully against all other vehicles as here on the Hudson.

It has been hinted that the *Clermont* was not the first watercraft to crawl these waters without oar or sail; that Livingston was negotiating with his own brother-in-law, John Stevens, to furnish the steamboats to ride the river under his legalized monopoly. This Stevens was a true son of the Hudson. He was born on its east bank in the city of New York, he lived all the significant years of his life on its west bank at Hoboken, on the rocky promontory which ever since has been known as Stevens or Castle Point; and the studies he conducted there saw their fruition as a result of experiments conducted on the waters between these two shores.

Indeed, when the *Clermont* first paddled her way up-river, that August afternoon in 1807, it had already been three years since James Renwick and his two companions from King's College saw, in May, 1804, what years afterward he thus described in a letter to Frederick DePeyster:

"As we entered the gate from Broadway, we saw what we, in those days, considered a crowd, running toward the river. On inquiring the cause, we were informed that 'Jack' Stevens was going over to Hoboken in a queer sort of boat. On reaching the bulkhead by which the Battery was then bounded, we saw lying against it a vessel about the size of a Whitehall rowboat, in which there was a small engine *but no visible means of propulsion.* The vessel was speedily underway, my late much-valued friend, Commodore Stevens, acting as coxswain, and I presume the smutty-looking personage who fulfilled the duties of engineer, fireman, and crew, was his more practical brother, Robert L. Stevens."

This boat was the *Little Juliana*. But "no visible means of propulsion" was what baffled the crowd on the Battery. They were not unaccustomed to Stevens's other experiments thereabout. But *how* was that boat driven, apparently without oars, sails or wheels? One recalls the mystification of the Chinese over the first cable-car: "No pushee, no pullee, go like hellee allee samee!" The key to the mystification, as to the *Little Juliana's* movement was under water. It embodied Stevens's long-held theory of "wheels in the stern." Actually what Renwick and his friends and the others in that crowd were witnessing was, according to Turnbull, the first-known successful application of steam to twin-screw propellers.

Stevens's genius was responsible for another incredible surprise in 1809, just two hundred years after the *Half Moon* sailed out of the river, and for two centuries no ship had gone hence except under wind-blown canvas. But midday of June 10, in the year 1809, the river, in a manner of saying, "opened its eyes." It was familiar with John Stevens's latest and biggest steamboat, the *Phœnix,* built and recently launched at the Hoboken waterside. But what, they asked, was Stevens going to do with it? The Hudson was locked against it by the Livingston monopoly. Perhaps, the imaginative conjectured, it was unwisely intended to breast the rougher waters of Long Island Sound.

"In the general view," wrote Turnbull, "the business of steamboating was wholly a 'flat-calm' affair. Hence, when the word was passed along the New York and Hoboken waterfronts that the *Phœnix* was to be sent 'outside,' it was received with cold disbelief or open sneers. Old-timers, sitting on the docks between cruises under topsails, took their pipes from their lips and spat derisively into the river. A steamboat on an ocean voyage? They would as soon volunteer for that as for an expedition to the moon."

And the first ocean voyage of a ship under steam actually began as the *Phœnix,* with the inventor's twenty-one-year-old son, Robert Livingston Stevens, as captain and engineer, stood off to the south and disappeared beyond Staten Island on its way down the coast and up the Delaware River to Philadelphia. It is significant that all the pessimists were confounded, for the gallant craft completed its voyage with flying colors. But it is incidental that it fought fogs first and then gales and "anchored at 9 O'clock, abreast Market St. Wharf, Philadelphia," according to its log, on the twenty-third day of the same month, one day short of a fortnight on its voyage between docks of departure and destination.

Within the passing of less than two other decades, after the steamboat became a part of life here, there happened another event momentous to the chronicle of the Hudson. The Erie Canal was completed, and then there began to appear on the river a new kind of craft without oars, without sails, without paddle-wheels, without steam, without any means aboard it for its own propulsion. That was the redoubtable canal-boat. The appearance of steamboats on the river was not, at the time, generally believed to have been of greater significance to the development and prosperity of these tidewater towns and cities than the appearance of the first fleet of canal-boats. Certainly the *Clermont* made her memorable maiden voyage to infinitely less acclaim than greeted the departure of the first fleet of canal-boats from Buffalo, on October 25, 1825, and continued robustly until they had passed Albany, the Highlands, the Tappan

Zee, the Palisades and Manhattan Island on their triumphant way to the river's mouth.

The historic flotilla was led out of Buffalo by the *Senaca Chief,* drawn by four powerful gray thoroughbred horses. Governor De Witt Clinton was aboard with a party of distinguished guests. Another boat in the long line of those following was called *Noah's Ark,* and its passengers were two of all the stranger species of birds and beasts obtainable in the newly opening hinterland. Cannon had been placed along the entire four hundred and fifty miles of the canal and river route, from the lakes to the ocean. As the canal was declared open, and the flotilla got under way in Buffalo, the announcement of it was made by the first cannon nearest, and those who manned the next gun, and the next and the next, discharged them as they heard the report from the west, until the whole chain of detonations had carried the memorable message forward, in what then seemed an incredibly few minutes, to the city of New York.

There were celebrations and pageants at all the important points along the route. At Albany the *Chancellor Livingston* and a squadron of other steamboats took the canal-boats in tow and drew them in triumph to the river's mouth. Here they were joined by crafts of every character current, which escorted the pudgy little heroes out on to the Atlantic. There was performed the symbolic ceremony of wedding the waters of the lakes to the sea as "Governor Clinton poured a Keg of Lake Erie's water into the Atlantic Ocean."

The ubiquitous, impotent, indispensable canal-boats have ever since been one of the distinguishing features of the tidewater Hudson picture. Though they appeared here a century and a half after the Dutch period, their squat sturdy build falsely suggests an heredity from the patroons and burghers anciently here, even if it were not that the Netherlands was the nursery and has ever been the principal home of this type of marine carrier.

The canal-boats lead a gregarious life on the river. None is ever found away from the pack. They huddle together as if in fear of what might happen to one of them if it were to detach itself and attempt an adventure on its own. They are herded, drilled and marshaled on their way by a lusty bullying tug, no bigger than any single one of them, which marches on ahead, straining at the tow-line as if a bulldog had in leash a flock of reluctant dachshunds.

Seen with a somewhat more practical eye, the canal-boat tows seem little floating villages, not least at night as the reflecting waters multiply the twinkles of their signal and window lights. A little house rises modestly astern each deck, curtains and flower boxes often ornament the tiny window openings and a miniature stove pipe reaching through the roof breathes out wisps of smoke which suggest snug comfort and a stewing supper down below.

Life aboard these canal-boats seems the last word in leisure, if it is not even the first syllable in luxury. As a rule the captain is accompanied by his wife, and they domesticate themselves and their children aboard. The period of their voyage spent under way on the river is, in a measure, a holiday for all on board. The deck is their front yard and their promenade. Here the captain lounges and smokes the day away. Here his wife comes, for a few moments of fresh air and sunshine and rest, with her mending or knitting or a pan of parings for the dinner.

The first day out of Albany is always wash-day and then every deck is aflutter with wind-tossed garments as if the flotilla had "dressed ship" for a festival. This first day is imperative for this fixed purpose, for it is the boat-*frau's* last chance to take fresh water aboard, as it floats south into brackish and then salt waters. The great care during this portion of the cruise are the horses which tow the boats along the canal. Generally they are brought aboard at Albany and are stowed below, and caring for them is the men's chief occupation as long as the canal-boats are in the river.

Up to the end of the Revolution land travel along the river was even more primitive than water travel. The latter had at least a broad, dependable road-bed. Paralleling this one the way had been blazed for roads for wheeled vehicles on both sides. But travel on them was as precarious as it was unorganized. The first "stage-waggon" was put on a route along the east shore between the cities of New York and Albany within a year of the close of the Revolutionary War. It made the round trip once a month. The vehicle is described as having been of the crudest type, without springs and without backs to the plank seats. Nevertheless, it so prospered that, the next year, another such wagon was added to this run. In 1785 the company operating this service secured from the Legislature the first transportation charter granted by the state of New York, and it was privileged "to erect, set up, carry on and drive stage-waggons between Albany and New York on the east side of the Hudson River for a period of ten years."

Its obligation was to maintain two covered wagons, each to be drawn by four able horses, the trip to be made once a week in each direction, and the company was "to make the land passage most easy and agreeable, as well as most expeditious, by performing the journey in two days, at three-pence a mile." This, however, was found to be "a break-neck speed," and a

ınkrupting rate of fare, so the time for the trip was extended
▸ three days and the fare to four pence a mile. By 1797 a daily
ʿrvice was maintained on this route over what has since become
ıown as the Albany Post Road.

The route paralleled the river without being more than oc-
ısionally in sight of it. It left the city of New York by the
ɛoadway and the Bloomingdale Road, crossed the Harlem
ıver over King's Bridge, and then rambled around and over
ɛ riverside hills to Tarrytown, Peekskill, Fishkill, Pough-
epsie, Rhinebeck, Red Hook, Hudson and Albany. Stops
ɛre made for a part of each of two nights at the ordinaries
Peekskill and Rhinebeck.

A continuous road along the west side of the river was linked
only in the beginning of the new century. It kept far inland
the first part of its northern course, touching Hackensack
·d Goshen; but after it reached Newburgh it was frequently
sight of the river on its way through Kingston and Catskill
·d so on to Albany. The stage line set up here soon proved a
ʿmidable competitor of the one across the river, although the
·er company led in the race by reducing the hours of transit
·ween the cities at either end of the tidewater down to fifteen
ıurs, in February, 1820.

·An amusing account of an 1831 winter trip on the west
ʿre line has been left us by Grant Thorburn, a New York
·dman:

'We left Hoboken with about fifteen passengers closely
·ked in a stage with wheels, and a very neat coach, and so
·lish was I and ignorant (never having travelled on land)
·ought this same fine close carriage would go through thick
·l thin with me all the way to Albany: in two short hours my
·s were opened. We stopped in Hackensack at a tavern gro-
·y grogshop and post-office all under one roof, for we carried

151

Uncle Sam's letter bags, which was another grievance, as we had to stop every few miles to change the mails. The keeper of the office began to bluster and swear he had neither carriages covered or uncovered to forward so many passengers. He said the Jockey Club in New York took all the money and gave him all the trouble. In short, says he, unless you remain here till four o'clock P.M. you must go on with such conveyance as I can furnish. We applied to our Hoboken driver. He said his orders were to drop us at Hackensack and bring back the coaches; and sure enough he turned about and back he went. I stepped into the barroom—a large place. In the centre stood a large old-fashioned tin-plate stove, surrounded by fifteen or twenty large lazy fellows. After waiting an hour' we were sent forward, vis. two in an open chair, four in an open wagon, and the remainder, eight I think, in a common Jersey farming wagon, all the machines being without covers. It now commenced raining, and by the time we got to the next stage, we looked like moving pillars of salt, our hats and coats being covered to the thickness of an eighth of an inch with ice transparents. At the town of Goshen we changed the mail, thawed our garments, and ate our dinner. As we got north the sleighing got better, so we were accommodated with a covered box and runners, but alas! it was like the man's lantern without a candle. The cover was of white wood boards placed a quarter of an inch apart without paint, leather, or canvas to protect them from the weather.

"We travelled all night. The rain and snow descending through the roof, our hats were frozen to our capes, and our cloaks to one another. In the morning we looked like some mountain of ice moving down the Gulf Stream. I thought the machine used at the Dry Dock would have been an excellent appendage to have lifted us bodily into the breakfast room; and this is what the horse-flesh fraternity in New York advertise as their *safe, cheap, comfortable,* and expeditious winter establishment for Albany."

The great merger came in 1835. There was room for improvement. Too, there was a suggestion of ominous rivalry for stage-coaches in the roarings of a new device called a locomotive, which had a few years before begun to haul trains out of Baltimore and, nearer, out of Albany. The Beaches, father and son, of Poughkeepsie gathered ownership of the two great north and south coach lines as well as several tributaries. The platform wagons were replaced by the safer and comparatively luxurious Concord coaches with four swift horses to each of them, a fresh relay of horses every fifteen miles, improved taverns and a dependable schedule of twenty-four or not more than twenty-eight hours. Such celerity and dependability won for the Beaches the contract for carrying the United States mails, a contract they held for more than thirty years.

Their united stage lines became a formidable affair. When the mail coach started off promptly at eight of the morning from its headquarters at the old Western Hotel in Cortlandt Street, it frequently led a line of five or six other coaches according to the bookings of passengers and baggage. On the high front seat, beside the coachman, invariably sat the armed government guard, who was there not only to protect the mails but to see that the schedule was kept.

In severe winter weather, when the upper river froze over to dependable thickness, the coach wheels were replaced by stout sled runners, and the troublesome dangerous frozen hill roads were abandoned for the swifter course over the level ice. Temporary relay stables and "tavern shanties" were set up along this alternate route, oftentimes out in mid-river.

One special winter trip provided by this line has taken its place in history. On account of the *Caroline* affair in the winter of 1837-38, General Winfield Scott was ordered with all possible speed to the frontier at Niagara. Mr. Beach undertook to put him through from New York to Albany in record time and with a maximum of comfort. On account of snow and ice a sleigh and four fleet horses were provided. The start from New

York was made at eight o'clock in the evening. For the dis
tinguished passenger's convenience the seats had been taken ou
of the sleigh and mattress, pillows and blankets were subst
tuted. According to General Scott's own statement he wa
asleep before he was out of the Bowery and did not awake be
fore morning. One account says:

> "The night was clear and cold; the roads were good; th
> river was frozen from Poughkeepsie northward; the rela
> were prompt; drivers and horses were on their mettle. At eig
> the next morning the door of the sleigh was opened at th
> hotel in Albany, and the proprietor greeted his distinguishe
> guest with the words: 'General Scott, your breakfast is served.'

The middle of the century saw the beginning of the decline
stage-coach travel. A steam railroad reached the river first
1831 when the Mohawk and Hudson Railroad drove its trai
into Albany. Ten years later the Erie Railroad reached th
river on the west shore of Tappan Zee at Piermont. Once th
development of railroads began here, it was rapid and extensiv
By 1851 the Hudson River Railroad had completed its wate
side railway between New York City and Greenbush, opposi
the city of Albany, where the transit of the river was made
first by ferry. The construction of the West Shore Railw
was not begun until 1881. Passenger service on this side b
tween Jersey City and Albany was first operated in the summ
of 1883.

The coming of the railroads completed the familiar pictu
of vehicular transportation here, until the automobile began
appear along the river's shores and the occasional aeropla
began to wing its flight high above water and mountains. T
railroads ruined the stage lines, which gradually abandoned
roads. They have, it is true, greatly prevented the river tra

rom expanding, but there is not, nevertheless, a watercourse f equal length which has so frequent and such luxurious teamer-boat service as the tidal Hudson. There is not, indeed, river of length equal to that of the tidal Hudson whose waters nd adjacent shores present a density of transport movement omparable to that presented here by the sailing craft, the anal-boat flotillas, the tugs, the shunting ferries, the steamoats and the ocean-going vessels of all classes on the surface f the waters; by the trains pounding the steel highways at ie water's edge on both banks; and, finally, by the processions f automotive traffic which thread their ways about the high anks of the same adjacent hills.

Coincident with this development of transportation, paraoxically created by it and yet creating it, arose a dense population along the river, culminating in the prodigious metrolitan unit at its mouth. Wealth came with such ease and in ch quantities as had before rarely come to others in the whole orld save to national monarchs by their success in armed conest. There arose here figures who became internationally mous largely if not wholly because of their vast bewildering alth. The Hudson became the home of the Astors, the anderbilts, the Goulds, the Stewarts, the Morgans and the ockefellers, at the head of a long line of others whose riches re only a little less bewildering. Riches were so abundant d so extensively distributed and so freely expended that the idas-touch appeared everywhere, and gave another and the esent domestic character to the hills behind the Hudson's idings.

Most of the early Dutch houses have disappeared, those few at remain are overshadowed in opulence, if not in interest, the results of that orgy of expensive building which dis-

tinguished the nineteenth century. The finer of the colonia
and early republican houses were easily counted and were so
detached that they dominated, though with a sincere and digni
fied reticence, each its own town or neighborhood.

In its latest expression, however, the river shores are so
packed with palaces that they are without much individuality
except to their owners and their intimates. With money so
plentiful, speed in building seemed so essential that there ap
peared to have been little time to wait on taste in architecture
The result has been that, surrounding some excellent modern
mansions, there grew up an overwhelming number of others of
an upstart indeterminate type which gave little regard to ap
proved models, to proportion, to balance or to other accepted
standards of taste. Such houses often seem not to have been
built from ordered drawings, or, when they were, then they
suggest a disordered memory which drew on scraps of styles
rather than units of any single standard.

By all the rules of radicalism the outgrowth of such artistic
anarchy should have been a new style and perhaps a better
The fact is, however, that out of the nineteenth-century Hudson
domestic architecture has survived but one well identified detail, the bracket. This ubiquitous unit appeared in legions,
everywhere, supporting eaves, balconies, door and window lin-
tels, and trimming angles wherever the upright met with the
horizontal.

If, in spite of the survival of chaster older specimens and of
some submerged modern models, the architecture of the Hudson's golden era has so often been disappointing, the same can
not be said of the environment furnished these houses. The
landscaping has been notable. The natural diversity of the
slopes, the nobility of the indigenous trees, the skilful intro-

MARTIN VAN BUREN

© *The New York Times Studios*

THEODORE ROOSEVELT   FRANKLIN DELANO ROOSEVELT

THREE PRESIDENTS OF THE UNITED STATES BORN ON
THE HUDSON

luction of exotic growths, the mellowing influence of ivy and other clinging vines, the harmonizing adaptation of drives to original contours, the sound selection of the spot where the earth best supports a house and where the house may best command the lovely water vistas, have all contributed to make the domestic ensemble here a thing of ravishing beauty.

But moneyed men did not dominate the scene to the exclusion of other conspicuous figures. The river valley was the birthplace or became the habitation of a notable list of statesmen, as well as of writers, painters and other creative characters.

In addition to three presidents of the United States—Martin Van Buren, Theodore Roosevelt and Franklin Delano Roosevelt—these seven vice-presidents of the United States were born or were domiciled here: Aaron Burr, George Clinton, Daniel Tompkins, Martin Van Buren, Schuyler Colfax, Levi P. Morton and Theodore Roosevelt; and these justices of the Supreme Court of the United States: Henry Brockholst Livingston, Smith Thompson, Samuel Blatchford, Rufus W. Peckham, Charles Evans Hughes and Harlan Fiske Stone. General Philip Sheridan was born at Albany. At the head of the bar, of too many distinguished figures for space to recount them here, stands the celebrated Chancellor Kent, whose Commentaries has stood unchallenged for more than one hundred years as "the foremost American institutional legal treatise."

Among the more conspicuous nineteenth-century writers most intimately identified with tidewater Hudson are Washington Irving, James Kirke Paulding, Edgar Allan Poe, William Cullen Bryant, John Bigelow, J. J. Audubon and Nathaniel Parker Willis, captains of a company only a little less famous, which included Charles Fenno Hoffman, George P. Morris, Frederick Swartwout Cozzens, Evert Augustus Duyckinck, Susan and

Anna B. Warner, Benson J. Lossing, Amelia E. Barr, Lyman
Abbott, Hamilton Wright Mabie, E. P. Roe and Joel Benton;
all of whom were precursors of a notable array of other writers
who have clustered here since New York City assumed its conspicuous position in the publishing world.

The Hudson River shares with Barbizon the distinction of
having a school of painting named after it. Indeed, "the term
Hudson River School came to include those landscape painters
in America working under the influences and conditions prior
to the advent of the Barbizon pictures in this country," and the
continuation of this influence. Among the last century's great
artists the river valley was the birthplace or the sometime studio
of George Inness, Thomas Cole, John F. Kensett, Albert Bier-
stadt, Emanuel Leutze, Robert W. Weir and J. Alden Weir.

So came the Hudson down to the present century, with no
material changes since that do not reflect the variations in population and building both ashore and afloat that were shared by
much of the rest of this country during the first third of this century. What is perhaps more significant of the enduring and
dominating character of the river is that, with all its superficial growth and change, it has never lost its primeval impres-
siveness.

Its first broad lower reaches push its banks apart so far that
the details of life here terraced toward the sky, when seen from
shore to shore, melt almost indistinguishable in mere sym-
phonies of color. The mountains of the Highlands have known
how to protect their scarpes and summits. Where the upper
valley ranges, between receding hills, Nature seems to prevail
still, for the manifestations of man reach back from the landings
on flat or gently tilted stretches, rather than along the water's
edge, and hide themselves behind one another or behind screens

of venerable trees, so that they are but suggestions of their populous selves. Thus the new life colors the old shores with scarcely any oppressiveness of detail. The units of the busy life here seem to punctuate Nature without prevailing over it. Nearly all that has come to it in three centuries seems to have enhanced its natural beauty and splendor.

CHAPTER VII

MANHATTAN ISLAND

UR course so far has been up the centuries since the discovery of the river, rather than up the river itself. It has been chronological rather than geographical. We have been viewing the background of the present, the setting against which the survivals stand and from which they derive their significance. Now our course will be along the river itself from its mouth to the end of its tidal reach.

The natural way to see a river is from a boat upon its waters. But in this way one sees little other than the scenery itself. The larger attraction for man, however, is man; the men settled on the banks behind the landings. So, to know the beauty of the Hudson we shall sail up its waters, but to know its rare historical survivals and to know the men and women who acted the story which gives them their allure we shall make continual landings on its shores, observing, inquiring, absorbing, until we have, if not all that makes this story significant to those whose lives and whose forebears' lives have been spent on its banks, at least most of what makes its beauty so inspiring and its record so essential to our national evolution and its chronicle.

The attention of any one entering the mouth of the Hudson is attracted inevitably and first by Manhattan Island. This is because, but not because only, of the bewildering city heaped upon it. From the beginning of the white man's adventures in these parts this land arrested his attention. As long as the white man has dwelt on the river, he has dwelt here on this island.

But the vision which confronts the traveler to-day is inexorably that of the present phalanx of man's contrivance. Original contours have been largely swept away by generations of blasting and shoveling and hauling and filling. The whole original area, once a great forest of green, has been obscured by mountains of gray fabrications of stone and steel, chiseled and piled, cleated and riveted and cemented; the past buried deep under their scores of stories and revealing itself only in a few green patches, here parks dedicated to the capering of the quick, and there cemeteries dedicated to the sleep of the dead; in a few churches, in a few buildings the span of whose years reaches barely beyond the beginning of the Revolutionary War.

There is but one engineer who can readily remove the accumulation of solid ordered litter which obscures the past, and that is imagination; there is only one archeologist who can outline the physiognomy of the past, and that is history.

Entering the river it is singularly at its very mouth, on its eastern lip, at the southern extremity of Manhattan Island, that nearly the whole procession of people out of the island's past would find themselves most at home in this neighborhood to-day, because there is here less apparent change than anywhere else on all the island.

This tip of land so long known as the Battery, in spite of

three centuries of incredible changes all about it, remains truest
to its original character. It is still, as it always has been, an
open area, with grass and trees and an unobscured outlook over
the water. Indeed, because of this outlook this point was first
called Schreyers' Hook, or Weepers' Point, as it was here that
little groups of the early Dutch settlers gathered to watch the
departing home-bound ships fade in the mist, or disappear
through the distant narrows.

Just here the earliest Dutch colonists made their first settlement on the island. If they returned now in the belief they
recognized their familiar Schreyers' Point, they could be told
that even this fragment of identity with the past is not quite
genuine. Only superficially is it the same, for the ground they
would be treading, believing it familiar ground, is actually all
made land which left the original point some distance inland.
The Custom House now stands where once the island ended.
Pearl Street was once the first street above the water's edge,
and the Dutch so named it because of the pearly shells found
along the shore by its side. As the land was reclaimed and
the river pushed out, Water and Front and South Streets
were successively added, and their names indicate that each
successively became the southern or shore boundary.

The first Dutch settlements were not precisely on the point
of land but some distance north of it, on higher land, estimated
to have been on ground now adjoining the west side of Broadway between Morris Street and Exchange Place. When these
settlements were made, and how, under examination remains
somewhat obscure. Until comparatively recently credit was
given to various statements which since have been proved to
be inaccurate. One of them is the fable that Adrian Block's
ship, *De Tijer,* was burned here at the mouth of the river in

the winter of 1613-14; that he built his new ship, *Onrest,* here, and during these operations he and his men built and lived in four houses on the adjoining shore of the island. There is no sound evidence to support these claims. On the contrary, there is strong circumstantial evidence to support the belief that Block spent that winter at the head of the tidal river and built his *Onrest* in sight of the present city of Albany. Another often-repeated statement is that Captain Samuel Argall came to the mouth of the river at this time and found four houses on the south tip of the island. The source of this fable, a statement in a document of 1648, is discredited by internal evidence.

There is no proof of a white settlement on Manhattan Island previous to 1624, though it is possible that some rude temporary habitations may have been erected here previously by the explorers and traders who frequented the river.

The first permanent white settlement known to have been made on Manhattan Island was that made in the spring of 1626, when Director Pieter Minuit arrived with two shiploads of settlers. It was at this time that he concluded the purchase of the entire island from the Indians for trinkets and implements and clothing of an estimated value of twenty-four dollars. This seems to have been at the time mutually satisfactory to the red man and to the white man, for there is no known complaint about the bargain except by some comparatively recent sentimentalists who repine over the fact that Minuit got for so little a tract of land to which is now attributed such fabulous values.

It was of conditions on the island at that time that Wassenaer wrote when he gave this first written description of the white man's settlement here:

"The colony is now established on the Manhates, where a

fort has been staked out by Master Kryn Frederycks, an engineer. It is planned to be of large dimensions. . . . The counting house there is kept in a stone building, thatched with reed; the other houses are of the bark of trees. Each has his own house. The Director and the *Koopman* live together; there are thirty ordinary houses on the east side of the river which runs nearly north and south. The Honourable Pieter Minuet is Director there at present; Jan Lempon *Schout;* Sebastian Jansz. Crol and Jan Juych, comforters of the sick, who, whilst awaiting a clergyman, read to the commonality there, on Sundays, texts of Scripture and the commentaries. François Molemacker is busy building a horsemill over which shall be constructed a spacious room sufficient to accommodate a large congregation, and then a tower to be erected where the bells brought from Porto Rico will be hung."

There is not less variety in the early spellings of the word we now know as Manhattan than there was in the spelling of most proper names three hundred years ago. And the interpreters have been equally facile and imaginative in explaining the meaning of it. The term Manhattan Island is in fact a curious bit of tautology, according to Fiske, who was, however, betrayed by the printers who typed this, his explanation of it:

"For the name Manhattan many explanations have been suggested, and among other things we have been told that the island was named after the tribe which inhabitated it. But this is getting the cart before the horse. These Indians were a branch of the great Lanni-Lenapé confederacy, afterwards known as the Delawares. Now in the Lenni-Lenapé language *Manatey* means 'island' and *Manhattanis* are 'those who dwell upon an island.' Evidently, therefore, the Manhattans were simply the island tribe of the Delawares. Throughout the seventeenth century the island was designated indifferently *Manatey* and *Manhattan.* When we say 'Manhattan Island' it is a case of unconscious tautlogy [sic]."

The town at the river's mouth was called New Amsterdam after the great city of the company's and the colonists' homeland,

and so it was known until the very end of the Dutch régime. The fort was called Fort Amsterdam. It was "at first simply a block house encircled by red cedar palisades backed by earthworks." Stretching from the fort along the East River rose the thirty one-story log houses with bark roofs which sheltered the greater number of the first inhabitants here. This row of dwellings made the first suggestion of a street, and that first street was called Pearl Street, and survives as the oldest thoroughfare in New York. At that time the waters of the North River came up to a line now roughly defined by Greenwich Street. The villagers used an open space just north of the fort as their playground. As the burghers' favorite pastime was the game of bowls, this spot took very early its enduring name of Bowling Green.

Fort Amsterdam was completed in 1635. Within its walls were the director's house, the barracks and a guard-house. New buildings erected outside, but near, the fort at this time were "a new bakery, a small house for the mid-wife, a goat-house behind the five large stone houses of the Company, a church with a house and stable behind it, a large shed where the ships were built having a sail-maker's loft above." A church had been erected, in 1633, on what is now 39 Pearl Street, the first building in the entire province devoted exclusively to religious worship; but nine years later it was referred to as "a mean barn." But by that time the burghers had begun a new stone church inside the fort and occupying almost one-fifth of the entire area inside the fortified walls.

The size of New Amsterdam in 1648 may be gaged roughly by the contemporary statements; one made by the Government that "nearly the just fourth of the City of New Amsterdam" consisted "of Brandy Shops, Tobacco and Beer houses";

the other, made by Dominie Backer, that at that time there were "seventeen tap houses here." The town would therefore seem to have been made up of about seventy houses outside the fort. The preponderance of houses of public entertainment is explainable by the fact that New Amsterdam was in the seventeenth century wholly supported by its international sea-trade, and naturally it catered to the appetites of the numerous sailors ashore there.

There is in the Royal Archives, at The Hague, a charming water-color drawing of New Amsterdam as it appeared about 1650. It shows, in the foreground, at the water's edge, two cranes either of which looks suspiciously as if it might be a gallows. However, no mention of such a gallows appears in the records; though there were stocks and pillory to discipline and chastise the wayward citizenry. The houses in this drawing are nearly all shown to have been two and a half stories high, and they huddle close together, sometimes with contiguous walls. They present their steep gable-ends to the front, and some of them have the stepped-gables so popular with the Dutch. The houses are placed in rows but with only a little suggestion of streets, and extend from the fort eastward directly to the East River. The palisades of the fort rise above the red roofs of the burghers' houses directly before it, and above its own walls, and from within their cincture, rise most conspicuously the gables and cupola of the church. The only other conspicuous thrust into the sky-line is made by the high wind-mill and its four great sails south of the fort, but at the eastern end of the town stands the detached square *Stad-Huis,* or City Hall, near Coentes Slip.

This sketch was made before the erection of the great wall which extended across the island, from river to river, on the north side of the little community, to protect it from the attack of its enemies, Indian and Puritan. The wall was completed in 1653, and consisted of a line of round palisades, six inches in diameter and twelve feet in height, strengthened at intervals of a rod by stout posts to which split rails were fastened at a height of ten feet from the ground. As long as it stood this barricade was known simply as the Wall. The location and direction of it have ever since been preserved by the street made along the line left when the wall was demolished, and which was called Wall Street.

·Behind the Wall was the New Amsterdam of Director Petrus Stuyvesant, a just man, but with a will of iron stouter than his wooden leg. It is estimated that in his little capital he lorded it over a population which, in 1656, numbered one thousand souls. The limits of the city remained south of the Wall until the English administration succeeded the Dutch in 1664.

The land of the whole island had meantime been reserved by the Company entirely in its own ownership. At first it let this land out in small lots, called *bouweries,* to tenant farmers, making a few exceptions, however, in cases where it worked the *bouwerie* on its own account with hired labor. On one such farm the Company maintained a brewery "covered with tiles." The sale of the island land to private owners began in 1638. In spite of the general rule of the Company we are not surprised, however, to find so facile a nest-liner as Director Wouter van Twiller, had secured a land grant to himself in 1629. He picked himself an attractive stretch of rich low land on the banks of the Hudson for his *bouwerie,* on the site of what had been an Indian village, about two miles north of the fort.

The coming of the English brought the little city nearer our ken, because the new administrators gave it that nomenclature which it has ever since retained. Now New Amsterdam was renamed New York. Fort Amsterdam became Fort James. Both names recall that James, Duke of York, who held title to the whole Province of New York by grant from his brother, King Charles II. *Heere Straet* or *Heere Wegh* (The Highway), which was the mid-island road through the city Wall, became Broadway, and marched northward to its destiny. When the English apprehended an attack by the French, in 1693, they established a line of ninety-two cannon across the open space behind Schreyers' Hook, and this they called the Whiteside Battery, or simply the Battery, and the Battery it has been ever since.

Among the first streets laid out north of the Wall was Maiden Lane which had been *Maagde Paat* or Maiden's Path, and curved along the bank of a brook in whose waters the Dutch girls and women "did" the family washing. A suburban community had developed on what had been Wouter van Twiller's farm, and this became Greenwich Village, which it continues to be, in name at least, though long since swallowed up in the sweep of the metropolis.

Early building tended to avoid the Hudson side of the island. Here, adjacent to the fort, there were open spaces including a small area known as Governor's Garden, but few houses were erected until near the end of the century.

Street developments north of the Wall are shown first in a plan of the town bearing date of 1695, and though the houses on them were comparatively few, the streets so charted covered an area more than half that of the little city south of the Wall. It is interesting to find that another plan, bearing date of only thirty-five years later, shows the city's growth meanwhile had reversed these proportions. By that time, the year 1730, streets

TRINITY CHURCH, NEW YORK CITY

SAINT MARK'S IN THE BOUWERIE, NEW YORK CITY

THE JUMEL MANSION, NEW YORK CITY

FRAUNCES TAVERN, NEW YORK CITY

had been developed as far as the north side of the present City Hall Park. The fortified Wall had vanished and in its place now appeared the name Wall Street, and the distance on the south from it to the Battery was only half that on the north from it to the last outskirts of the town.

New York City now ranked third in population among the cities of the English colonies along this Atlantic coast. It was exceeded in size by both Boston and Philadelphia. The estimated number of its inhabitants about this time was only eight thousand six hundred and twenty-four. But sixty years later, in 1790, with a population which then numbered thirty-three thousand one hundred and thirty-one, it had outstripped both its rivals and took a numerical supremacy among American cities which it has held ever since.

Meantime, the development on the Hudson front had lagged. On the west side of Broadway, between Maiden Lane and the still somewhat distant Greenwich Village, there were almost no developments other than farm buildings. An exception to them, and the outstanding buildings along this shore, were then the house and brewery of Anthony Lispinard. A decided change came during the next three decades. In 1799 streets had been developed as far north as Christopher Street, and Greenwich Street formed a continuous artery of travel, just back of West Street, as far north as the developing city then extended. From the beginning of the nineteenth century the Hudson water-front developed by leaps and bounds until, before the end of the century, it was built solid from the Battery to Spuyten Duyvil, and its water-line was toothed with docks over nearly all the same distance.

The city at the mouth of the Hudson, sharing the political and social history of the province, shared a similarly varying mode of life under Dutch, English and American régimes as was found elsewhere along the river, always, however, with an urban and cosmopolitan accent. It was at first a Dutch town, a simple imitation of remembered bits of towns in Holland. The English erasure of the name New Amsterdam, and the substitution of New York for it, was a prophecy and a symbol of their erasure as well as of the Dutch aspect of life there. They gave it a wholly English aspect, gradually replacing the stepped gables on the old houses with severe rectangular façades, retiring the primitive Dutch churches to make way for churches with columned porches and high supported spires reminiscent of London's ecclesiastical architecture, and setting up other public and private buildings equally reminiscent of the city of Christopher Wren and Inigo Jones.

To-day one seeks in vain for any visual survival of the Dutch era. The centuries have divested the island of every vestige of New Amsterdam. The new city, which is nevertheless the heir to the old city's Dutch traditions, gives no evidence of the fact, no evidence of sentiment where such an heirloom is concerned. It would seem as if even the memory of the past had followed the old city into oblivion. The new city has not set up anywhere on the entire island any memorial to Hudson who started the current of world's interest to this spot, or an effigy of any single Dutchman of New Amsterdam. The new city has indeed shown on its surface little evidence of historical self-consciousness. Sentiment has almost everywhere here succumbed to commercial expediency. The rising tide of land values has swept away nearly all the souvenirs of the island's notable place in our national history.

The modern city's builders seem to have gone everywhere for their models except into its own architectural beginnings.

Although such accents were removed in the first instance under the English régime, it is somewhat ironical that the eighteenth-century English erased Dutch New Amsterdam with scarcely more thoroughness than the nineteenth-century Americans erased English New York.

This is not to say that each period did not improve on its predecessor. Old New Amsterdam left little evidence that it was a place over which to repine. Simple, primitive and a little picturesque it was, but it was the product and the expression of a pioneer period and a people whose virtues were many, of which sociability was not the most conspicuous. The English brought with them the tradition of a gayer life. They added clubs and theaters, and public pleasure gardens patterned after their own Vauxhall and Ranelagh in London. The very scarlet of the British soldiers' tunics, so conspicuous during the twelve decades that New York was an English garrison town, was significant of the bright note of color that had been added to the mode of living and to the environment of the people.

No other great city has, in so brief a span of its life, made itself over so many times. The search for the realistic expression of the past here discloses little else than significant street names down in the southern area on both sides of the line where once ran the Wall. These at least, in many instances, remain as they were at first, still eloquent in their significance, for those who can interpret them, suggesting people and events, conditions and locations of very early days.

But when one comes to search for the original houses that stood along these old streets, houses of great national traditions in many cases, one finds little other evidence of them than markers indicating their sites. Historic Manhattan Island is visually a matter of sites and tablets, for of all the city built here before the Revolutionary War only three structures survive. They are Fraunces's Tavern, Saint Paul's Chapel, and the Morris or Jumel Mansion.

Fraunces's Tavern now nestles at the foot of the sky-scrapers at the corner of Pearl and Broad Streets, but at the time it was built it stood out boldly near the water, easily seen from the decks of ships entering the river. It is the oldest structure on the island, and thanks to its latest intelligent restoration, it bravely carries something of its earlier days.

It dates from the year 1719 when it was built by Stephen Delancey as his town residence. In 1762 it passed into the ownership of Samuel Fraunces who converted it into a tavern, known variously as the Queen Charlotte, the Queen's, and the Queen's Head. It became the most resorted and most fashionable tavern of its day. Fraunces was a notable host. He was also proprietor and host of the Vauxhall Gardens, and when he closed them he took from them his collection of wax figures and set them up in his tavern. He had a mind to sell it in 1781 when his advertisement gave this description of it:

"An elegant three story and a half brick dwelling house, situate in Great Dock Street [merged into Pearl Street in 1792] at the corner of Broad Street, the property of Mr. Samuel Fraunces, and for many years distinguished as the Queen's Head Tavern; in which are nine spacious rooms, besides five bedchambers, with thirteen fireplaces, an excellent garret in which are three bedrooms well furnished, an exceeding good kitchen, and a spring of remarkable fine water therein; a most excellent cellar under the whole, divided into three commodious compartments; a convenient yard, with a good cistern and pump, and many other conveniences too tedious to mention; the whole in extraordinary good repair, and is at present a remarkable good stand for business of any kind, and will upon the reestablishment of civil government be the most advantageous situation in this city, from its vicinity to the North River and New Jersey."

But no one seemed to be willing to advantage himself of such an "elegant" and "extraordinary good" house, with its "spring of remarkable fine water" in the kitchen. Mine host, Fraunces, continued to cater there, and his tavern's great day came just two years later on that celebrated occasion of the dinner at which Washington bade farewell to his officers. This, however, was not the only association between the General and this famous tavern-keeper. Seven years previously, in 1776, his daughter, Phoebe Fraunces, acted as housekeeper for the General when he made his headquarters in New York, and to her is given credit for having saved his life when she divulged the plot in which Hickey, her lover and Washington's body-guard, was to have assassinated his master. It was probably not more in grateful memory of this act than in recognition of Fraunces's excellence as host and caterer that President Washington made him his steward in 1789 while in residence at the then seat of government.

The old tavern led a varied and somewhat precarious existence during the nineteenth century. One time it degenerated into "a German tenement house with a lager-beer shop on the ground floor." But through it all it has survived to be known, in memory of its best days, as Fraunces's Tavern. It was restored in 1910 to its present excellent estate, and is open to the public as an historical museum.

The second oldest building on the island is Saint Paul's Chapel, which was built between the years 1764 and 1766, except for its spire which was added in 1794. This "chapel" is in size the equal of many a "church," but it is so called because it is a dependency, one of six chapels attached to Trinity parish.

It served for a time, indeed, as parish church, after the burning of near-by Trinity Church in 1776. At the time of its erection, Saint Paul's stood in a wheat-field and its adjacent lands stretched down to the near-by Hudson, the view from it uninterrupted except by groves and orchards. The choice of its site was much criticized, at that time, as being "too far out of town." But its isolation had this advantage in its earlier days, that ferry-boats timed and advertised their schedules in crossing the Hudson "by Saint Paul's Church clock."

During and immediately after the Revolutionary War, Saint Paul's was in effect the church of state, for the destroyed parish church of Trinity had not yet been replaced. While the British troops held New York, it was here that Lord Howe came to worship, as did his officers, including Major André and a certain young midshipman of the Royal Navy, then in his teens, who later sat on the British throne as King William IV. President Washington, after the ceremonies of his inaugural, in Federal Hall on Wall Street, came in procession with the members of Congress up to Saint Paul's, and here listened to service conducted by Bishop Provoost, the chaplain of the Senate.

The third of those three survivals of colonial New York, Mount Morris or the Jumel Mansion, is the junior of old Saint Paul's by only one year. It stands on one of the highest points on Harlem Heights, where the distance between the Hudson and the Harlem Rivers is less than a mile, and its lands originally extended from river to river. This house was built in 1765 when its surroundings were wholly rural, and when the view of the two rivers from its lofty pillared portico was uninterrupted in any direction except by the horizon. It is easy to understand why in its earlier days this place was regarded as one of the finest seats on the Hudson.

The builder, Colonel Roger Morris, was born in England and came to the American colonies in 1752 on the staff of General Braddock, and accompanied him on his campaign against the French and Indians in the West. In this service he was associated with young Colonel George Washington who had been invited to become aide-de-camp to the British General. The paths of these two young men often met thereafter. Morris fell in love with Mary Philipse, daughter of Frederic Philipse of Philipsborough Manor, and a tradition has been handed down that Washington's interest in this celebrated beauty was such that he proposed to her on one of his early visits to the Hudson. She married Morris, however, and became the chatelaine of his mansion on Harlem Heights. He was a loyalist and so found it inconvenient to remain at his house and welcome Washington when the General occupied it as headquarters in 1776. Later, when the Americans were forced to retreat northward after the battle of Harlem Heights, Sir Henry Clinton occupied the house as his headquarters, and it was so occupied by British officers at intervals until the end of the war. Morris and his wife then retired to England, and the mansion was confiscated and sold as enemy property. Thereafter, according to an advertisement of 1784, it was for a time used as a tavern by Talmage Hall "for the accomodation of his Eastern and Northern stages" with "ready and obedient servants, and the best fare the country and town affords," also "genteel lodgings, stabling and pasture," and in the same connection, it is noted that "The Octogan Room is very happily calculated for a turtle party."

Washington returned to this house of so many memories again while he was in residence in the city during his first term as president. He noted the occasion in his diary, as of July 10,

1790, in his customary terse terms, but it is not difficult to read into the few lines of the entry what a distinguished occasion they recorded:

"Having formed a Party, consisting of the Vice President, his lady, Son and Miss Smith; the Secretaries of State, Treasury and War, and the ladies of the two latter; with all the Gentlemen of my family, Mrs. Lear & the two children we visited the old position of Fort Washington and afterwards dined on a dinner provided by Mr. Mariner at the House lately Colo Roger Morris, but confiscated and in the occupation of a common farmer."

The gentlemen referred to were Vice-President John Adams, Secretary of State Thomas Jefferson, Secretary of the Treasury Alexander Hamilton, and Secretary of War Henry Knox.

The house left its lethargy again after 1810, in which year it was purchased by Stephen Jumel, a rich French wine merchant, whose wife made herself one of the most discussed social characters of New York early in the nineteenth century. Jumel came to New York from Santo Domingo and, defiant of the opinions of a small conservative American city, he established himself with a mistress, one Eliza Brown, whom he found here. She was a pretty and ambitious baggage, and her unconventional history was only too well known in New York. She could not move social New York, not in the direction of her house at least. She could move old Jumel, however, and induced him to make her his wife, believing that thus, removing the cause of the prejudice against her, she could remove the social barriers that prejudice had set in her way. It was then Jumel purchased Mount Morris, restored it to its original beauty and filled it with beautiful furnishings. The invitations went out; but the guests would not come in, at least not those guests whom Madame Jumel coveted.

In 1815 the Jumels went to Europe where people were unacquainted with her history or, if they knew it, they were indifferent to it. Jumel's money and Madame Jumel's beauty achieved a success for her that she so much desired. This was the single satisfying period of her life. And it was brief. The Jumels returned to New York and were soon separated. She retained possession of the house her career had made known as the Jumel Mansion, and when Jumel died, she married her attorney, a very old gentleman with a story of his own, and thus she became Mrs. Aaron Burr. Burr had wished to mend his fortunes by the marriage to the rich widow. It is not conceivable that the ambitious Madame Jumel envisaged herself as the wife of a man many years older than she, and a character already in political and social eclipse. They started to make their home in her famous house, but the two wills soon clashed, there was a separation and she ended her days alone, many years after, in 1865, in an environment of neglected faded finery and in a tottering mental state which begot ambitious hallucinations which she mistook for realities.

This famous house is now owned by the city and is maintained as a museum. One finds the atmosphere reestablished there more suggestive of the days when it was known as Mount Morris and was the home of the aristocratic Mary Philipse, but its later history clings to it and so does the name, at least one of the names, of the picturesque woman who gave it its later fame, for it is now almost universally referred to as the Jumel Mansion.

Other buildings erected on the island in the eighteenth century, but after the Revolutionary War, once visible from the decks of ships sailing up the Hudson, though now, in all instances save one, partly or wholly obscured by other structures, are the former Eastern Hotel, at the corner of Whitehall and South Streets; Number Seven State Street; Claremont on Riverside Drive; and the Dyckman Farmhouse. Number Seven State Street is now a mission for immigrant girls, but in its youth was one of the centers of fashionable New York. The old building near by, which in its heyday was the Eastern Hotel, was built before 1790, and derives its interest from its once distinguished entertainments and from its notable list of guests, among whom were Robert Fulton, Daniel Webster, P. T. Barnum and Jenny Lind. One of Barnum's most remunerative frauds was his celebrated Cardiff Giant, a "petrified man," of supposed prehistoric origin, which was the subject of much discussion among scholars and scientists, and the object of much curiosity by the multitude who paid to see it. Barnum had it removed from his museum every evening and placed in his own apartment in the Eastern Hotel. This, he allowed it to be believed, was in order that it might better be protected from theft, but actually it was to prevent any one from learning that the "giant" was merely a statue carved out of gypsum, as later became known, when was disclosed the whole story of how it had been buried near Cardiff, in upper New York State, in order that it might be, as it was, "discovered" by men digging a well there.

No one who has sailed up the Hudson since the earliest days of the Republic but could see, high on its banks, where One-Hundred-and-Twenty-Third Street now terminates, the white mansion-tavern which is called Claremont. It was so named by an early owner, Michael Hogan, after the Surrey home of Prince William, afterward King William IV of England, with whom Hogan had served as midshipman in the Royal Navy. Later distinguished residents of Claremont were the mysterious

Courtenay and Joseph Bonaparte, ex-King of Spain, who made it his home when he came to the Hudson after the battle of Waterloo. Courtenay was an Englishman. He lived the life of a recluse here, and one of the many bizarre traditions attached to his memory is that he inherited the title and estates of the Earl of Devon.

Less impressive than Claremont, even though that house's original lines are somewhat hard to find behind its cincture of utilitarian piazzas, but charming in its aspect of unspoiled oldness, is the Dyckman Farmhouse which clings to its rock at the corner of Two-Hundred-and-Fourth Street and Broadway. It was built in 1783 and shows the Dutch tradition as still having influenced the builders nearly a century and a half after the Netherlands flag disappeared from the river. One seeks in vain for mention of it in any of the old chronicles. Its story is a private matter, and the house is none the less dignified for being of interest for just what it is, a valued example of a vanished period and neighborhood.

Historically interesting Manhattan contemporaries of these eighteenth-century houses, but never Hudson riverside houses as these once were, are the Gracie, the Prime and the Towle houses on the island shore of the East River.

The Towle house, built, in part at least, before 1795, derives a particular interest from the fact that it was once the home of Colonel William S. Smith, Revolutionary soldier and aide-de-camp to General Washington, and of his wife, Abigail, daughter of President John Adams and his wife, Abigail Adams. He was the "Son" of the Vice-President mentioned as one of "A Party" which accompanied Washington that day when they "dined on a dinner" provided them at Mount Morris.

The Gracie house comes down to us attached to an alleged

royal witticism. It derived its name from its builder, Archibald Gracie, an eighteenth-century ship-owner, whose hospitality drew to his table some of the most celebrated characters of his period. Among them tradition includes Louis Philippe, when in exile in America in 1799 and not yet for some years to become King of France. As the story goes, there was considerable interest among the members of the Gracie family in the coming of this royal personage, which rose to excitement in the case of the younger members. But when they had seen him drive up in their father's "coach and four," there was a moment of disillusionment, for one of the little girls exclaimed:

"That's not the King. He has no crown on his head."

Louis Philippe overheard her and, humoring the child in her confusing of royal princes with kings and coronets with crowns, replied laughingly:

"In these days kings are satisfied with wearing their heads without crowns."

Other less venerable Manhattan structures, whose lives nevertheless span a century, are Trinity Church; the so-called Monroe house in which ex-President James Monroe died in the year 1831, situated at the corner of Lafayette and Prince Streets; Saint-Mark's-in-the-Bouwerie; and Hamilton Grange standing in the northern end of the island.

Trinity Church, begun in the year 1830, is the youngest building of this group, but its site is long renowned, for it is the third church edifice on the same site since the first one was erected here in the year 1696. Throughout its lifetime here on the rise of land at the head of Wall Street, its spire has been a landmark for those passing on the river. Saint-Mark's-in-the-Bouwerie derives its hyphenated name from its position on the site of a chapel of the Dutch Reformed faith, raised by Gov-

From the Manors and Historic Homes of the Hudson Valley, by Harold D. Eberlein,
Published by J. B. Lippincott Company

THE DYCKMAN HOUSE, NEW YORK CITY

Courtesy of The American Science and Historic Preservation Society

ALEXANDER HAMILTON'S GRANGE, NEW YORK CITY

THE PALISADES

On the New Jersey shore of the Hudson River

ernor Petrus Stuyvesant on his own *bouwerie*. The corner-
stone of the present church was laid in the year 1795, so that,
with the exception of Saint Paul's Chapel, Saint Mark's is the
oldest ecclesiastical structure on the island. On its outer eastern wall is a tablet with this inscription:

In this vault lies buried
PETRUS STUYVESANT,
Late Captain-General and Governor-in-Chief of Amsterdam
in New Netherland, now called New York, and the Dutch
West Indies Islands.
Died August, A. D. 1682, aged 80 years.

One of the other houses here, in the mazes of mid-town,
though less venerable than those mentioned, has even more historic significance than some. It is a brownstone house, in
East Twentieth Street, where President Theodore Roosevelt
was born. It is preserved as a museum and as an enduring
monument to "T.R."

The house now known as Hamilton Grange stands on high
ground at the corner of One-Hundred-and-Forty-First Street
and Convent Avenue, a little removed from its original site.
It is a simple, dignified, rectangular frame dwelling which was
built, in the year 1801, by Alexander Hamilton, for his use
as a country house.

At that time the city was eight miles from it, and it commanded glorious views of the East River, of the Hudson River,
of the Palisades, and, indeed, even of that distant spot on the
New Jersey shore of the Hudson where he was to meet his
tragic death at the hands of Aaron Burr. Hamilton named his
country house after the home of his grandfather in Ayreshire,
Scotland.

181

Although Hamilton was born in another colony, he came to New York as a youth, spent all the rest of his life here, and married Elizabeth, daughter of General Philip Schuyler of Albany. He is generally considered as New York's first citizen. This is a little because of his military service in the Revolutionary War; most because of his brilliant career in the civic and official life of the young Republic; and only a little less for the sentimental reasons thus described by an anonymous writer:

"The genuine New Yorker seems always to have had a certain regard for the memory of Hamilton, ascribable perhaps to his untimely taking off, to a sentiment of having been, as it were, robbed of the services of a great man, and to the strong light thrown upon the contrast between his traits and those of his distinguished and brilliant antagonist. He had faults, but they were very human ones, while those of his adversary tended towards the incarnation of selfishness. His career is probably more familiar to the people than that of any of the other characters connected with the State of New York during the Revolutionary era."

This regard in which New York holds its greatest citizen is expressed on the island in seemingly every possible form of civic memorial.

The way might seem to lead on across Spuyten Duyvil Creek and so directly up-river. But the Manhattan Island shore of the Hudson is paralleled by an even greater length of shore opposite, whose historic roots are quite as deep in the past. That is the New Jersey shore of the Hudson which extends from the western lip of the mouth of the river at Powles' Hook, up so far as this state extends along these waters at the northern terminus of the Palisades.

CHAPTER VIII

NEW JERSEY'S HUDSON SHORE

Berkeley and Carteret's Grant—Michael Pauw—Powles' Hook—The Conservatism of Communipaw—How the Dutch Lady Saved the Sinking Boat—"Lighthorse Harry" Lee's Adventure at the Hook—Old Bergen—On the Route to Philadelphia—A Canny Boniface—Survivals in Jersey City—Hoboken—Colonel John Stevens and Castle Point—First Experimental Passenger Steam Railway—The Elysian Fields—The Mystery of Mary Rogers—Weehawken and Its Duels—Aaron Burr and Alexander Hamilton—Bull's Ferry and André's Ballad of *The Cow Chase*—Fort Lee—The Palisades.

HE western shore of the river, for the first twenty-one miles above its mouth, is New Jersey soil. But what one sees least of here is just soil. It is a thickly populated area, yet one sees few habitations. Along the entire Jersey shore is a screen hiding the life behind it.

Over the first five miles this screen is made up of docks and wharves and piers, ocean liners, tramp steamers, ferry-boats, train barges, lighters, tugs, canal-boats, and seemingly every size and variety of water vehicle. The sky-line is a jagged uneven sequence of masts and funnels. It is not high. It is not higher than the similar sequence along the shore of Manhattan Island opposite. But New York rises behind its shore-line in clusters of titanic architectural stalagmites, far toward the firmament, dwarfing the fringe of marine life along its margin. On the Jersey shore, however, the scene stretches in three simple parallel bands of water, shipping and sky, for the land is low behind it.

The extension of this screen northward rises, after a short

interval of varying bluffs, to the sheer precipice, famous as the Palisades, which walls the river here for another twelve miles. It is sublimely elemental like the water at its feet and the sky above it. Here the shipping seems not to exist except as a decorative hem on this great fabric of stone. In places clusters of great trees rise up before its face, but the cliffs diminish them to the aspect of moss. Man has crept to the edge of this precipice and there has built for himself many beautiful habitations, but seen from the river the distance reduces them to mere points of color, mere decorative dots of yellow and white and pink and gray.

The early political history of this portion of the west bank of the river is, in its larger aspect, identical with that of the bank opposite. The Dutch administration, with its director in the little town of New Amsterdam, extended across the Hudson and beyond. Manhattan Island would, indeed, seem even to have taken its name from this western shore. Juet, in his entire journal of the cruise of the *Half Moon,* mentions only one place name in connection with the river, and that is when he referred to "that side of the river that is called Manna-hata." The sense of the text locates it on the west shore. Any one who is dubious of Master Juet's intention may find this interpretation confirmed on an English map, dating from 1610, on which the name "Manahata" appears on the west side of the mouth of the river, and the word "Manahatin" on the east side.

But both sides of the river were New Netherland throughout the Dutch régime, until the English came into political control in 1664. Governor Andros then gave his attention to the west shore and he called it Albania. That was before news reached across the sea that, at the same time, the Duke of York had divided the Province of New York into two parts. That portion along the first twenty-one miles of the west shore because a part of the province which the Duke granted Berkeley and Carteret and by him then named "New Cæsarea or New Jersey" in honor of Carteret who had been governor of the Isle of Jersey. For about a year, 1688-89, it was annexed to New England, and between the years 1702 and 1738 the royal governor of New York was also the royal governor of New Jersey. Since then, as colony and state, it has had its own governor.

This whole sector, from the mouth of the river to a point opposite Spuyten Duyvil, is a peninsula, nowhere wider than Manhattan Island opposite, for the Hudson is paralleled to the west by the Hackensack River, and their waters meet in the Kill van Kull between New Jersey and Staten Island. Although, in the present state of the water-front, there is from the river no evidence of high land on the southern reach of the peninsula, its spine rises from a height of one hundred feet near the mouth of the river to two hundred feet where these higher lands reach the river shore, and then farther to three hundred feet where the bluffs merge into the Palisades. The first reach of this peninsula on the river is "made ground." The shore whence the Indian launched his canoe and where the first white settlers here drew their boats upon the beach are now hidden beyond the artificial shore-line, which has pushed the original water-line thousands of feet inland.

Originally the now unseen heights were in full view from the river, across marsh-land out of which rose a few low sandy hills that at high tide were almost entirely surrounded by water. On the most southerly of these dunes rose the town of Bergen from which grew Jersey City. Farther north on another hill which terminated in a rock at the water's edge rose the houses that were the beginning of Hoboken.

To-day along the shore, as one travels north, contiguous and almost indistinguishable from one another, are Jersey City, Hoboken and Weehawken. Farther north our interest is engaged by the stories of Bull's Ferry and Fort Lee, which cling close to the Palisades.

In the early days when these shores were green and the sand-hills were visible without even obscuring the higher ridge behind them, the peninsula as far north as the Palisades was a part of a purchase from the Indians made in 1630 by Michael Pauw, and was by him called Pavonia. On the lips of his successors Pauw's name gradually became Paulus, Pawles and Powles. From this original owner of the land came the name Powles' Hook which until well into the last century described the point at the mouth of the river.

The first settlements at Powles' Hook were made "on the maise land behind Communipaw," when Jacques Cortelyou was ordered to lay out a village there in 1660. We know what a sizeable town New Amsterdam, across the river, had become by this time, so that if we are to believe the chronicles of Diedrich Knickerbocker, as thoroughly as we enjoy them, history has left out a great gap which only he supplies, thus:

"Among these favored places, the renowned village of Communipaw was ever held by the historian of New Amsterdam in especial veneration. Here the intrepid crew of the Goede Vrouw first cast the seeds of empire. Hence proceeded the expedition under Oloffe, the Dreamer, to found the city of New Amsterdam, vulgarly called New York, which, inheriting the genius of its founder, has ever been a city of dreams and speculations. Communipaw, therefore, may truly be called the parent of New York, though, on comparing the lowly village with the great flaunting city which it has engendered, one is forcibly reminded of a squat little hen that has unwittingly hatched out a long-legged turkey.

"It is a mirror also of New Amsterdam, as it was before the conquest. Everything bears the stamp of the days of Oloffe, the Dreamer, Walter, the Doubter, and the other worthies of the golden age; the same gable-fronted houses, surmounted with weathercocks, the same knee-buckles and coats, and multifarious breeches. In a word, Communipaw is a little Dutch Herculaneum or Pompeii, where the reliques of the classic days of the New Netherlands are preserved in their pristine state, with the exception that they have never been buried.

"The secret of all this wonderful conservation is simple. At the time that New Amsterdam was subjugated by the Yankees and their British allies, as Spain was, in ancient days, by the Saracens, a great dispersion took place among the inhabitants. One resolute band determined never to bend their necks to the yoke of the invaders, and, led by Garret Van Horne, a gigantic Dutchman, the Pelaye of the New Netherlands, crossed the bay, and buried themselves among the marshes of Communipaw, as did the Spaniards of yore among the Asturian mountains. Here they cut off all communication with the captured city, forbade the English language to be spoken in their community, kept themselves free from foreign marriage and intermixture, and have thus remained the pure Dutch seed of the Manhattoes, with which the city may be repeopled, whenever it is effectually delivered from the Yankees."

That all communication with the burghers across the river was cut off seems to have been a part of the good Knickerbocker's suspected tendency to exaggeration, for another, and probably not less dependable "historian," more than hints at such intercourse. It appears in his account of an occasion when, as a Communipaw Dutchman with his *vrow* and family were returning home from market, "an immense fish in its gambols leaped from the water, and, accidentally landing in the boat, crashed through the bottom. Whereupon the good-wife, drawing about herself her voluminous petticoats, calmly seated herself in the hole, effectually stopping the inflow of water, and enabling all to reach shore in safety. A striking example of her presence of mind and general adaptability."

Before the Revolution Powles' Hook enjoyed such distinction as attaches to having a popular race-track. It attracted thoroughbred racers and a promiscuous attendance from both sides of the river. The *New York Mercury* for October 14, 1771, carried an advertisement for a horse-race "round the new course at Powles' Hook" between "Booby, Mug, Bastard, and Quicksilver." The purse was thirty dollars, the horses were to run twice round to a heat, they were to carry "catch riders," and the meet was to start at two o'clock. If one is to judge by the purse, this race was small fry compared to those at another meet here reported in the same paper of June fifteenth next following. On the latter occasion the purses had risen to fifty pounds for one race, wherein "Mr. Water's Horse Auctioneer" outran "Mr. Cornell's Horse Richmond, Mr. Elsworth's Horse Quicksilver, and Mr. Cornell's Horse Columbus"; and to ninety pounds for a race in which "Mr. Bud's Horse Liberty" won over "Mr. Cornell's Horse Tulip, and Capt. DeLauncey's Horse Poppet."

At the outbreak of the Revolutionary War General Washington caused a fort to be built on Powles' Hook by which he sought, in conjunction with the Battery across the Hudson, effectively to control the mouth of the river. Soon after the British captured New York a part of their fleet came up the bay, on September 23, 1776, and subjected the Powles' Hook fort to a cannonading during a full half-hour. General Hugh Mercer was in command of the fort. He soon found it untenable, and abandoned it in favor of a retreat westward. Thereafter it remained in British control until the end of the war. But their "peaceable adverse possession" did not go unchallenged.

In one of the most daring exploits of the war the fort was

captured in August, 1779, by Major, afterward General, "Lighthorse Harry" Lee; although it was abandoned immediately. The project and performance were wholly Lee's. The only object was, by means of an unexpected descent, to reach the fort, dismantle it, destroy all stores possible, withdraw at once with all prisoners, and thus by a brilliant stroke infuse new courage into the spirits of the colonists and their army. Although he had learned that the fort was negligently guarded by a garrison of not more than five hundred soldiers, its position and natural protection made its capture a hazardous operation. Washington Irving, in his *Life of Washington,* thus describes Lee's exploit:

"A creek, fordable only in two places, rendered the Hook difficult of access. Within this, a deep trench had been cut across the isthmus, traversed by a drawbridge with a barred gate; and still within this, was a double row of abatis extending into the water. The whole position, with the country immediately adjacent, was separated from the rest of Jersey by the Hackensack, running parallel with the Hudson, at the distance of a very few miles, and only traversable in boats, excepting at the New Bridge, about fourteen miles from Paulus Hook.

"Confident in the strength of his position, and its distance from any American force, Major Sutherland had become remiss in his military precautions; the lack of vigilance in a commander soon produces carelessness in subalterns; and a general negligence prevailed in the garrison.

"All this had been ascertained by Major Lee, and he now proposed the daring project of surprising the fort at night, and thus striking an insulting blow 'within cannon shot of New York.' Washington was pleased with the project; he had a relish for signal enterprises of this kind. He was aware of their striking and salutary effect, upon both friend and foe, and he was disposed to favor the adventurous schemes of this young officer. The chief danger in the present case, would be the evacuation and retreat, after the blow had been effected, owing to the proximity of the enemy's force at New York.

"In consenting to the enterprise, therefore, he stipulated that Lee should not undertake it unless sure from previous observation, that the post could be carried by instant surprise. When carried, no time was to be lost, in attempting to bring off cannon, or any other articles, or in collecting stragglers of the garrison who might skulk and hide themselves.

"He was 'to surprise the post, bring off the garrison immediately, and effect a retreat.'

"On the 18th of August, 1779, Lee set out on the expedition at the head of three hundred men of Lord Stirling's division, and a troop of dismounted dragoons under Capt. McLane. The attack was to be made that night. Lest the enemy should hear of their movement, it was given out that they were on a mere foraging excursion. The road they took lay along that belt of rocky and wooded heights, which borders the Hudson, and forms a rugged neck between it and the Hackensack.

"Lord Stirling followed with five hundred men, and encamped at the New Bridge on that river, to be on hand to render aid if required. As it would be perilous to return along the rugged neck just mentioned, from the number of the enemy encamped along the Hudson, Lee, after striking the blow, was to push for Dow's Ferry on the Hackensack" (foot of present St. Paul's Avenue) "not far from Paulus Hook, where boats would be waiting to receive him.

"It was between two and three in the morning, when Lee arrived at the creek, which rendered Paulus Hook difficult of access. It happened fortunately that Major Sutherland, the British Commander, had the day before, detached a foraging party under Major Buskirk, to a part of the country called English Neighborhood (now Englewood). As Lee and his party approached, they were mistaken by the sentinel, for this party on its return.

"The darkness of the night favored the mistake. They passed the creek and ditch, and had made themselves masters of the fort before the negligent garrison were well roused from sleep. Major Sutherland, and about sixty Hessians, threw themselves into a small Block House, on the left of the fort, and opened an irregular fire.

"To attempt to dislodge them would have cost too much time. Alarm given from the ships in the River, and the forts at New

York, threatened speedy reinforcements from the enemy.
"Having made one hundred and fifty prisoners, among whom
were three officers, Lee commenced his retreat without tarrying
to destroy either barracks or artillery. He had achieved his
object, a 'Coup de main' of signal audacity. Few of the enemy
were slain, for there was but little fighting, and no massacre.
His own loss was two men killed and three wounded.

"Lee's retreat was attended by perils and perplexities.
Through blunder or misapprehension, the boats which he was
to have found at Dow's Ferry, on the Hackensack, disappointed
him, and he had to make his way back with his weary troops, up
the neck of land behind that river, and the Hudson, in imminent
danger of being cut off by Buskirk and his scouting detachment. Fortunately, Lord Stirling heard of his peril, and sent
a force to cover his retreat. Washington felt the great advantage of this hardy and brilliant exploit."

The Congress passed resolves highly complimentary to the
young officer, thanking him for "the remarkable prudence,
address, and bravery" displayed by him, and ordered a gold
medal, emblematic of the affair, be struck and presented to him,
a distinction which, it is said, "no other officer below the rank
of general received during the war."

The village which Cortelyou laid out at Powles' Hook, in
1660, was called Bergen, and so it was known until the year
1820 when it was included in the newly incorporated Jersey
City. It has since been best known to the general and otherwise
unobservant traveler for its ferries. From the beginning of the
white man's sojourn on this side of the Hudson Powles' Hook
seems to have been a landing for those who wished to cross the
river. At first those crossings were made by the settlers in
their own boats, but in the year of the founding of Bergen, one
William Jansen established a legalized ferry between New
Amsterdam and the protected waters on the south side of
Powles' Hook. When the horse-manned catamaran type of

ferry was put into service, that traffic was somewhat independent of wind and tide, and the boats made their landings on the side of Powles' Hook inside the mouth of the river.

The "ferry stairs" at Powles' Hook were the eastern terminus of the stage route between Philadelphia and New York. Its New York terminus was, at least as early as 1764, at "Mesier's Dock at the foot of Cortlandt Street." The trip between these two greater cities required three days.

There were tricks in the ferry trade even from the first. One of the traditions is that the wily owner of the stage line, who owned also an inn at the Powles' Hook landing, started his stage off to Philadelphia at dawn, and refused places to any who had not crossed the Hudson before dark the afternoon before, so helping to fill not only his stages but his bedrooms as well. Another dodge experienced by Charles William Jansen, about 1793, was thus described by him in his *The Stranger in America:*

"Journeying towards the south, the traveller may proceed to Philadelphia by the stage-waggon, or by Amboy, which is chiefly performed by water-carriage, at much less expense. I took a place in the waggon, wishing to see the Jerseys. I was directed to the coach-office in the Broadway, in New York, where I paid the full fare, five dollars, and was desired to attend at nine the next morning, with my luggage. I did so, and found other passengers waiting; when, to my infinite astonishment, we were directed to cross the water at the confluence of the East and Hudson, or North River, which appears nearly a league broad, and were informed that we should find the stage on the other side, at Paulu's Hook, in the state of New Jersey; and to add to this imposition, we each paid our own ferryage. Thus, though the stranger pays for his place from New York to Philadelphia, he, in fact, is carried only from Paulu's Hook to the latter city."

It was over this route from Powles' Hook, in his own coach to be sure, that General Washington started back to Mount Vernon after bidding farewell to his officers across the river in Fraunces's Tavern. The New York *Gazette,* incidental to its account of this last memorable day of the General in New York, reported that:

"The Corps of the Light Infantry was drawn up in a line, the Commander in Chief, about two o'clock, passed through them, on his way to Whitehall, where he embarked in his barge for Powles Hook. He is attended by General Le Baron de Steuben, proposes to make a short stay at Philadelphia, will thence proceed to Annapolis, where he will resign his commission of General of the American Armies into the hands of the Continental Congress, from whom it was derived; immediately after which, his Excellency will set out for his seat, named Mount Vernon, in Virginia, emulating the example of his model, the virtuous Roman General, who, victorious, left the tented field, covered with honour, and withdrew from public life, *otium cum dignitate.*"

Back of its screen of shipping, Jersey City has a few remnants of the earlier days. They are, naturally, not far from the old square which was the heart of the little village of Bergen from the time it was laid out on its slight rise of ground back of Powles' Hook. They are on sites of earlier houses for the most part, but some of them still bear names indicative of their Dutch ancestry; such as the Van Horn house and the Van Wegenen house. Most venerable of all, with a beginning attributed to 1666, is the Sip house, no longer on its original site but moved into the suburbs where it is preserved in excellent condition.

The line between Jersey City and Hoboken is imaginary. The hems of both cities are of the same pattern. But if one looks sharp among the shipping one may discover a solitary waterside elevation crowned with an imposing old building. This is Castle Point and about it lies Hoboken. This old community derives its name from one of the earliest land transactions on the river, Michael Pauw's purchase from the Indians more than three hundred years ago. His lands were described thus:

"Aharsimus and Arresick extending along the river Mauritius and island Manhattan on the east side and the island Hobocan Hackingh on the north, and surrounded by Marshes Serving sufficiently for distinct boundaries."

Courtiers of Lady Nicotine will be interested to know that those who are wise in the Indian languages say that these are Indian words; that Hackingh means "land" or "territory," and that Hobocan means "tobacco" or "tobacco pipe." But Hoboken, or Hobocan, is no longer an island for its marshy inlets have long since been filled and the evidences of them are buried under the accumulations of the white man's civilization.

To Henry Hudson and his men it had loomed a white-green cliff, on its first appearance in history, in Robert Juet's account of their voyage. They reached this neighborhood on October second, and the chronicler said they:

"Anchored in a Bay, cleere from all danger of them [Indians] on the other side of the River, where we saw a very good piece of ground; and hard by it there was a Cliffe, that looked of the colour of a white greene, as though it were either Copper or Silver Myne: I think it to be one of them, by the Trees that grow upon it."

Thirty-five years later, in 1643, it was the scene of one of the blackest tragedies of the Dutch-Indian conflicts. In the course of a feud between the Indians on the west side of the river and the Dutch on Manhattan Island, a number of the whites had been murdered by the red men, and the settlers resolved to be avenged. Soon the fierce Mohawks came down from the north, reddening their path with murder and encamped on Hobocan Hackingh. The Dutch stole across the river at night, attacked the Indians in their sleep, massacred almost a hundred of them, and drove others off the point to perish in the freezing waters of the river.

This point and the land about it was, during the greater part of the eighteenth century, before the Revolution, the property and home of the Bayards. This family went "loyalist," however, and their estate was confiscated and sold by the Government to John Stevens in the year 1787. He and his descendants have given this neighborhood its greatest distinction.

Colonel John Stevens's biographer epitomizes him in this graphic paragraph:

"John Stevens was a genius of steam. We accept a modern President's message on Transportation as axiomatic, because John Stevens steadily preached and Practised the same text a century and a half ago. As the leading steamboat man of 1800, Stevens built craft that preceded all others of importance on the Hudson and embodied a design destined, thirty or forty years later, to alter the whole science of steam navigation. On land, he began twenty years ahead of his American contemporaries a single-handed fight for the recognition of steam. In the face of skepticism and ridicule, he gained one great objective in that fight by building and operating the first 'steam-carriage' ever run upon rails on the American continent. To any truly progressive plan for passenger-travel or freight-haul he gave his support with unflagging enthusiasm and with all the mental or material means at his command."

Castle Point was the scene of most of John Stevens's experiments. Most picturesque of them was perhaps that steam passenger railway he put in commission around his house, the first such railway in America, in the years 1825 and 1826. He had made an earlier experiment in building "a steam carriage" in the year 1795, but he abandoned it as too "cumbersome." He resumed this experiment when he was nearly eighty years old.

He then laid out a circular track on the lower lawn at Castle Point, and the locomotive which thereon drew the carriage is preserved in the Smithsonian Institution, in Washington. According to Carl Mitman's official description of it:

"The locomotive consists of a four-wheel platform truck upon which is mounted a vertical tubular boiler inclosed in a circular sheet-iron casing terminating in a conical hood that holds the furnace door, and upon the hood rests the smokestack. The furnace and its grate are circular and are placed inside of the circle formed by the boiler tubes and thus are inclosed by them. The grate rests on the projecting ledge of the lower part of the boiler. A single horizontal cylinder with valve chest on top is situated alongside the boiler and transmits its power to a crank shaft on which is mounted a gear wheel. This gear engages a second and larger gear vertically beneath it, which in turn meshes into a rack rail situated midway between the rails and about on a level with them. Four vertical posts extending downward from the floor of the truck near each corner and terminating in rollers in contact with the inner surface of the rails, guide the truck on the track."

Describing an experiment on the circular track at Castle Point, in 1826, the *New York Commercial Advertiser* said:

"The curve of this article is very rank, much more so than can be possibly required in pursuing the route of a road. This great deviation from a straight line gives rise to an enormous friction, the greater part of which, however, Mr S. has contrived to obviate.

"His engine and carriage weigh less than a ton, whereas those now in use in England weigh from eight to ten tons. His original intention was to give the carriage a motion of sixteen to twenty miles an hour, but he has deemed it more prudent to move, in the first instances, with a moderate velocity, and has accordingly altered the gearing, which renders it impracticable to move fast."

Nevertheless, declared Turnbull, referring to Steven's enthusiasm in demonstrating his practical experiment in steam locomotion by road, "Gentlemen must cram their beavers a bit tighter on their heads; ladies must gather their wide skirts about them and clutch the handles of their tiny parasols. At the appalling speed of six miles an hour, one and all must try the first American steam railroad."

In the first half of the last century, before the wharves had crowded the land off the river, the grassy and wooded shore between Hoboken and Weehawken was famous on both sides of the Hudson as the site of a pleasure resort known as the Elysian Fields. It was the scene of one of P. T. Barnum's early fiascos. He prepared "a grand Buffalo Hunt" to be held here. He was a master of ballyhoo and so it is not surprising that he gathered an enormous crowd. But he was not a master of the inscrutable buffalo, so it is probably no more surprising that something in the air on the Elysian Fields produced such an effect on the "wild untamable brutes" that "they refused to be disturbed in their meditations," and the only hunt was for refreshments and the way out.

The Elysian Fields is generally ascribed as having been the scene of one of the most baffling murders of the early nineteenth century. It was translated from the Hudson to the

Seine by Edgar Allan Poe and thrillingly told and ingeniously solved by him in his *The Mystery of Marie Roget*. Marie Roget was a thin disguise for Mary Cecelia Rogers, a young girl who worked in a New York tobacco shop. She was a popular young beauty and made the shop the resort of many admirers. One day she disappeared. When it was believed that she had been dealt with foully the police took up the case. There were few enough clues. She had last been seen on a ferry crossing the Hudson toward the Elysian Fields. In a few additional days her scarcely recognizable body was found in the river between Hoboken and Weehawken. The police sought a solution of her death with all their resources. Enormous rewards were offered for the conviction of the murderer. The newspapers made it the *cause celèbre* of the day. But the mystery of the death of Mary Rogers and of the identity of her assassin, if she reached her end by foul play, baffled all the detectives, professional and amateur. Time was about to fold up Mary Rogers, and public interest in her, in forgetfulness, when Poe revived the case in the terms of his celebrated mystery tale and immortalized the New York tobacco-shop girl as the Parisian Marie Roget.

History has consigned Weehawken to fame as the scene of many duels, in the days when offense was wiped out with weapons on "the field of honor." The dueling ground was on the river shore, some distance south of the present ferry landings, at a point precisely opposite the western end of Forty-Second Street, New York City. The encounters all date back to the days before the advent of the railway at a time when this was a sylvan and secluded shore. Among the duels fought here, and authenticated by local historians, were:

September 2, 1799. Aaron Burr and John B. Church. Neither hurt.

November 22, 1801. Eaker and Price. Neither hurt.

November 23, 1801. Eaker and Philip Hamilton. Hamilton killed.

December 25, 1801. John Langstaff and Oliver Waldron, Jr. Neither hurt.

December 25, 1801. Augustus Smith and A. M. Cocke. Neither hurt.

August 1, 1802. John Swartwout and DeWitt Clinton. Swartwout wounded.

November 21, 1803. Robert Swartwout and Richard Riker. Riker wounded.

July 11, 1804. Aaron Burr and Alexander Hamilton. Hamilton killed.

July 8, 1815. Gouverneur and Maxwell. Gouverneur killed.

May 12, 1816. Price and Green. Price killed.

October 19, 1818. John Heath and Oliver Hazard Perry, the hero of Lake Erie. Neither hurt.

November 28, 1827. Graham and Barton. Graham fell.

Oct. 19, 1835. Aitkin and Sherman. Arrested before firing.

May 16, 1837. A Spaniard and a Frenchman. One wounded.

September 28, 1843. Names unknown. Seconds loaded with cork bullets. No harm done.

It will immediately be recognized that the most famous of these duels was that of July 11, 1804, between Aaron Burr and Alexander Hamilton. It may be observed, also, that Alexander Hamilton fell wounded unto death on the same relative spot as that on which his son Philip had three years earlier been shot dead in his encounter with Eaker. It is a further coincidence that the identical brace of pistols used in the meeting of 1799, between Burr and Church, were used in 1801 by Eaker and young Hamilton, and again in 1804 by Hamilton and Burr.

There have been varying accounts of Hamilton's meeting here with Burr, some romantically heroic in their interpretation of Hamilton's attitude. The best authenticated is that of Hamilton's grandson, Alexander McLean Hamilton:

"Col. Burr arrived first on the ground, as had been previously agreed. When Gen. Hamilton arrived the parties exchanged salutations, and the seconds proceeded to make their arrangements. They measured the distance, ten full paces, and cast lots for the choice of positions, as also to determine by whom the word should be given; both of which fell to the second of Gen. Hamilton. They then proceeded to load the pistols in each other's presence, after which the parties took their stations. The gentleman who was to give the word then explained to the parties the rules which were to govern them in firing. . . . He then asked if they were prepared; being answered in the affirmative, he gave the word *present*, as had been agreed upon, and both parties presented and fired in succession—the intervening time is not expressed, as the seconds do not agree on that.

"The fire of Colonel Burr took effect, and General Hamilton fell almost instantly. Colonel Burr then advanced toward General Hamilton, with a manner and gesture that appeared to General Hamilton's friend to be expressive of regret, but without speaking, turned about and withdrew, being urged from the field by his friend. . . . No further communication took place between the principals, and the barge that carried Colonel Burr immediately returned to the city."

Hamilton was carried across the river, and was taken to the home of his friend, William Bayard, at numbers 80-82 Jane Street near the corner of Greenwich Street. A courier was dispatched to Mrs. Hamilton who was at the Grange, ignorant of what had occurred, and she joined her husband by noon. Later they were joined by their children. Hamilton died at about two o'clock the next day.

At two miles above Weehawken is Shadyside, famous in Revolutionary times as Bull's Ferry; and at about six miles is

Fort Lee, a point now easily recognized as the western terminus of the George Washington Bridge.

The Bull's Ferry neighborhood was made up largely of Tories. The patriot families about them complained that these Tories seized and held their cattle. In this the marauders were protected by the garrison of a British blockhouse erected in a strong position above the ferry. Washington directed Anthony Wayne to storm and capture the blockhouse and restore the cattle to their owners. Wayne and his men made a gallant effort in late July, 1780, but the enemy's position was too strong and Wayne's own ammunition was too weak for him to attain his objective. It was said, however, that at the moment the assault was given up the British had only one round of ammunition remaining.

The incident attracted an enormous amount of attention at the time, owing to the British adulation of the defenders of the fortification on the heights, but the memory of it will perhaps be given a longer life by reason of the poetic caricature of it written by Major André in a comic ballad of seventy-two quatrains, after the manner of the English ballad *Chevy Chase,* and entitled *The Cow Chase.* Two of the verses are sufficiently suggestive of the other seventy:

> "O ye whom glory doth unite
> Who Freedom's cause espouse
> Whether the wing that's doomed to fight
> Or that to drive the cows.

> "Ere yet you tempt your further way
> Or into action come,
> Hear, soldiers, what I have to say,
> And take a pint of Rum."

The three cantos of *The Cow Chase* were published in three

installments in *Rivington's Gazette*. An ironic significance, unpremeditated by André, was given this, his final quatrain:

> "And now I've closed my epic strain
> I tremble as I show it,
> Lest this same warrior-drover, Wayne,
> Should ever catch the poet."

On the very day that the *Gazette* published those lines, Major André was arrested near Tarrytown as a spy in connection with the treason of Arnold, and there was poetic justice, later, in the fact that the commander of the troops from whom was chosen the guard which accompanied the "poet" to the scaffold, on this same bank of the Hudson, and only fifteen miles from Bull's Ferry, was the "warrior-drover," Anthony Wayne.

The patriot Americans had a further last word to say on the subject of this poem, for on a manuscript copy of it there appears, beneath André's signature, this endorsement:

> "When the epic strain was sung
> The poet by the neck was hung.
> And to his cost he finds too late
> The dung-born tribes decide his fate."

Fort Lee was, during the Revolutionary War, the complement of Fort Washington, on the heights opposite on the east side of the Hudson, for the defense of the river against the British shipping. It was from this point that Washington watched the battle, across the river, which, against his expressed belief that the fort should be abandoned as untenable against the surrounding enemy, resulted in the fall of the fort named in his honor. The ultimate fate of the fort on the west bank was thus sealed, but the American troops held it until Lord Cornwallis landed six thousand British troops on the shore five miles above under the protection of the Palisades, with the obvious intention of cutting the garrison at Fort Lee off from the rest of the American Army. Washington saw this as clearly as he foresaw the fate of Fort Washington. In the earlier instance he expressed an opinion in which, for some unknown reason, he indulged his officers' disinclination to concur. He expressed no indecision about Fort Lee. He ordered the troops away from it and the abandonment of the position.

The columnar range of the lofty Palisades, from this point to their termination, twelve miles to the north of it, march on almost unbroken. They rise practically from the water's edge, perpendicularly except where erosions, made by man as well as by Nature, heap up at their base, to heights varying from three hundred to five hundred feet. In places the rocky wall has been riven by the torrents of the ages, but the scars of these narrow gorges have been healed by the ministering foliage of the forests. Its face, seen close up and in detail, is made fantastic by the peculiar hexagonal jointing of the rock, an unusual geological formation which is known to exist in only two other important instances, the Giant's Causeway on the north coast of Ireland, and Fingal's Cave on the island of Staffa on the west coast of Scotland.

The value of the miles of broken rock at the foot of this precipice was found to afford such ready material for making macadam roads, and as the road makers were availing themselves of it with a freedom which menaced this great natural wonder, the state bought the property and dedicated itself to the care of the Palisades as a public park. Or, in the words of one of the reports promoting this end:

"The events from the advent of man to the assault on the

Palisades may, for present purposes, be covered in a few words. Adam discovered the earth. Columbus discovered America. John McAdam, a descendant of the old Adam, discovered how to construct roads with crushed stone. Carpenter Brothers, quarreymen, discovered the Palisades. And the people of New York and New Jersey discovered that one of the most beautiful features of the Hudson scenery was being ruined to supply road material."

From the river crest of the Palisades the view embraces an enormous horizon, which includes the mouth of the Hudson and New York Bay; the whole of Manhattan Island and glimpses of Long Island Sound and the Connecticut shore beyond to the east; westward down its own slopes gradually descending into the valley of the Hackensack River; and north up the broadening waters of the river to the mountainous barrier of the Highlands.

It is in this direction that interest next beckons us, to that Westchester shore of the Hudson opposite nearly all the upper reach of the Palisades, then along both shores of those wide waters where the Hudson is broadest, and beyond to the gates of the Highlands. Sailing on, in our approach, the congestions of commerce behind and forgotten, the majesty of Nature asserts itself. The shores of the river, seen from its surface, are two green bands converging indefinitely ahead. Between them the broad blue path which is the lordly river entices us on to the misty distance, which we must penetrate and try to make clear.

CHAPTER IX

TAPPAN SEA AND HAVERSTRAW BAY

Spuyten Duyvil—Philipsborough Manor and the Philipse Family—Confiscation of Loyalists' Estates—Jonkheer Van der Donck Gives His Name to Yonkers—Philipsborough Manor House—George Washington and Mary Philipse—Roger Morris's Marriage—A Prophecy—Jan Dobs and Dobbs Ferry—Tappan Sea—Water Lore—The Unresting Oarsman—The Mysterious Storm Ship—Tappan Village—DeWindt House—Major André's Prison—His Trial and Execution—The Indian's Sin of Being Found Out—Sunnyside and Washington Irving—Tarrytown—Sleepy Hollow—*Ichabod Crane and the Headless Horseman*—The Old Dutch Church and Its Yard—Castle Philipse—Sing Sing—Ossining—Croton River—The Van Cortlandts and Their Manor House—Haverstraw Bay—The Treason House—Stony Point—Peekskill—Cortlandtville—Old Saint Peter's Church and Its Hillside Burying-Ground—Israel Putnam and the Spy of Gallows Hill.

HE shore of the Hudson opposite the Palisades and above Spuyten Duyvil Creek was once a part of the manor of Philipsborough, which extended north along this shore twenty-two miles to the confluence known as the Croton River.

The origin of the name Philipsborough rests on the unimaginative foundations of fact; that of Spuyten Duyvil rests on the more colorful fable of Diedrich Knickerbocker, who ascribes it to the last heroic exploit of Stuyvesant's trumpeter, Antony Corlear, who was deputed to ride forth and trumpet the countryside to war:

"It was a dark and stormy night when the good Antony arrived at the famous creek (sagely denominated Haerlem *river*) which separates the island of Manna-hata from the main land. The wind was high, the elements were in an uproar, and no Charon could be found to ferry the adventurous sounder of

205

brass across the water. For a short time he vapoured like an impatient ghost upon the brink, and then, bethinking himself of the urgency of his errand, took a hearty embrace of his stone bottle, swore most valorously that he would swim across, *en spijt den Duyvel* (in spite of the devil!) and daringly plunged into the stream.—Luckless Antony! scarce had he buffetted half way over, when he was observed to struggle most violently as if battling with the spirit of the waters—instinctively he put his trumpet to his mouth and giving a vehement blast—sunk forever to the bottom!

"The potent clangour of his trumpet, like the ivory horn of the renowned Paladin Orlando, when expiring in the glorious field of Roncesvalles, rung far and wide through the country, alarming the neighbours round, who hurried in amazement to the spot—Here an old Dutch burgher, famed for his veracity, and who had been a witness of the fact, related to them the melancholy affair; with the fearful addition (to which I am slow of giving belief) that he saw the duyvel, in the shape of a huge Moss-bonker with an invisible fiery tail, and vomiting boiling water, seize the sturdy Antony by the leg, and drag him beneath the waves. Certain it is, the place, with the adjoining promontory, which projects into the Hudson, has been called *Spijt den duyvel,* or *Spiking devil,* ever since."

Philipsborough Manor derives its name from the less apocryphal Frederic Philipse who rose in an astonishingly short time from the office of carpenter to be one of the greatest landholders on the Hudson. His family became one of the most distinguished of the colonial period and souvenirs of them survive in many places on and near what was once his great manor.

Earlier, that part of the manor land adjacent to Neperhan Creek had been the patroonship of another extraordinary colonial, Jonkheer Adriaen Van der Donck, who bought it from the Indians in 1646. Van der Donck was a cultured young Dutchman from Breda, a doctor of laws, who came to New Netherland to serve as sheriff of Rensselaerwyck, and received his grant of land from the West India Company in acknowledgment of his services as peacemaker between the red men and Director Kieft. He laid out a farm for himself on the banks of the Neperhan not far from its mouth on the Hudson, and there he dammed the creek and erected a sawmill.

Jonkheer Van der Donck was the first lawyer on the Hudson. But he was not permitted to practise, and for a curious and perhaps unmatched reason. When he made application to practise law in New Netherland the directors of the Company refused to permit him to plead because they did not know "of there being any other of that stamp" in the colony, and hence none "who can act and plead against Van der Donck in behalf of the other side." They compromised by permitting him to give legal advice.

Frederic Philipse, who bought Van der Donck's estate after that gentleman's death and to it united other lands north and south of it along the Hudson, was born in Bolswaert, Friesland, and was the grandson of the Viscount Philipse, a Bohemian noble who had fled from his native land to Holland, and he came to New Netherland probably in 1647. Although he was referred to in early documents as the Company's "carpenter," if he was, indeed, a mere manual journeyman, his skill and character very soon raised him to a much higher professional plane, probably best expressed by the term "architect-builder."

In his thirty-first year Philipse was made a burgher or freeman of New Amsterdam, and thereafter his name reappears in increasingly important positions of public trust and service. He speculated in wampum; he exhibited a real genius in his operation as a fur trader; in addition he had his interest in and took his profits from mills, lands, the foreign as well as river shipping and trade, which included "privateering," believed to have been a polite term for the then winked-at profession of piracy;

until in his forty-seventh year he was listed as New Amsterdam's richest citizen. His fame, in fact, extended overseas to the court circles of London, for in the royal commission of Governor Dongan, the Duke of York directed his representative, upon his arrival in New York, "to call together Fredericke Philipps, Stephen Courtland, and so many more of the most eminent inhabitants of New Yorke, not exceeding tenn, to be of my Councill."

Philipse continued to add to his lands on the Hudson, about the Neperhan, until in 1693, in his sixty-seventh year, he owned the entire east shore from Spuyten Duyvil Creek to Croton River, a distance of twenty-two miles. It was in this year, too, that these lands were, by a royal charter in the name of William and Mary, erected "into a Lordship or Manor of Philipsborough in free and common soccage according to the tenure of our Manor of East Greenwich within our County of Kent in our realm of England, yielding, rendering and paying therefor, yearly and every year, on the feast of the Annunciation of the Blessed Virgin Mary, at our fort at New York, unto us, our heirs and successors, the annual rent of £4 12s. current money of our said Province."

His manor hall rose on the high point between the Neperhan and the Hudson at a short distance from the Post Road to the east and the great river to the west, with a range of view along the latter which extended up and down beyond the Palisades in both directions. In addition to this house he built another, known ever since as Castle Philipse, on the banks of the river at Slapershaven, or Sleepy Hollow, Creek, eleven miles north of the manor hall.

Frederic Philipse, founder of the manor of Philipsborough, seems to have had a penchant for widows. He was twice married and both times to seasoned mates. His first marriage, in 1662, was to Margaret Hardenbrook, widow of Peter Rudolphus de Vries, a distinguished Dutch colonial trader; his second, in 1692, was to the widow of John Derval, Catharine, daughter of Oloff Stephanus Van Cortlandt. He died in the year 1702. The Philipse line descended from the first marriage, as there were no children by the second venture.

His grandson, Frederic Philipse (1695-1751), was the third and last lord. This Frederic Philipse was scarcely the counterpart of his immigrant grandfather. His estates, his fortune, and his social position had been created for him. His uneventful career indicates that he conceived his full duty was to do little else than to maintain them. He is variously spoken of: by the historian Hall as "the courtly and scholarly gentleman of the old school"; by Timothy Dwight, president of Yale College, as "a worthy and respectable man, not often excelled in personal and domestic amiableness"; and by Chief Justice John Jay as "a kind benevolent landlord," with "a taste for gardening, planting, etc." In one respect at least the last lord of Philipsborough did resemble his distinguished grandfather, the first lord, for like him he married a widow, the twenty-four-year-old relict of Anthony Rutgers. But he and his wife seldom appeared in the same carriage together, for his girth grew with his amiability until it attained "such large dimensions that there was not room for both in the family chariot." One of his sisters, Susannah, married Beverley Robinson of the Highlands, whom we will meet later; and another was the Mary who married Roger Morris for whom Mount Morris, now known as Jumel Mansion, was built. The last generation of this celebrated family in America consisted of the ten children of this last lord of the manor.

He and his family were Tories and withheld from any association with the patriotic American party. Such was the suspicion of his "hostility or equivocal neutrality" in 1775, that he was arrested and was taken to Hartford, Connecticut; but in about a fortnight was there released on his parole to return when required, and in another six months he returned to his manor on the Hudson. Thence he went to his town house in New York City. In September of the next year he was summoned to return to Hartford, and, although it has been said in his defense that he did not receive the summons, he was, by his failure to return, later, in 1779, adjudged to have broken his parole. His real and personal estates were confiscated under an act of the State Legislature which declared him "guilty of felony," and if he should be found in any part of the state he should "suffer Death . . . without Benefit of Clergy." With him, under this ban, fell his sisters Susannah and her husband, Beverley Robinson, and Mary and her husband, Roger Morris. Thus vanished the manor of Philipsborough.

The Philipses remained in New York City until the treaty of peace was signed at the termination of the Revolutionary War, when the late lord of the manor, "humiliated in spirit, blind of sight, and broken in health," took himself and his family off to England where they ended their days.

Sailing this flank of ancient Philipsborough Manor, the green hills bank back to a height of over two hundred feet. They are flecked everywhere with the colorful outcroppings of the roofs and towers of suburban houses. As we approach Yonkers, the most interesting detached house is Font Hill, almost but not quite eclipsed by the foliage and by the background of the buildings of Mount Saint Vincent Academy of which it is now a part. It was built by the actor, Edwin Forrest, for his country home, and is an interesting specimen of the English castellated style, having six towers, the highest of which reaches seventy-one feet from the ground.

Yonkers suggests nothing else so much as that it is a piece of upper New York City, broken from that island unit, and in some inscrutable way lodged here in terraces rising three hundred feet between river and sky. The town derives its name from the familiar title of the first patroon of these shores, the Jonkheer Adriaen Van der Donck, for sometimes his property was called the Jonkheer's Land, from which it became the "Yonnckers Land," and finally Yonkers. Van der Donck left another name in this neighborhood, Saw Mill River, the modern name of the Neperhan, derived from those sawmills which he first put here about 1646.

It was in the waters off this shore that Hudson anchored the *Half Moon* for the third time on his way up-river, on September thirteenth. "Then there came four Canoes aboord," chronicled Juet, "but we suffered none of them to come into our ship. They brought great Store of very good Oysters aboord, which we bought for trifles."

It is here begins that line of country estates, each with its vast and splendid house, which earned for this bank of the Hudson its nineteenth-century distinction as "Millionaire's Row." The house of first historic import in this neighborhood is the manor hall of Philipsborough. Once it commanded an extensive view east and west. To-day it is hemmed in at the heart of Yonkers where it is cared for by the state in a condition excellently representative of its best traditions.

The manor house has the shape of a right angle which presents its short side to the south and its long side to the east. Its general effect is impressive, but less pleasing than its detail, which is handsome, dignified and significant. The observer is at once struck by the fact that its long side is built of brick and its short side of stone. This is indicative of its history.

The first lord built his manor hall of stone and facing south; it is reasonably supposed, about the year 1682. This ancient building survives, incorporated in some part of the south façade of the present building whose long east front was erected about 1745. The door and window spacing on the east façade is irregular and hence this side is less pleasing than the south façade where the placing of the door and the windows at least appears well balanced. The interior details reflect the best taste of eighteenth-century English building and decoration.

A wholly real if somewhat romantic interest attaches to the hall by reason of the birth, courtship and marriage here of Mary Philipse, sister of the third lord of the manor. This Miss Philipse was esteemed one of the most beautiful and accomplished young women among the river families. The traditions of the hall are rarely referred to without citing the details of her wedding here; and that occasion is seldom described without a reference to the tradition that no less a personage than George Washington once sought her hand in marriage.

Washington made his first visit to the Hudson in the year 1756, on his way to Boston to consult General Shirley, Commander-in-Chief of His Majesty's forces in America. He was then in his twenty-fourth year, a bachelor, and had recently become the master of Mount Vernon on Potomac. On that occasion he stopped for seven February days the guest of his former Virginia schoolmaster, Beverley Robinson, at his New York City house. Washington had already been more or less in love with Mary Carey, Lucy Grymes and Betsy Fauntleroy,

PHILIPSE MANOR HOUSE, YONKERS

SUNNYSIDE

Washington Irving's Home, Tarrytown

so it is not wholly improbable, especially in view of related evidence, that on this occasion he was susceptible to the attractions of Mary, sometimes called "Polly," Philipse, who was at the time a guest in the home of her sister, Mrs. Beverley Robinson.

On his return from Boston Washington renewed his visit at the Robinson house, and when he departed he was sufficiently interested in Miss Philipse to request his friend, Joseph Chew, to keep him informed of her. The main support of the belief that Washington may have looked to her as the future mistress of Mount Vernon is this letter from young Mr. Chew, written in the year next after Washington's visit to New York:

"As to the Latter part of your Letter what shall I say? I often had the Pleasure of Breakfasting with the Charming Polly. Roger Morris was there (don't be startled) but not always; you know he is a Lady's man; always something to say, the Town talk't of it as a sure & settled Affair. I can't say I think so, and that I much doubt it, but assure you I had Little Acquaintance with Mr. Morris and only slightly hinted it to Miss Polly; but how can you be Excused to Continue so long at Phila. I think I should have made a kind of Flying march of it if it had been only to have seen whether the Works were sufficient to withstand a Vigorious Attack—you, a Soldier and a Lover.... I intend to set out to-morrow for New York where I will not be wanting to let Miss Polly know the sincere Regard a Friend of mine has for her and I am sure if she had my Eyes to see thro she would Prefer him to all others."

Washington's rival, as we have already seen, was his old friend and companion in arms, Roger Morris. Washington left no written evidence that he acted further on young Chew's warning or that he did anything other than to allow Morris "to urge his suit unrivalled and carry off the prize," which he did.

Mary Philipse and Roger Morris were married in the

drawing-room of the manor hall on January 19, 1758, surrounded by a company of brilliant social contemporaries dressed
in the height of the colorful fashions of the middle of the
eighteenth century. Hall thus describes the culmination of the
occasion and a portentous after-event:

"Presently a premonition of the approaching bridal party
sent a magnetic thrill through the company, and about half-
past three the bride and groom with their attendants entered.
Miss Barclay, Miss Van Cortlandt and Miss De Lancey were
the bridesmaids, and Mr. Heathcote, Captain Kennedy and Mr.
Watts were the groomsmen. Acting-Governor De Lancey, son-
in-law of Colonel Heathcote, Lord of Scarsdale Manor, assisted. Standing under a crimson canopy emblazoned with
the golden crest of the family—a crowned demi-lion issuing
from a coronet—the ceremony was performed, the bride's hand
being bestowed by her brother. The latter, the Lord of the
Manor, was superbly dressed and wore the gold chain and
jeweled badge of the ancestral office of Keeper of the Deer
Forests of Bohemia.

"Following the ceremony there was a grand banquet. In
the midst of the feast, it is said, a tall Indian, closely wrapped in
a scarlet blanket, appeared unannounced at the door of the
banquet hall and with measured words said:

" 'Your possessions shall pass from you when the Eagle shall
despoil the Lion of his mane.'

"Then he vanished as mysteriously as he had appeared. The
sensation produced by this message can be imagined. For years,
it is said, the bride pondered on this strange prognostication,
and never understood its significance until the magnificent domain of which she was a part owner was confiscated during the
Revolution."

Beyond Yonkers the shore reverts to the mottled green of
suburban loveliness, after five other miles mounting to a height
of four hundred feet about Dobbs Ferry, which is so much
richer in historic memories than in survivals to recall them.
It owes its name to a ferry operated here in the eighteenth cen-

tury by a descendant of *"Jan Dobs en zyn huys vrou, Abigail,"* who were settled here in 1698.

Beyond this point the natural aspect of the river presents its first marked change. The Palisades rise in one final lofty reach and then dip, almost abruptly, and disappear in the low billowy greenery below Sneden Landing. Opposite, the higher hills lift their summits nearly two miles east from the water. The beauty of the scene is milder as the banks lose their abruptness, the surface of the water widens, and we sail into what appears to be a hill-cinctured lake, but what in that part of the Hudson is known as the Tappan Sea.

This water takes its name from one of the Mohegan tribes of Indians who inhabited its shores. Over the twelve miles of its length, from the end of the Palisades to Croton, sometimes called Teller's Point, it averages from two to three miles in width. But we are no sooner in the Tappan Sea, and its panorama develops, than we realize that in places here the shores rise to heights unattained farther south. Due north they present a wall six hundred feet high. The west side rises gradually to equal and even greater heights, and culminates, near the sea's north end, at Verdrietege Hook (Grievous Point) in the bald brown precipitous flanks of Hook Mountain, whose crest is seven hundred and thirty feet above the water.

The Dutch imagination, frightened by the unfamiliar heights, with their ominous night shadows, has peopled this sea with its own share of the specters which are attached to the river. Two of those most familiar in local folk-lore are The Unresting Oarsman and the not less mysterious Storm Ship.

The oarsman was once a hearty youth of Spuyten Duyvil named Rambout Van Dam. Word had reached him of a Saturday-night frolic in one of the Dutch villages in the hills back of Verdrietege Hook, and with the native intrepidity of a true if somewhat unreal hero, he braved current and tide and weather to row all the eighteen miles from his home to the party. There he danced and drank in high spirits until long after midnight, when the party waned and his thoughts turned to home, down-river. His friends warned him of the dire consequences visited by Dutch theology on those who had broken the Sabbath. But his was a reckless mettle, and disregarding all advice, he sped his boat off across the black waters toward Spuyten Duyvil. There is no record that he ever arrived. Indeed, reports are all to the contrary. These same reports say, as dipping oars hint the presence of an oarsman indistinguishable in the darkness, that it is young Van Dam doomed to row on eternally.

The Storm Ship legend harks back to the early days before the English came to bedevil the Dutch calm on the river. Then a mysterious ship, flying the Netherlands colors, is said to have been seen entering the river with sails bellied by winds nowhere else apparent, riding forward against a strong ebb tide. The astonished burghers signaled a command to her to stop and show her papers; but the ship sailed on. Then a gun at the Battery sent a ball thundering toward her. But "her hull did not stop the ball, nor did the ball check her course." On she sped past the Palisades, straight up the Tappan Sea, around the frowning heights of Verdrietege Hook, until she disappeared from sight and for ever. She was never seen to pass down-river and out to sea. But that is not the last of her here, as many a Tappan fisherman has attested, for she is the Storm Ship, says Bacon, "that makes mysterious journeys, never heeding shoal or headland, tacking when the wind is fair and running free in the teeth of a gale, with never a concession to any weather that mortals give heed to. Into the moonlight she comes suddenly, from some unknown quarter and as suddenly, while the eye is fixed upon her, vanishes completely as a bubble that floats for a moment where a wave has broken, and then, in a twinkling, is dissipated."

As we enter the Tappan Sea the most conspicuous artificial object is a long pier reaching out from the western bank nearly half-way across the river. It is Piermont Landing and it invites us ashore to follow the road inland just behind the Palisades, an easy two miles, to the village of Tappan. This village is modest enough in its modern appeal, but it has its particular survivals of an historic past. Tappan grew up in the midst of land which was granted in 1686 to sixteen Dutch farmers, some of whom were already resident there. It came into the national picture, as has already been indicated, during the Revolutionary War.

Here, for four brief periods, General Washington had his headquarters in the home of Johannes DeWint. He stopped here from August 8 to 23, 1780; from September 28 to October 7, 1780; from May 5 to 8, 1783; and from November 11 to 13, 1783. Two of these pauses of Washington were marked among the outstanding events of the Revolution. While Washington was at the DeWint house on his second visit to Tappan in 1783, he here approved the findings of the court martial which tried André, thus signing the British spy's death-warrant. He came here in May, 1783, because he found it a convenient residence while conducting the parleys, at Dobbs Ferry, with Sir Guy Carleton in relation to the evacuation of British troops then on American soil.

The DeWint house still stands, the oldest surviving building which was occupied by Washington as his headquarters during the Revolution. The date 1700 appears in brick built into its walls and this is presumed to be the year it was erected. This house, a one-story-and-a-half structure, is now attached to a larger and more modern dwelling.

Another of Tappan's historic houses is the old stone house in which André was imprisoned during his trial and until his execution. It was, at the time, the inn of a Mr. Mabie. From it André marched to and from his trial in the old brick church which has long since been destroyed. The house was built in 1755. Not only did Mabie use it as a tavern, but such it continued to be until about 1857; and such in a modest way it is again to-day, hugging the roadside invitingly. Its walls are built of gray and brownish stone with some brick trim. The house is squat and solid, and reflects a Dutch tradition, with no nonsense.

André left this house for the last time a little before noon on Tuesday, October 2, 1780, to march to the place of his execution, about one mile distant on a hilltop west of the village. The way thither on that day was lined by crowds of curious spectators.

As the cortège moved from the prison André walked arm-and-arm between two subalterns, flanked by two others. These four officers carried drawn swords. A captain's command of thirty or forty men surrounded the central group of five, and these in turn were surrounded by an outer guard of five hundred infantrymen, who later formed a hollow square at the place of execution. Neither General Washington nor a single member of his staff appeared, but at the head of the procession was nearly every field officer of the army mounted on horseback.

André believed he was to be shot like a soldier, so that when he reached the hilltop and saw a gallows there, he was seized first with surprise and then with a great loathing which he expressed in his manner rather than words. He recovered a measure of composure and must have at least affected the bravado shown as he "leaped lightly" on to the baggage-wagon drawn beneath the cross-tree, took his position on the lid of his own coffin, threw his hat aside, removed his stock, loosened his shirt collar, snatched the rope from the hangman's hand, adjusted it about his neck and then bound a handkerchief over his eyes. When, finally informed that he might speak, he said firmly and with dignity:

"All I request of you, gentlemen, is that you will bear witness to the world that I die like a brave man."

A moment later he murmured in an undertone: "It will be but a momentary pang." Almost immediately the wagon moved swiftly away and the sentence of death had been executed.

That night Thatcher made entry in his Military Journal:

"Major André is no more among the living. I have just witnessed his exit. It was a tragical scene of the deepest interest. During his confinement and trial, he exhibited those proud and elevated sensibilities which designate greatness and dignity of mind. Not a murmur or a sign ever escaped him, and the civilities and attentions bestowed on him were politely acknowledged. . . . The fatal hour having arrived, a large detachment of troops was paraded, and an immense concourse of people assembled; almost all our general and field officers, excepting his Excellency and his staff, were present on horseback; melancholy and gloom pervaded all ranks, and the scene was affectingly awful."

He was buried at once in a grave at the spot of execution. Forty-one years later the grave was opened and his remains were removed and transported to England to be buried in the south aisle of Westminster Abbey. Over his first grave, within a circular iron paling, there is a modest memorial granite stone with a generously worded inscription detailing its purpose.

Among the many traditions of Tappan, some nearer the border-land of legend than that of fact, is one illustrative of Indian character in the days when the red man still hovered in the neighborhood. According to the story, a whipping post was set up there during the Revolution for the punishment of military prisoners, and on one occasion a young Indian, caught at thievery, was sentenced to receive a lashing on the bare back while bound to the post. According to the local historian:

"The Indian's father was present and begged the officer in command to permit him to administer the punishment to which his son had been condemned. The officer hesitated to consent as he suspected the old Indian naturally would lay on the lash with only too gentle a hand. He decided, however, to grant the father's wish with the reflection that if he performed the task too tenderly, some of the soldiers could do the job over and thus teach both the natives a needed lesson. But instead of gentleness, the Indian father displayed the utmost savagery, dealing his son blows that brought the blood with each cut of the whip, and as he swung the whip lash, he cried with every stroke:

" 'Bad Indian! Steal! *And get caught!*'

"The latter consideration—getting caught—being, according to the code of the red men, the only reprehensible feature of the whole proceeding."

On the eastern shore of the Hudson, about one-third the reach of Tappan Sea, where it is widest and where the towns of Nyack and Tarrytown face each other across its waters, is Sunnyside, the home of Washington Irving, the genial and imaginative presiding genius of most of the river's lore. If this river surpasses all other American rivers in the fame of its myths, it is owing to the creator of its legendary aristocrats, Rip Van Winkle, Ichabod Crane, Wolfert Webber and the redoubtable chronicler, Diedrich Knickerbocker.

More fortunate than most other celebrated houses of the lower Hudson, which have been divested of their original setting by the upward sweep of population and development, Sunnyside retains its rural charm and its rustic seclusion, alone with its hills, its glades, its forests and its waterside. The old stone house is not less true to itself to-day than when described by Irving as "made up of gable ends, and full of angles and corners as an old cocked hat. It is said, in fact, to have been modeled after the hat of Peter the Headstrong, as the Escurial of Spain was fashioned after the gridiron of the blessed St. Lawrence." He spoke of it affectionately as Wolfert's Roost, a name deriving from the fact that it owed its beginnings in 1656, to Wolfert Acker, and given it, as Irving suggests, "probably from its quaint cockloft look, and from its having a weathercock perched on every gable."

One may say of it now, as did Irving fourscore years ago:

"The Roost still exists. Time, which changes all things, is slow in its operations on a Dutchman's dwelling. . . . Odd rumors may gather about it, as they are apt to do about old mansions, like moss and weather-stains. The shade of Wolfert Acker still walks its unquiet rounds at night in the orchard; and a white figure has now and then been seen seated at a window and gazing at the moon, from a room in which a young lady is said to have died of love and green apples."

Irving purchased the house in 1835, but his diplomatic appointments in Europe and his literary occupations on this side the Atlantic kept him from this home, except at intervals, until 1846. Thereafter he was more continually at Sunnyside until he died here, November 28, 1859.

The community which stretches along the shore near by Sunnyside commemorates him in its name, Irvington, but it melds imperceptibly into Tarrytown which is, indeed, more nearly the center of the Irving tradition here, for not only is Sunnyside at its southern extremity, but at its northern extremity is Sleepy Hollow, scene of the brook, the bridge and the church famed in Irving's account of the legend of *Ichabod Crane and the Headless Horseman.*

As long as this tale is retold, and it bids fair to be retold for ever, so long will be true what Irving said of Sleepy Hollow: "There was a contagion in the very air that blew from that region; it breathed forth an atmosphere of dreams and fancies infecting all the land."

In order to be scrupulously exact about such important matters it must be recorded that the little low schoolhouse where Ichabod taught the youngsters of this neighborhood has long since disappeared, and even the bridge of to-day is not the same bridge as that across which the schoolmaster and choir-singer fled on Van Ripper's nag, old Gunpowder, when madly pursued by the horseman who carried his head in the crook of his elbow. Indeed, there are people so querulously particular as to say that the bridge does not stand in the same place as the one which rattled under the hoofs of the mounts of the haunted Ichabod and his spectral pursuer. But no one has yet been found so brave as to question the identity of the brook or the church, or the old graveyard by it where the headless rider "tethered his horse nightly among the graves."

The old stone Dutch church stands on the slope of Sleepy Hollow, just where the Post Road crosses the brook. It was built in 1699 by Frederic Philipse. At that time it was the only church on the river between New York and Kingston, and it was the only church between Yonkers and Peekskill for over a century. It retains its original lines which distinguish it particularly by a half hexagon bay at the east or pulpit end, by the graceful curve of its hipped roof, and by the belfry and its adornments. These last are the original weather-vane marked V. F. (Verdyk Flypse) there since 1700, and the old bell cast in Holland by command of the donor, the lord of the manor of Philipsborough, and bearing this inscription: "Si · Deus · Pro · Nobis · Quis · Contra · Nos · 1685." It is still rung for the Sunday afternoon services in September and October. The old church stands staunch and conservative, looking its age which it wears like a decoration, yet facing the future with a hearty fortitude.

The interior is much altered. The pulpit, the oak communion table, and the two beakers and the baptismal bowl of solid silver originally used here, were, like the bell, and probably the weather-vane, made in Holland by command of the same donor. The table and the communion silver are in use in the First Reformed Dutch Church of Tarrytown.

In the old yard about the church nestle the toppling tombstones of the Van Tassels, the Van Werts, the Eckers, the Swartwouts, the Beekmans, the Buckhouts and many other Dutch families; some stones dating back to 1704. A little way north of the church, on a slope which descends toward the Pocantico, are the graves of the Irvings. The plain headstone of Washington Irving does not differ from that of any other of the family, and records simply his name, his parents' names, the date of his death, and his age. Pilgrims come to the Sleepy Hollow churchyard to see Irving's stone who are heedless of the monuments of the Dutch aristocrats who sleep about him.

Standing a little nearer the river, and facing the old church across the Post Road, is Castle Philipse, also built by the first lord of Philipsborough Manor, whose original lands extend seven other miles to the north. The date of the building is attributed to the year 1683. Its original character is much obscured by modernization. When the first lord died he left this house to his son, Adolphus, who made his home here and made it the seat of administration of that portion of the manor under his control. When he died, in 1750, this house and its lands were inherited by the second lord of the manor, who lived at the manor hall to the south, and there again united the administration of all Philipsborough. When, in 1776, the Assembly or Convention of New York was forced north from the Manhattan Island, one of its stops is said to have been made here at Philipse Castle.

In and about Tarrytown are other arresting points. The spot where André, on his ride south along the Post Road to regain the security of British controlled territory, was apprehended by John Paulding, David Williams and Isaac Van Wert, is traditionally believed to be near that marked by a marble monument commemorating that roadside episode, which was so significant in its effect on the trend of our national destiny.

Here and hereabout have lived, among many other distinguished public characters, Commodore Oliver Hazard Perry, who was not only the hero of Lake Erie but was also so instrumental in opening Japan to the influences of the Western World; General John C. Frémont, "the Pathfinder," and John D. Rockefeller. The neighborhood about, and especially east of Tarrytown, was the scene of many of the episodes of *The Spy* by James Fennimore Cooper, who made his home for some time in the center of what is now Scarsdale, not far away. The local recurrence of the Beekman name, notably in the case of Beekman's Forest, is one of the reminders that this family succeeded the Philipses as the early great landowners here.

Less than five miles above Tarrytown the riverside green has been shaved away and the shore is stark as a sterile rock. In this bleak patch rises a heterogeneous group of bold, angular, garish, high-walled, fortresslike buildings, which are the prison known as Sing Sing.

High above it, and as it were wrapping its terraces in a green mantle apart, are the roofs and spires of Ossining. The names, Sing Sing and Ossining are two forms of a single Indian root word variously written *Sin-sing, Sing Sing, Sin Sinck* and *Sink Sink*. Ossining means "place of rock," and refers alike to the stout hills on which the place is built and to the vast munition of ancient boulders which guard its shore-line.

Just above Ossining the Croton River enters the Hudson, between hills which are a continuation of an even loftier hinterland. There, for some miles behind the Croton Dam, extend the marvelously beautiful waters of Croton Reservoir, its shores bent in every direction by the impregnable flanks of the green hills round about it. Once this reservoir was the main water supply of New York City, and it is still a mighty contributor to the vast metropolis's cleanliness and to assuaging its thirst. The name Croton is believed to derive from an Indian word meaning wind or tempest.

The stream marks the dividing line between the vast original domains of the manor of Philipsborough south of it, and Van Cortlandt Manor north of it. The latter stretched along this bank of the Hudson a full twelve miles to the farther side of Anthony's Nose at the gateway into the Highlands.

Van Cortlandt Manor was erected by royal charter in the year 1697. It contained eighty-three thousand acres. The charter conveyed the rights to hold courts-leet and -baron, and the extraordinary privilege of sending its own representative to sit in the Provincial Assembly. Its obligation to the Crown was the payment of an annual rental of forty shillings on the Feast of the Annunciation of the blessed Virgin Mary.

The first Van Cortlandt in America was Oloff Stephanus who reached the river in 1637 and resided in New Amsterdam where he became one of the richest and most powerful burghers. He was Colonel of the Burghery, President of the body called the "nine men," *Schepen* of the city, and eventually its burgomaster, an office he filled uninterruptedly from 1655 until the end of the Dutch régime.

His son, Stephanus Van Cortlandt, who became the first lord of the manor, was an equally dominating figure in the social and political life of the province. He was born in New York City in the year 1643, and at the early age of thirty-four became the mayor of the city, its first American-born mayor. Later, among many services and distinctions, he was Chief Justice of the province and a member of the Governor's Council. He died in the year 1700, leaving behind him eleven children who intermarried with the DePeysters, DeLaunceys, Beekmans, Schuylers, Skinners, Bayards, Johnsons, Van Rensselaers and other distinguished river families. During the Revolutionary War, the Van Cortlandts were fervently devoted to the American cause.

The Van Cortlandt manor house still stands near the foot of a hill which protects it from wintry blasts, on the west side of the Croton within a few hundred yards of its confluence with the Hudson, a view of whose wide waters it still commands in spite of the semi-suburban character of the modern environment in which it finds itself. Lawns surround it in all directions. To the east, the paths lead off to the old gardens, still colorful and fragrant with flowers and shrubs, and beyond them

226

the walk leads on to the old ferry landing and a dwelling which once was the quarters of the keeper of the ferry.

The house is one of the most venerable mansions on the shores of the Hudson. It was built by Johannes Van Cortlandt, eldest son of the first lord, and never since has it been out of the ownership of the family. In its present excellent state of preservation, the result of unremittingly generous and intelligent care during the more than two and a quarter centuries of its life, it is an admirable expression of the sound utilitarian dignity of the better buildings of the end of the seventeenth century.

When it was built, utility rather than style or beauty motivated the builder. This house, then so far from New Amsterdam and from any other protective settlement, was erected to serve the threefold purpose of country house, administration building and fort. Its solid walls of gray stone, with door and window trim of brick, are three feet thick, and are pierced on every side with loopholes for defensive musketry. Not all these loopholes have yet been sealed up. Originally it had a flat stone roof which, with the passing of danger from the Indians, gave place to a gable roof pierced by dormer-windows. In this and other ways the house has been changed somewhat through the centuries, yet its simplicity and charm and distinction remain, to carry back unmistakably to the days of its distant youth.

It is built on the rise of the hill, and is so masked with galleries and lattice and vines, that its front presents a suggestion of a mere story-and-a-half house. Actually, it consists of a spacious rambling main floor set above a high basement and under a dormered upper story. The front door consists of one wide perpendicular leaf, Dutch fashion split transversely in half. Above it, in the branches of a pair of antlers, is a bow said to have been the possession of the Indian chief from whom was purchased a part of the land on which the manor house stands.

Within, the rooms ramble off on each side of the central hall which extends through from the south front to the north front. The hall and main reception rooms are, wholly or in part, paneled with oak, some of which it is believed dates to the earliest days of the manor. The house is full of family treasures, of which two at least are of general interest. One is the little writing table at which De Witt Clinton died. The other is the dining-room table, brought, along with other pieces still treasured by the family, from Holland, by Oloff Stephanus Van Cortlandt when he came to the Hudson in 1637. It is probably one of the earliest pieces of mahogany furniture to have reached America, for this wood was rarely used in the seventeenth century. It is a tradition in the family that every colonial governor of the province dined at this table, to which may be added assurance of the strong probability that the list of such a company might be extended to include members of all the distinguished families who have resided on the Hudson and many of the celebrated visitors who have come to the river since Van Cortlandt manor house was built.

There is an intimate association between this house and two other Van Cortlandt dwellings, one of which we will find presently near the river at the northern extremity of the manor lands, and the other which stands in Van Cortlandt Park, Borough of the Bronx, New York City, about one mile east of the Hudson. Jacobus Van Cortlandt, brother of the first lord of the manor, and founder of what is called the Yonkers branch of the Van Cortlandt family, married the so-called Eva Philipse, adopted daughter of the first lord of the manor of Philipsborough, and was the first of his family to own the property now incorporated in Van Cortlandt Park. His son, Frederick Van Cortlandt, built the handsome house which stands there, about the year 1749.

Beyond the mouth of Croton River, the long low westward reach of Croton Point cuts the width of the Hudson in half. In the lee of the tip of the peninsula was anchored the British sloop-of-war, *Vulture,* when she brought Major André up the Hudson on his fatal errand with Benedict Arnold. As we round the tip of this point, to pass out of the long sweep of Tappan Sea, it is to come to another link in the chain of charming variations which distinguish the great river. Here is another of those hill-locked reaches which makes the Hudson seem a succession of lakes.

It is called Haverstraw Bay, and though its length from Croton Point to Stony Point is only six miles, here the river attains its greatest width anywhere between its mouth and its tidal head, measuring more than three miles across from Waldberg Landing at Long Clove to the eastern shore opposite. This eastern shore rises gradually from the water to summits of five and six hundred feet within a mile of the shore-line. The western shore rises to equal heights, however, in bold precipices mounting directly from the water's edge, culminating in High Tor, which has an altitude of eight hundred and thirty-two feet, the highest mountain encountered so far in this progress from the sea. To the north the hills seem to curtsy, so that across them we may see the horizon lifted high by the misty purple flanks of still loftier Dunderberg. Nothing below this stretch compares with it in the beauty produced by the breadth, variety, grace, dignity, distance, heights and colors here.

In the precipitous hills inside the bay on its west side are two cloves, the Long Clove and the Short Clove. The word *clove* is one which recurs in Hudson nomenclature, and it derives from the Dutch word *Kloof,* meaning a cleft, gap, or ravine. The Long Clove is of interest because Joshua Hett Smith brought Major André to it from the *Vulture,* and on this point of the shore Arnold awaited his co-conspirator. From it André's and Arnold's way led them through the flat green-tipped village of Haverstraw at the foot of High Tor, on to Smith's house about two miles north of the village, where Arnold consummated the details of his treason. From that house Arnold set off in his barge for his headquarters opposite West Point, and André crossed the Hudson at King's Ferry near by on his fatal effort to reach the British lines. The house still stands.

Thus Tappan Sea and Haverstraw Bay compass most of the scenes of the drama of the Arnold-André drama, and they are included in the marvelous panorama which unrolls for the eye when seen from the summits of the hills behind and about Ossining. At the right is the mooring stop of the *Vulture,* beyond it are Long Clove where Arnold awaited André, above Haverstraw is the house where the treasonable understanding was concluded, farther on the site of King's Ferry where André embarked to cross the Hudson, the east shore where he landed, the long stretch of shore which he traveled on his way south along the Post Road to the left as far as Tarrytown where he was apprehended by Paulding and his companions, and, across from it, the valley opening behind the Palisades, where is Tappan which witnessed the British officer's trial and execution.

We pass out of Haverstraw Bay between the high lighthouse on the projecting nose of Stony Point, scene of General Anthony Wayne's celebrated exploit, which won for him the soubriquet of "Mad" Anthony, and Verplanck's Point, scene of those post-war military fêtes in honor of our French allies.

Again the course of the river, beyond the four miles in sight, can merely be conjectured by the traveler without a chart. It is only when one is opposite the point of Dunderberg that one sees that it is round it that the channel disappears into the embrace of other high mountains. In the watery elbow opposite Dunderberg is Peekskill, a considerable community which of preference retains the civic status of a village, and as such claims to be the largest village in America, its houses modestly climbing the lofty hills behind a lacy veil of green foliage.

Peekskill was in General Washington's path many times for, during the Revolutionary War, it was an important post and supply base of the Continental Army. As such it was the object of British attention, and on one occasion the enemy sacked and burned the American camp here.

The village was the birthplace of André's captor, John Paulding, and among the many personages more recently associated with the village were Peter Cooper, who spent a portion of his youth here; Henry Ward Beecher, who resided here in his later years; and Chauncey M. Depew, who was born here and is memorialized here by his home, his statue and the hilltop park named for him.

Peekskill takes its own name from Peekskill Creek which enters the river half a mile above it and is so called after Jan Peek, one of the early traders who sailed his ship into this *kil,* or creek, having mistaken it for the northern extension of the Groote Rivier, and built himself a habitation on its banks and spent a winter here. At the head of the creek's navigable waters, and now practically a suburb of Peekskill, is the village of Cortlandtville where are the upper Van Cortlandt manor house, Saint Peter's Church and Gallows Hill.

This Van Cortlandt house, two miles from the mouth of the

creek, was one of the subsidiary homes of the manor of that name. As one sails into the creek, one may see it above the waterside where originally it had its own landing. It is much altered by additions and modernization, but in the new block one may still pick out many of the lines of the original house which seems to have combined dignity with comfort. A tablet attached to its east wall recites that "General George Washington with his Aides slept in this house many nights while making Peekskill their headquarters in 1776, 1777 and 1778."

Cornelia, daughter of Pierre Van Cortlandt and wife of Gerard G. Beekman, made this house her home for a time and it is said that while here she unconsciously played a part in shaping the André drama. Eberlein gives this version of the incident:

"Lieutenant Jack Webb, acting aide to General Washington, came to the house one evening and left with Mrs. Beekman for safe keeping a bag containing a new uniform and some gold, asking her to send it to him 'at Brother Sam's' when he sent word. One evening, about a fortnight later, Joshua Hett Smith appeared at the house and asked for the bag, saying that Jack Webb was in Peekskill and had asked him to come and get it. Mrs. Beekman was on the point of handing over the bag, but suddenly thought better of it and declined to do so. Smith was insistent and urged that as Mrs. Beekman knew him well it must be all right to let him have the uniform. To this Mrs. Beekman promptly replied that she knew Smith so well that she didn't trust him. There was nothing for him to do but go away greatly disappointed.

"This was just the time that Smith was trying to get Major André back within the British lines. In some way he had learned of the whereabouts of Lieutenant Webb's new uniform and hoped to get it for André, knowing that André and Webb were about of a size. Had he succeeded in persuading Mrs. Beekman to give it up, André, in all likelihood, would never have been captured."

On the hillside beyond the road is the little old parochial church of Saint Peter in the midst of its ancient venerable graves and stones. This quaint and humble structure was erected in the year 1766 on land donated by Catherine Van Cortlandt, daughter of the first lord and the wife of Andrew Johnson. The frail building has been reverently protected in the interval, but it awaits the generosity of some patron to be restored to its original estate.

In its yard are buried most of the members of the Van Cortlandt family not interred under Trinity Church in New York City. The principal burial ground of this family originally was near the manor house at the mouth of Croton River. In recent years the encroachments of increasing population robbed that yard of its privacy and peace, with fear of worse to come. It was then that the surviving members of the family deemed it more reverent and protective to remove their forebears to the hillside cemetery about Saint Peter's at Cortlandtville, where they rest still, however, in the acres of the original manor. Among their stones we find those of the Honorable Pierre Van Cortlandt and his wife, Johanna Livingston Van Cortlandt; General Philip Van Cortlandt; Catherine, daughter of Vice-President George Clinton and wife of Colonel Pierre Van Cortlandt; Anne, Stephen, Gilbert and Gertrude Van Cortlandt; and Gerard Beekman, husband of Cornelia Van Cortlandt. Here, too, within the shadow of the church is a shaft which marks the grave of John Paulding.

Across the creek is Gallows Hill, which derives its gruesome name from the hanging here, in August, 1777, of the British spy, Edmund Palmer. General Israel Putnam was in command of the Continental troops in this area at the time of the capture of this officer, and Sir Henry Clinton, in command of the

British troops, sent to him under a flag of truce a "demand" for the surrender of the prisoner. In reply Putnam made his laconic and historic rejoinder: "He has been tried as a spy, condemned as a spy, and shall be executed as a spy; and the flag is ordered to depart immediately:" to which was added this brief postscript: "He has been accordingly executed."

Sailing down and out of the Peekskill, we find ourselves face to face with the water gate into that section of the Hudson known as the Highlands, a portion apart, unique in the course of the river, and as such the subject of its own portion of this chronicle.

CHAPTER X

HIGHLANDS OF THE HUDSON

The Appalachian Chain Crosses the Hudson—The South Gateway to the Highlands—Dunderberg and Anthony's Nose—A Sanctuary of Elemental Beauty—Its Varying Charms—Legendary Characters—Origin of the Fireflies—The Dutch Goblin of the Dunderberg—How a Beam from Trumpeter Anthony's Nose Killed a Mighty Sturgeon—Bear Mountain Bridge—Philipse's Highland Patent—Garrison—Saint Philip's Church—West Point—The United States Military Academy—Constitution Island—A Tunnel Eleven Hundred Feet under the Hudson—Crow's Nest—Storm King—Breakneck Ridge—The North Gateway of the Hudson.

S WE enter the Highlands in putting Peekskill behind us, so, having passed through them, we will leave them as Newburgh and Beacon appear on the shores ahead.

The south gateway to the Highlands is formed by the high front of Dunderberg, rising eleven hundred feet above the water on the west side, the highest mountain encountered so far on the river, and Anthony's Nose opposite, which appears almost as high because its scarp is more abrupt. Twelve miles beyond is the north gateway guarded by two other mountains, Storm King on the west side, only a little off perpendicular to its summit at nearly fourteen hundred feet, and Breakneck Ridge on the east side, nearly as high as that on its first rise adjacent to the river and then mounting, immediately beyond, another two hundred feet higher.

These mountains at the two gateways, and those along both sides of the twelve miles of river between them, have a much more impressive altitude than is usually associated with equal heights. The reason is that every foot of their rises toward the horizon counts. The altitude of mountains is computed in feet above the level of the sea. But it is generally customary for an observer, when looking up at a mountain from its base, to be standing on the land out of which they rise, land which itself is, in most instances, high above sea level, and the altitude of this land, being included in the given altitude of the mountain observed, by so much diminishes the apparent height of that mountain. The Highlands of the Hudson rise from the water level, a level of salt sea water, so that not a foot of these mountains is absorbed in their bases, and every foot of their measured flanks is visible between base and summit, between water and sky. They are a part of that vast agglomeration of heights which stretch in one continuous flight from northern Alabama on the southwest to the shore of the Saint Lawrence River on the northeast. Collectively these mountains are known as the Appalachian system. Among its more conspicuous groups are the Blue Ridge and Alleghanies to the west of the river, the Green and the White Mountains to the east of it.

This Appalachian system is a wall paralleling the Atlantic coast. Over most of its length this wall lies discreetly distant from the ocean. It is nearest to the sea where it crosses the Hudson, for here it ventures within fifty miles of the Atlantic. And just here the ocean found a vulnerable point where it could push its waters through. There are other points along the Appalachian system, points called "gaps," where fresh-water rivers rush through from greater heights, down to the sea, but its cleavage here in the Highlands is the only place between the Saint Lawrence River and the state of Alabama where the sea itself penetrates the long mountain wall and pushes its waters beyond it.

The river between the two gateways bends, around the rocky knees of these mountains, into three sectors, each resembling a long mountain-bound lake. Just within the south gate, low Iona Island thrusts itself out from the west bank to narrow the channel of the river to less than half of a mile, and the width of the river scarcely exceeds this until, beyond Constitution Island, under lofty Crow's Nest and Storm King, the steep shores relent a little, grudgingly to add a mere few hundred feet between the margins of the water. When it is narrowest there are only sixteen hundred feet between shores.

But what the imprisoned river loses in width it gains in depth. Its channel bed south of the Highlands, generally averaging a depth of about fifty feet below the surface, doubles that within each gateway, sinking to one hundred and nine feet off Dunderberg, and to one hundred and nineteen feet at Little Stony Point. The river bottom is farthest from the surface between West Point and Constitution Island, where it sinks to a depth of two hundred and sixteen feet.

There is an awesome beauty in the unfolding panorama as we sail through the narrow aperture admitting to the Highlands. The exhilarating effect of an entrancing variation of line and light and color is subdued by the generally unspoiled primeval character of Nature here, by the expanses of mountain-flank, by the silence of the currentless water, by the protective blue sky which the crowding summits rob of its dome-like spread and narrow to a strip of sheltering blue canopy.

The high shores seem sparsely peopled, for here man dwells reticently, somewhat screened by the forest. Occasionally a great house, set up near the horizon, looks down from its aerie like an Old World castle, and curiosity lingers over the problem of driving to such heights. There is no city within the gates;

and there are only two considerable but inconspicuous villages, Highlands Falls and Cold Spring, which peep out at certain angles for a brief visibility. The one conspicuous fabricated unit here is the massive group of stone and granite which is the United States Military Academy.

The Highlands are a sanctuary of a great and elemental beauty which gives the fulness of its manifold treasure only to those who linger and contemplate. For they have one beauty of the morning, when the dawn dissolves the lingering gray shadows in its bath of sunlight; another of noon, when the sun stands high overhead, and lines and colors are vivid in literal splendor; and another of night, when the waters are black, and the mountains lose definiteness and mystery hangs broodingly over the inscrutable scene, unless, perchance, the moon drifts from behind a crest to dissolve the opaqueness in its soft effusion and make the hushed hour lyric even in its silence.

They have one beauty of the opulent summer, when the mountains are lush with varying greens; another of autumn, when the frosts nip their flanks and, from shore to summit, they flame the whole gamut of yellow and scarlet, as if consumed by an epic fever; another of winter when, such fires having burned them black and the ice having locked the waters motionless as in death, the silent blinding storms shake out their snowy draperies, obscure all but their own shimmering fleece, and then part to reveal only mountains of soft silent miraculous white about the curves of a firm river of bright metal; and yet another of spring, when, under the rays of a strengthening sun, the icy manacles crack with a report as of musketry and break up under the pressure of the freshets and of the recurring tides, to dissolve into their elements or float down to the sea, leaving the blue waters laughing again, for joy of the returning greens, and white hulls and sails, and choirs of birds on its margins.

There is one beauty in the very silence which is the pervading mood of the river here, when the lap of the waters against the piles of the landings is softly audible and the call of a bird seems to be Nature's loudest note. There is another beauty even in man's intrusion with his contrivances: the muffled splash of the side-wheeler; the long blast of the steam whistle echoing from wall to wall; and the reverberations of the railway trains pounding their metals on either flank as they approach with the perfected crescendo and pass on and away with the perfected diminuendo of a master musician.

But no other beauty here is so arresting as that of the storm, when winds rise to whip the river into fields of whitecaps and the gathering tempest lashes the forest, and out of the lowering black clouds the artillery of heaven threatens to split the mountaintops as its detonations crash from peak to peak, multiplying in endless echoes, until they beat themselves out or are beaten out by other and mightier volleys.

Small wonder that out of such natural wizardry has sprung a world of supernatural wizards who rule the Highlands as well as much of the river above and below them. Irving confirms the presence of these legendary characters out of the mouth of Heer Antony Van der Heyden, for the benefit primarily of truant Dolph Heyliger, but for our benefit, too:

"The circumstance of Dolph's falling overboard led to the relation of divers disasters and singular mishaps that had befallen voyagers on this great river, particularly in the earlier periods of colonial history; most of which the Heer deliberately attributed to supernatural causes. Dolph stared at this suggestion; but the old gentleman assured him it was very currently believed by the settlers along the river, that these highlands were under the dominion of supernatural and mischievous beings, which seemed to have taken some pique against the Dutch colonists in the early time of the settlement. In consequence of this, they have ever taken particular delight in venting their spleen, and indulging their humors, upon the Dutch skippers; bothering them with flaws, head-winds, counter-currents, and all kinds of impediments; insomuch, that a Dutch navigator was always obliged to be exceedingly wary and deliberate in his proceedings; to come to anchor at dusk; to drop his peak, or take in sail, whenever he saw a swag-bellied cloud rolling over the mountains; in short, to take so many precautions, that he was often apt to be an incredible time in toiling up the river.

"Some, he said, believed these mischievous powers of the air to be evil spirits conjured up by the Indian wizards, in the early times of the province, to revenge themselves on the strangers who had dispossessed them of their country. They even attributed to their incantations the misadventure which befell the renowned Hendrick Hudson, when he sailed so gallantly up this river in quest of a northwest passage, and, as he thought, ran his ship aground; that they affirm was nothing more nor less than a spell of these same wizards, to prevent his getting to China in this direction."

Even the myriad of fireflies that sparkle "like gems and spangles on the dusky robe of night" are here accounted for by another misty bit of lore. These, according to the tradition recited by Trumpeter Corlear, "were originally a race of pestilent sempiternous beldames, who peopled these parts long before the memory of man; being of that abominated race emphatically called *brimstones;* and who for their innumerable sins against the children of men, and to furnish an awful warning to the beauteous sex, were doomed to infest the earth in the shape of these threatening and terrible little bugs; enduring the internal torments of that fire, which they formerly carried in their hearts and breathed forth in their words; but now are sentenced to bear about forever—in their tails!"

One encounters stories of the elves and gnomes from the very moment of passing into the Highlands around Dunderberg, for Irving tells of a particular goblin who haunts the river but is believed to dwell above it on this mountain:

"It is certain, nevertheless, that strange things have been seen in these highlands in storms, which are considered as connected with the old story of the ship. The captains of the river craft talk of a little bulbous-bottomed Dutch goblin, in trunk hose and sugar-loafed hat, with a speaking trumpet in his hand, which they say keeps the Dunderberg. They declare that they have heard him, in stormy weather, in the midst of the turmoil, giving orders in low Dutch, for the piping up of a fresh gust of wind, or the rattling off of another thunder-clap. That sometimes he has been seen surrounded by a crew of little imps, in broad breeches and short doublets, tumbling head over heels in the rack and mist, and playing a thousand gambols in the air, or buzzing like a swarm of flies about Antony's nose; and that, at such times, the hurry-scurry of the storm was always greatest. One time a sloop, in passing by the Dunderberg, was overtaken by a thunder-gust, that came scouring round the mountain, and seemed to burst just over the vessel. Though tight and well ballasted, she labored dreadfully, and the water came over the gunwale. All the crew were amazed, when it was discovered that there was a little white sugar-loaf hat on the mast-head, known at once to be the hat of the Heer of the Dunderberg. Nobody, however, dared to climb to the mast-head, and get rid of this terrible hat. The sloop continued laboring and rocking, as if she would have rolled her mast overboard, and seemed in continual danger either of upsetting, or of running on shore. In this way she drove quite through the Highlands, until she had passed Pollopol's Island, where, it is said, the jurisdiction of the Dunderberg potentate ceases. No sooner had she passed this bourne, than the little hat spun up into the air, like a top, whirled up all the clouds into a vortex, and hurried them back to the summit of the Dunderberg, while the sloop righted herself, and sailed on as quietly as if in a millpond. Nothing saved her from utter wreck but the fortunate circumstance of having a horse-shoe nailed against the mast, a wise precaution against evil spirits, since adopted by all the Dutch captains that navigate this haunted river.

"There is another story told of this foul-weather urchin, by Skipper Daniel Ouslesticker, of Fishkill, who was never known to tell a lie. He declared that, in a severe squall, he saw him seated astride of his bowsprit, riding the sloop ashore, full butt against Antony's nose, and that he was exorcised by Dominie Van Gieson, of Esopus, who happened to be on board, and who sang the hymn of St. Nicholas, whereupon the goblin threw himself up in the air like a ball, and went off in a whirlwind, carrying away with him the nightcap of the Dominie's wife, which was discovered the next Sunday morning hanging on the Weathercock of Esopus church steeple, at least forty miles off. Several events of this kind having taken place, the regular skippers of the river, for a long time, did not venture to pass the Dunderberg without lowering their peaks, out of homage to the Heer of the mountain, and it was observed that all such as paid this tribute of respect were suffered to pass unmolested."

The more literal-minded pundits have striven to connect the name of the adjacent mountain, Anthony's Nose, with that holy man for whom Portuguese Gomez called the river San Antonio. But such a notion has long been extinguished under Knickerbocker's more alluring attribution of it to the rotund trumpeter of New Amsterdam:

"And now am I going to tell a fact, which I doubt me much my readers will hesitate to believe; but if they do, they are welcome not to believe a word in this whole history, for nothing which it contains is more true. It must be known then that the nose of Antony the trumpeter was of a very lusty size, strutting boldly from his countenance like a mountain of Golconda; being sumptuously bedecked with rubies and other precious stones—the true regalia of a king of good fellows, which jolly Bacchus grants to all who bouse it heartily at the flaggon. Now thus it happened, that bright and early in the morning, the good Antony having washed his burley visage, was leaning over the quarter-railing of the galley, contemplating it in the glassy wave below—Just at this moment the illustrious sun, breaking in all his splendour from behind one of the high bluffs of the Highlands, did dart one of his most potent beams full upon the refulgent nose of the sounder of brass—the reflection of which shot straightway down, hissing hot, into the water, and killed a mighty sturgeon that was sporting beside the vessel! This huge monster being with infinite labour hoisted on board, furnished a luxurious repast to all the crew, being accounted of excellent flavor, excepting about the wound, where it smacked a little of brimstone—and this, on my veracity, was the first time that ever sturgeon was eaten in these parts, by christian people.

"When this astonishing miracle came to be made known to Peter Stuyvesant, and that he tasted of the unknown fish, he, as may well be supposed, marvelled exceedingly; and as a monument thereof, he gave the name of *Anthony's Nose* to a stout promontory in the neighbourhood—and it has continued to be called Anthony's nose ever since that time."

Advancing into this sector of the river with a more appraising eye for realities, we find our interest engaged at once by the high single span of Bear Mountain Bridge, swung between the mountain from which it takes its name and Anthony's Nose, its roadway at a height of one hundred and eighty-five feet above the water, twenty-two hundred and fifty-seven feet long, its central span alone sixteen hundred and thirty-two feet in length. One's first impression of this vast network of wire and cables, seen from the river on a misty day, is that of a vast cobweb spun between the mountains. The view from its roadway, far above the pale blue ribbon of river, encompasses all of the crests in the Highlands. Seen from this high point, equidistant from each shore, the parelleling gray and purpling mountains march northward like a procession of fabulous pachyderms.

The eastern shore beyond Anthony's Nose as far as Fishkill Creek under the north flank of Breakneck Ridge, practically the whole eastern shore of the Highlands, and extending east to the Connecticut line, was known, at the end of the seventeenth and the beginning of the eighteenth centuries, as the great Highland Patent of the Philipse family of Philipsborough Manor below. It was never erected into a manor. This portion of the holdings of the "loyalist" Philipse family was forfeited to the state in common with their other property during the Revolution. Tangible souvenirs of the Philipses are rare here. There is a township called Phillipstown whose length is almost coequal with the river boundary of the old patent; there is a Philipse Brook which enters the Hudson near Garrison; and Saint Philip's Church, on the banks of the river near by, named for the Adolphe Philipse to whom was granted the Highland Patent.

It was on this shore, at the foot of Sugar-Loaf Mountain, that stood the Beverley Robinson house, which was Benedict Arnold's headquarters and from which he fled down-river to the British man-of-war *Vulture,* when he learned of André's arrest. The house was destroyed by fire in 1892. It took its name from the son of John Robinson, who was president of the council of Virginia in 1734. While Beverley Robinson lived in the South he and George Washington became friends. He moved to New York and married Susannah Philipse, the eldest sister of the third lord of Philipse Manor, and it was at his town house, in New York City, that young Washington met Mary Philipse, Mrs. Robinson's sister. The Beverley Robinsons left for England at the end of the war and he died there.

The neighborhood above the site of the Robinson house is known as Garrison's, a name which derives from one of the older local families, and along the flanks and near the crests of the hills here are some of the finest modern houses on the Hudson. Not far from the landing at Garrison is St. Philip's Church which cherishes, among other traditions, a story that on one occasion, when General Washington was riding past it, one of his staff remarked, "That is a Tory church;" to which the General is reported to have replied, "It is my Church."

At the foot of Bear Mountain, on its north side, Popolopen Creek comes to the river through a precipitous ravine. This

© White

The United States Military Academy at West Point

West Point and the Upper Highland, Photographed from the Air

was the site, during the Revolution, of Forts Clinton and Mont-gomery. Fort Clinton stood on the south lip of the ravine and Fort Montgomery on the north lip. After their capture by Sir Henry Clinton they played no further part in the war.

From the moment of turning Anthony's Nose, into the middle-lake sector of the Highlands, the most conspicuous arti-ficial object in the view is West Point at its far end. One recognizes it by the agglomeration of buildings, on a plateau one hundred and fifty feet above the river, which are the national military academy, for the training of commissioned officers for the national army. They seem to rise out of the high shore, as if some titanic hand had brushed the forests away, and out of the bared rock had carved the gray walls and turrets and towers of the vast buildings, one of the most spectacular artificial features of the upper Hudson, their gray mass accented by the almost unbroken green of the mountain slopes of the Highlands about them.

During the Revolution the only works here were Fort Clin-ton, on the point near the river, and Fort Putnam, placed high above it on the mountainside, to defend it. President Wash-ington, as early as 1793, proposed the establishment of a national military academy, but it was made a reality only by an act of Congress, in 1802, which directed that it should be located on the Hudson at West Point. It has ever since been the cradle of the personnel of the command of our military establishment. Its graduates performed the most distinguished services in the Mexican War, and in every military war or emergency since. But not less distinguished were two of its cadets who were virtually expelled from the academy, one the poet, Edgar Allan Poe, and the other the artist, James McNeill Whistler.

On these shores, above and below West Point, but not far from it, have been the homes at times of the historical painter, Emanuel Leutze, John Bigelow, William Cullen Bryant, Lyman Abbott, George P. Morris, E. P. Roe, John Pierpont Morgan, Nathaniel Parker Willis and Robert W. Weir.

Opposite West Point, on the north side of the Hudson, where it briefly flows from west to east, is Constitution Island, a mass of gray rock and green forest, low, compared to the surrounding mountains, but formidable. At one place here the river is narrower than anywhere else in the Highlands and it was here during the Revolution the great chain was stretched from shore to shore to block the way of British war-ships.

To the Dutch navigators this was known as Martelaer's Island, and the reach between it and Storm King Mountain was called Martelaer's Rack or Martyr's Reach. The word "Martyr" in this connection is merely a corruption of Martelaer, which in turn is believed by some to be merely a pure Dutch word, indicative of the difficulty of navigating this reach, and by others to be a misspelling of Martelaire, the name of the members of a French family who are said to have resided on the island about the year 1720.

The present name of the island does not refer to the Constitution of the United States but to that of Great Britain, for the name is derived from Fort Constitution, built on it in 1775, before the United States or its constitution had come into existence. On Constitution Island in the last century lived the Misses Warner, who achieved some ephemeral reputation as writers of fiction.

Two of the greater wonders of the Hudson are just here, one visible and the other invisible. The visible wonder is the road high on the shoulder of Crow's Nest, which commands one of the most comprehensive vistas on the river. The invisible wonder is buried eleven hundred and fourteen feet below the surface of the waters. It is the syphon aqueduct which carries, from the west to the east side of the Hudson, the New York City water supply from its sources in the Catskill Mountains forty-five miles north of this point. This water-bearing tunnel is cylindrical in shape, fourteen and a half feet in diameter, and is bored through the solid rock supporting the weight of the waters of the river, which immediately above it are nearly two hundred feet deep.

As we advance, through the last reach of this great fiord-like waterway, these mountains at the north portal of the Highlands are its loftiest. No anticlimax here. On the west side Crow's Nest rises thirteen hundred and ninety-six and Storm King thirteen hundred and forty feet. Opposite them Bull Hill rises fourteen hundred and twenty-five and Breakneck Ridge sixteen hundred and thirty-five feet. The green and gray scarpes draw themselves up to their highest like the receding folds of doors opened to let the ships pass, but in their towering presence no ship passes through these portals that does not, by comparison with them, seem somewhat puny.

CHAPTER XI

Newburgh Bay to Kingston

Polopel Island—Camp-Grounds of the Continental Army—General Knox's Headquarters—New Windsor—The Temple or New Building—The Palatines—Newburgh—Washington and the Hasbrouck House—The Room with Seven Doors and One Window—Curious Fireplaces—Clinton Country—Fishkill Landing and Beacon—Fishkill Village—The Verplanck House and the Organization of the Society of the Cincinnati—Danskammer—Jew's Creek and Gomez's Mill-House—Poughkeepsie—Vassar College—Crum Elbow—Kingston—Old Houses—John Vanderlyn—Old Hurley—New Paltz and the Twelve Men.

ITH the mountains behind us, we pass out of the Highlands as if into another world. It is one other evidence of the striking variety of this great river. The epic elements melt into a gentler, friendlier expanse of broadening waters. The shores rise in low bluffs, backed by occasional rises which are higher on the western side. It is a smiling, alluring vista which stretches due north another eight miles. Locally these waters are spoken of as Newburgh Bay.

The roofs and spires of Newburgh and Beacon rise ahead on either side, but nearer at hand a picturesque detail dots the foreground of the river's surface. It is a rock emerging stark out of the water and crowned with a castellated medieval-looking building. Its name is Polopel Island, though sometimes it is called Bannerman's after the man who, until his death, owned it and here stored a strange collection of second-hand arms and war material sold by the Federal Government after the Spanish American War.

248

The North Gateway of the Highlands

Storm King Mountain on the left, Breakneck Ridge on the right, Polopel Island in the middle distance, and, beyond it, Newburgh Bay

THE SENATE HOUSE AT KINGSTON, THE STREET FRONT

THE SENATE HOUSE AT KINGSTON, THE GARDEN SIDE

Legend hangs thick about this rock, and on its adjacent shores are supposed to dwell the goblins which ride the storms in the Highlands. In sailing days it was the custom for the older sailors to toss apprentices overboard here, ostensibly in the belief that the ducking made them immune from the sorcery of the storm goblins.

On the immediate left, in the shadow of Storm King, is the village of Cornwall, and beyond it the Moodna Creek comes down into the river. It was on this shore of the Hudson, for three miles north of the Moodna, that George Washington spent such a long time. Here the Continental Army was encamped from 1779 until it was disbanded on August 18, 1783, save a six months' absence during the campaign which culminated in Cornwallis's surrender at Yorktown.

General Washington established his headquarters in the Ellison house, on the hill on the south side of the village of New Windsor, overlooking the Hudson, on June 22, 1779, and remained here until July twenty-first when he moved to West Point, where he remained until the end of November. He returned to New Windsor about December 1, 1780, and this time he stayed on until the June twenty-fifth following. Generals in command of divisions of the army made their headquarters in several different houses in this neighborhood.

The most interesting survival of the old houses known to the Revolutionary soldiers is another Ellison house, about two and a half miles southwest of the village of New Windsor, which goes by the name of General Knox's Headquarters. It is a pleasant, rambling, roomy, old stone house, and was at different times occupied by Generals Knox, Greene and Gates, and Colonels Biddle and Wadsworth. But General and Mrs. Knox lived here longer than the others and distinguished their occupancy by many famous, though simple, social functions, and so it is Knox's name in particular that attaches to the house to-day.

The Edmonston house, at Vail's Gate near by, is spoken of as having been the headquarters of Generals St. Clair and Gates, though "without tangible evidence," but the Brewster house, with a shade more probability, is spoken of as LaFayette's headquarters. The most interesting building connected with the stay of the army in this immediate neighborhood was built of wood and has long since disappeared. It was situated on Temple Hill near the Knox Headquarters, and was an assembly and recreational house for the army, and was sometimes referred to as the Temple and sometimes as the New Building. Here was held the assembly called and addressed by Washington on the subject of the Newburgh Letters. Of this occasion Lossing said:

"This spot is consecrated by one of the loftiest exhibitions of true patriotism with which our revolutionary history abounds. Here, love of country and devotion to exalted principles, achieved a wonderful triumph over the seductive power of self and individual interest."

And Washington said of that meeting: "Had this day been wanting, the world had never seen the last stage of perfection, to which human nature is capable of attaining." But before he began to read the address which closed with those stirring words, it was on this occasion that he reached for the spectacles which David Rittenhouse, the Philadelphia astronomer, had ground for him and remarked to the assembly: "You see, gentlemen, that I have grown not only grey but blind in your service."

Beyond New Windsor, and eclipsing that modest village, the city of Newburgh rises from the river on a series of terraces which lift its sky-line three hundred feet above the water. The first settlement here was made at least as early as 1709 by Germans from the Palatinate on the Rhine, who gave it the name of Palatine Parish by Quassaic. After two-score years so many Scots and Englishmen had come in that they were able to change that name to Newburgh, after Newburgh in Scotland. It played its part in the national drama toward the end of the Revolution, during the long armistice succeeding the surrender at Yorktown.

Here was the Headquarters of the Continental Army, under the command of General Washington, from March 31, 1782, until the last days of August, 1783. General Washington spent some of the most anxious moments of his whole life here endeavoring to preserve and consolidate all that had been won in the preceding campaigns, before the English should outwit a seemingly inept Congress and an indifferent people; and before his "victorious" troops should yield to a strongly developed disposition to rebel against such ineptitude and indifference. Here were circulated the Newburgh Letters urging the army to rebel to redress the withholding of their pay; here the Continental Army was formally disbanded; and here Washington received the Nicola letter which proposed that he become king of the liberated colonies, and wrote his reply to it; and here he disbanded and bade farewell to the army.

Washington made his residence and headquarters in Newburgh in the home of Jonathan Hasbrouck, which stood, and still stands, on a large open square, on the south side of the city, on the first terrace above the river.

The house is somewhat dour and austere and it suggests the

solid and simple tastes of even the rather distinguished builder
who gave the house his name. It is built of stone, on a rectangular floor plan, and such is the sweep of its quaint roof that
it would pass as a rather squat house, if one did not observe
it carefully and discover that, above a commodious basement-
cellar rise a full first story, a somewhat more restricted second
story, and even a third story of a few additional rooms under
the ridge-pole.

The interior is simple and compact with only nine windows
for the eight rooms on the first floor. There could have been
little privacy as between the occupants of such a house, for every
room seems attainable only by entry from another room, so
that nearly every one of them has to serve as a passage. Indeed,
the large central room, on the river front, which appears to have
been the sitting-room or common room of the house, though it
measures eighteen by twenty-three and a half feet, has only
one window; but it has seven doors leading into five other rooms,
to the upper floor and to the out-of-doors.

That the General and Mrs. Washington must, nevertheless,
have hallowed this room with sympathetic souvenirs for their
friends is attested by this anecdote, told one hundred years ago
by Colonel Nicholas Fish:

"The distinguished Secretary of Legation from France to
this country, during the Revolution, Mabois, was the guest of
Washington at Newburgh, and was very much impressed with
the hospitality of his host, and of his quarters. More than half
a century afterwards he gave a dinner, at his own magnificently
furnished house in Paris, to which LaFayette, then an old
man, was invited to meet the American Minister, with several
of his countrymen. The dinner was served in Parisian style,
and everything was in excellent taste, so as to excite the admiration of the party. The repast being over and the evening
far spent in agreeable and joyous conversation, the guests were

invited in to supper, and were introduced into a room which contrasted strangely with the elegantly furnished apartments they had just left. There was a large open fireplace, and plain oaken floors; the ceiling was supported with large beams and whitewashed; there were several small-sized doors and only one window with heavy sash and small panes of glass. The furniture was plain and unlike any then in use. Down the centre of the room was an oaken table covered with dishes of meat and vegetables, decanters and bottles of wine, and silver mugs and small wine glasses. The whole had something the appearance of a Dutch kitchen. While the guests were looking around in surprise at this strange procedure, the host, addressing himself to them, said, 'Do you know where we now are?' LaFayette looked around, and as if awakening from a dream, exclaimed, 'Ah! the seven doors and one window, and the silver camp goblets such as the marshals of France used in my youth. We are at Washington's Headquarters on the Hudson fifty years ago.' "

Another curious feature of this curious house are the vast fireplaces, two of them measuring three feet by eight, but, in any conventional sense, they are not fireplaces at all. They are not built into the walls. Each fireplace consists simply of a stone hearth laid in the floor of the room, but up against the wall, and with an opening in the ceiling above it to receive the smoke and to carry it off through the chimney beyond. The fire built on such a hearth is not built in a fireplace, but literally out in the room. Huge cranes thrust out their arms from their anchorage in the wall to hold pots and kettles over the coals. And it has this advantage over the conventional fireplace set into the wall, that it may be enjoyed on three sides instead of merely one, and so entertains a larger and more approachable family circle.

When Washington resided here the ground and gardens spread out in all directions and there was between the house and the water nothing to disturb the natural outlook. The house stands high and the panorama of the river spreads out in a way which must have recalled to him his own superb panorama at Mount Vernon. Here, as on the Potomac, the turns in the river produce the effect of a long lake, but at his own home he was accustomed to a milder beauty for, instead of the long flat reach of Maryland to a low horizon, here, opposite the Hasbrouck house, rises Breakneck Ridge to a horizon more than ten times as high as that on the Potomac.

The country back of Newburgh, about the village of Little Britain, was the home of the great family of Clintons. Charles Clinton was the first of this name to come here. His two sons, both born here, were General James Clinton, who fought at Frontenac, at the forts in the Highlands, and at Yorktown; and that George Clinton, who was a member of the Continental Congress, the first Governor of the State of New York and then Vice-President of the United States. James Clinton's son, De Witt Clinton, statesman, philanthropist and savant, was also born at Little Britain. Only three miles north of Little Britain is Coldenham, which takes its name from that great scholar Cadwallader Colden, who patented three thousand acres of land here in 1729.

Facing Newburgh, across the river, is the much younger city of Beacon. It came into being as recently as 1913 by the merger of the villages of Fishkill Landing by the water and of Matteawan on the higher ground. It takes its name from the beacon which was lighted on Breakneck Ridge from time to time during the Revolution to signal the movements of the enemy. The beacon-pyres were rectangular and as they rose they diminished in pyramidal form. They were made of logs and were filled with brush and other inflammable materials; and they were often built to a height of thirty feet. One of the largest

and most important of these fiery Hudson Valley signals stood
on one of the highest points on the ridge, called Beacon Hill,
immediately above the city.

Fishkill Landing was established near the mouth of Fishkill
Creek, at an early day in the settlement of the river. It attained importance during the Revolution because it was the
river terminus of the upper or "inner" road which the armies
and couriers used between the Hudson and Boston. The lower
road had its terminus at King's Ferry, between Verplanck's
Point and Stony Point. The southernmost road between the
Hudson and New England, the Boston Post Road, had its
terminus in New York City, and so was not available to the
Continental troops.

Among the characters who gave distinction to Fishkill Landing was Catharyna Rombout or Madame Brett, whose home,
known as the Brett Teller house, stands reticently on an inconspicuous corner at the eastern end of the present city.
Catharyna Rombout was born in New York in 1687. While
still a minor she fell heir to a vast tract extending east from the
Hudson and north from Fishkill Creek, "on the north side of
the mountains." This was but a part of an even vaster tract,
extending sixteen miles east from the Hudson and north from
Fishkill Creek for nearly thirteen miles, which her father and
Gulian Verplanck had bought from the Indians in 1682. The
tradition is that Rombout bargained with the red men for "all
the land he could see." When they agreed to this, it is said
that he climbed to the top of Breakneck Ridge and so claimed
the vast expanse there envisioned and which went into the deed.

When only sixteen years of age Catharyna Rombout married
Roger Brett, a lieutenant of the English Navy, and these two
young scions of civilization came up to their Fishkill property

and here made their home. She survived her husband and died in 1764.

Madame Brett is not remembered for any single act of either daring or bravery, but she must have been a strong character, for after nearly two centuries she lives in the traditions and the consciousness of the neighborhood. The Indians leaned heavily on her advice. Her own progress over the old roads in her coach and four is remembered as one of great state. She is buried under the old Reformed Church in Fishkill.

This village of Fishkill, which gave its name to Fishkill Landing, lies three miles up the creek on the great north and south highway, on this side of the Hudson, which is known as the Albany Post Road. In the village is the old Dutch Reformed Church, where the itinerant convention sat at one stage of its flight from New York City to Kingston. Near the village is the Van Wyck house, which was used by Israel Putnam and other Revolutionary generals as headquarters and is generally ascribed as the Wharter House of Cooper's *The Spy,* and several old Brinckerhoff houses, one of which was used as headquarters by General Washington.

About a mile north of Beacon, and on a hundred foot rise above the river, stands the gaunt charred ruin of the Verplanck house, which was destroyed by fire in September, 1931, after a distinguished lifetime of nearly two hundred years. The property on which it stands has never been owned by any other than a Verplanck. The first of that name here was Gulian Verplanck who took title by grant from King James II and by covenant with the Indians in the year 1683. Baron Von Steuben made his headquarters here. The greatest distinction which attached to this house, however, came to it in connection with the organization of the Society of the Cincinnati.

A kind of bloodless battle has for many years raged across the Hudson at this point as to whether this society came into being at the Verplanck house or at the Temple, just beyond Newburgh. The facts appear to be that in the spring of 1783, the officers of the Continental Army, which was then concentrated along these shores of the Hudson, anticipating demobilization and desiring to establish some expedient to continue their contacts, proposed the organization of a society whose membership should be limited to the commissioned personnel of the army. The earliest written suggestion in this connection which survives is a paper, in General Knox's handwriting, entitled "Rough Draft of a Society to be formed by the American officers, and to be called the Cincinnati," and dated April 15, 1783, at West Point. A meeting was held on May tenth following, at which a committee was appointed to revise and consolidate the proposal. The report of this committee was made and accepted at a meeting held May thirteenth at Baron Von Steuben's quarters in the Verplanck house, on which occasion the organization of the Society of the Cincinnati was effected.

General Heath, in his memoirs, tells us that on the June nineteenth following, "A number of officers of the army, viz. several general officers, and officers commanding regiments and corps, met at the New Building, and elected his Excellency Gen. Washington, President General; Gen. M'Dongal, Treasurer; and Gen. Knox, Secretary, *pro tempore*, to the Society of the Cincinnati."

The up-river course of the tides is blocked four miles beyond Newburgh and Beacon by a wall of green shore, but the turn is indicated by a white lighthouse at the waterside. This is Danskammer Light. Danskammer is a very old name on the river. Originally it was Teufel's Danskammer, or Devil's

Dance Hall, and a local tradition that Henry Hudson's men gave it this name when on their voyage up-river, alleges they paused at the point now marked by the light, and were entertained by the savages in one of their wild war or ritual dances. Certain it is that this point was favored by the Indians for just such dances, and it had its present name at least as early as the year 1640, for DeVries, in his record of his voyage along the river in that year, wrote in his journal:

"At night came by the Danzkammer, where there was a party of Indians who were very riotous, seeking only mischief, so that we were on our guard."

Another Dutchman, Lieutenant Couwenhoven, coming this way in 1663, anchored his sloop off the Danskammer, and he noted that "the Indians who lay thereabout on the river made a great uproar every night, firing guns and Kintikaying so that the woods rang." Kintikaeye was the name given one of the dances. These dances were finally discontinued by the English Government, but the memory of them still lives in the name of the site devoted to them.

To-day the plateau above the lighthouse is crowned with a ruin, a striking ruin of one of the stateliest classic homes these shores have seen, a veritable Grecian temple. The house was built of stone early in the last century by William Armstrong, a Scotsman, who had married Sarah Ward of Charleston, and he perpetuated the old Dutch name in calling his house Danskammer. Later it was for a time the home of Warren Delano, but he and others of the Delano family built homes of their own on both sides of the river in these reaches above the Highlands. Danskammer house eventually fell on evil days of emptiness, neglect, abuse and finally plunder. But in all its structural essentials it still stands, a suggestion, here above the Hudson, of Pæstum on the Tyrrhenian Sea.

The river straightens around Danskammer Light and reaches due north, without a deviation, to the horizon where water and sky are seen to meet under, but far beyond, the web of metal which is the high bridge at Poughkeepsie, nine miles away. For the first time the sense that the Hudson is a series of lakes is absent. Here, as far as the eye can see, it is river, direct and obvious, long and narrowed to an average width of about half a mile.

The first opening in the west bank is an inlet which admits the waters of Jew's Creek. This creek tosses its way north and, just before it reaches tidal level at the inlet, its waters were caught long ago by a dam at the side of which rose a mill and mill-house, built in the year 1711. The builder appears in the records as "Mr. Gomez," and also as "Gomez the Jew," and he it was who gave his name to Jew's Creek more than two hundred years ago. The sturdy stone house still stands, its walls three feet thick. From this base Gomez did such a thriving trade with Dutch and Indians, and prospered so on the trade he carried on, in his own ships, with Spain and Portugal, that he came to be accounted one of the richest men in New York.

Soon after the year 1772 Gomez's house rose in the world, after a manner of speaking, for then it took on a handsome upper story laid in alternating courses of all-heads and all-lengths. This was put on by Wolfert Acker, grandson of the Wolfert Acker who built the beginnings of Irving's Sunnyside and whose name Irving familiarized to us in his *Wolfert's Roost*.

The old Mill-House is tucked away from the river, behind a hill, so that, sailing this way, one does not see it, or even guess of its presence, without a detour on shore. What does attract the eye here are the orchards and vineyards, above and behind which peep out the eaves and dormers of the tidy little village of Marlboro. These terraced hillsides are the precursor and promise of the altered character of the life on the banks of this northern stretch of the Hudson.

The west shore for many miles is abrupt and high, piling back in places to five hundred feet. Here, where the forests yield clearings, are repeated stretches of orchards and vineyards. The east shore reaches back in long sweeps to heights of scarcely more than one hundred and fifty feet, and on this side orchards alternate with fields of grass and grain. Here we recall that these are almost the first evidences of an agricultural life seen so far along the Hudson's shores. From here north, however, as far as the tides flood, the land comes to the water in a yielding, fruitful mood.

Just ahead, in the midst of this smiling valley, raised on its own platform two hundred feet above the river and backed by higher hills, is the city of Poughkeepsie, the largest city on the Hudson between New York and Albany. The word "Poughkeepsie" is of Indian origin and derives, with various changes, according to the studies of Edmund Platt, from "Pooghkepesingh," and means "where the water breaks through or falls over," referring to the junction of the Fall Kill with the Hudson within the present limits of the city. It began to take form as a settlement shortly before the year 1717. Two houses of the community's earlier days survive. One is known as the Clear Everitt, or Governor George Clinton house, and was possibly one of the houses which he occupied while here. The other is the old Noxon house, altered beyond any suggestion of its age.

The blue for the first of our national flags to undergo fire was furnished by the Continental uniform of Captain Abraham Swartwout of Poughkeepsie. This flag was made hurriedly on August 2, 1777, by the defenders of Fort Stanwix or Schuyler, which stood where Rome, New York, now stands. When re-enforcements came to the fort on that day, with the news of the official adoption of the "stars and stripes," a flag was immediately improvised; the white stripes being furnished by the shirts of the soldiers, the red stripes by the petticoat of the wife of one of the men, and the blue field for the stars was supplied by Captain Swartwout's blue cloak. The evidence of this is the vouchers of the United States Treasury which reimbursed Swartwout for the loss of his cloak.

The single event of national significance which appears in the city's annals was the meeting here, in June, 1788, of the convention to decide whether New York should adopt the Federal Constitution and become one of the United States. The eyes of the other twelve states were focused anxiously on this meeting, not only because of the significance of the decision to them as well as New York, but because of the great characters who led the debate, among whom were Alexander Hamilton, George Clinton, John Jay and Chancellor Livingston.

A more wide-spread fame has come to the city, however, by its association with the name of Vassar. Matthew Vassar, who came to Poughkeepsie with his father in 1796, was born in England. The father founded a brewery here, which the son carried on with success. The beer produced here was the basis of the great fortune out of which Matthew Vassar gave nearly a million dollars for the foundation here of the Vassar Female College. The brewery died a natural death many years ago. But the college has survived to achieve an eminence which is historic.

The early records of the east shore of the Hudson contiguous to Poughkeepsie on its south side bring the name of Schuyler into the story of the river. Colonel Philip Schuyler was the first of his family here as appears from his patent of the year 1688. This, however, was but one of his vast holdings. Another, farther north and patented in the same year, reached from Magdalen, now Cruger's, Island for many miles northward along the river's shore. Beyond this second tract were the lands of the Beekmans.

In more recent years the inventor of the electric telegraph, Samuel F. B. Morse, lived at Locust Grove, his seat, south of the city. Above the city in the shore neighborhood known as Hyde Park are homes of other famous Americans. Here in the early years of the nineteenth century lived James Kirke Paulding, at his place called Plancentia. Paulding's fame is dim now, but it was bright enough during his lifetime, when he was famous as Washington Irving's collaborator in the publication of *Salmagundi* and in other literary enterprises. He became Secretary of the Navy in 1837, and it is a little curious that the best remembered policy of this son of the river of Stevens and Fulton was his opposition to the introduction of steam-driven vessels into the Navy. Here for several generations have been Roosevelt homes, and it is the latest distinction given the Hudson that one of these has been the lifelong home of Franklin Delano Roosevelt, third son of the Hudson to become President of the United States. The conspicuously handsome white stone mansion on the shore north of the village of Hyde Park stands on a portion of the estate which first bore the name Hyde Park, from which the town took its name. This house was built by Frederick W. Vanderbilt. On the opposite shore the naturalist and writer, John Burroughs, spent many active years of his long life at Riverby on the heights near West Park.

In these upper reaches of the river its waters sometimes, in severe winters, freeze solidly from shore to shore. The steam tug and the steam ferry have, however, seldom been found unequal to the task of keeping a navigable passage open. Not so before their advent, in the sailing days. Then when the ice king laid his stiffening hand on the river the sail or the horse ferries were forthwith out of commission. Then this same ice became a bridge across which the horse-drawn sleds and sleighs passed from shore to shore; at times it became a course over which were run sleigh races even from the early Dutch days. Then, too, the skaters found the river an incomparable natural rink, and the ice boats were raced and tacked over the silver surface. Such scenes are rarely witnessed now.

Between Poughkeepsie and Hyde Park the river deflects slightly west of north past an inconspicuous point known to mariners as Crum Elbow, an anglicization of Krom Elleboog, or crooked elbow, as, with a sly sense of exaggeration, it was called by the Dutch sailors. Crum Elbow reappears on the east shore as the name of a creek, of a small post-village, and of President Franklin Roosevelt's home. The resumption of a due northerly course discloses ahead the low green point of Esopus Island fairly bisecting the river. The short stretch beyond is one of the quietest and most primitive on the river. The comparatively low shores are ribbons of almost unbroken green punctuated at infrequent intervals by white dots where great country houses look out upon the river. There is no city here, no hamlet even that shows itself from the water, and, in the peace we are reminded that trains have roared along the track at both watersides almost continually on this progress northward, for here momentarily both railroads have retired a little way inland. Then, where Vandenberg Cove widens the river a little, and another lighthouse charts the course, the waterway bends a little to the left, and we are in another "lake," and the way ahead is crossed by the heights in whose embrace is locked the deep channel of Rondout Creek and the community which is the little city of Kingston. As one approaches there is no evidence of city, however. A single white spire lifts its finger through the dense green. There is no other suggestion of a community. It is only when one comes opposite the mouth of Rondout Creek and the riverside hills are fairly separated, that one sees the first evidence of a city reaching from its own modest water-front back over the western hills.

The ground covered by modern Kingston is adjacent to the Hudson at the mouth of Rondout and to two fresh-water creeks, the Esopus and the Wallkill, which flow through long fertile valleys. It presented an ideal base for the traders with the Indians and later, as these valleys were settled and cultivated, for a civic and commercial center. Indeed, just here Europeans erected one of their earliest defenses on the Hudson, or, indeed, in America. The precise date does not document. But it must have been before 1615 for, in 1665, their High Mightinesses, the States General of the Netherlands, declared: "It is more than fifty years since we are in possession of Forts Orange and Esopus."

There were settlers in these valleys before 1655 for in that year the Indians made such terrorizing and devastating raids here that the victims appealed to Petrus Stuyvesant, "director-general of New Netherland, Curaçoa, Bonaire, Aruba, and dependencies thereof," and he came up-river in person, "with sixty or seventy men to guard his person," and directed the erection of a fortified village, which was forthwith accomplished and was called Wiltwyck, in commemoration of the fact that the soil was the free gift of the Indians. But it was not called Wiltwyck for long. Before the end of another decade the English had taken possession of the river, and they changed the name of the little town to Kingston.

Here the Provincial Convention, having moved from Fishkill for greater security from the British, adopted the Constitution of the state of New York, April 20, 1777; and here George Clinton was inaugurated first governor of the state of New York, on July thirtieth next following. The British answer to such "rebellious insolence" was to send General John Vaughan "with thirty sail," up the river, in the October following, with directions to burn the village, which he did. Some of the houses had been built of stone, however, and those were not damaged beyond repair. It is to this fact that Kingston owes its distinction for possessing so many colonial survivals. Prominent among them are the house, built in 1676 by Colonel Wessil Ten Broeck, where the convention sat and which is now known as the Senate House; the old Academy; the Schoonmaker house; the Van Steenburgh house; the Sleight or Tappan house; and the Hoffman house. They were built by the Dutch or their descendants and in general reflect the Dutch colonial type of dwelling.

Kingston's most notable contribution to the personnel of our national life was probably the artist, John Vanderlyn. He was born here in 1776, and died here in 1852; but the longer portion of his life was spent in New York City, Paris and elsewhere. His pictures are in many galleries. Among them the most notable are *Ariadne* in the Pennsylvania Academy, Philadelphia; *Marius amid the Ruins of Carthage;* his self-portrait, in the Metropolitan Museum, New York City; and

The Landing of Columbus, in the Capitol of the United States, which may be found engraved on the United States five-dollar bank notes.

There are other interesting specimens of Dutch colonial dwellings at Old Hurley, now a suburb of Kingston, which has remained more thoroughly Dutch, in all but name, than any other community in the Hudson Valley. The old houses of near-by New Paltz are sometimes spoken of as Dutch specimens although they were built by Huguenot settlers.

New Paltz is the offspring of Old Hurley. The Huguenots had first established themselves at Hurley, but in 1663, the Indians attacked that settlement, burned it, and on their retreat carried away some of the women and children of Colonel Louis Dubois. The colonel was one of the rescue party who set out after the Indians. Their way led up the valley of the Wallkill, which parallels the course of the Hudson on the western side of the hills that rim the river. On their return, these French did not forget this lovely valley, and in 1677 they purchased from the Indians thirty-six thousand acres of land, whose eastern boundary was the Hudson itself, from a point nearly opposite the present city of Poughkeepsie up nearly to Kingston. For this they paid the red men "40 kettles, 40 axes, 4 adzes, 40 shirts, 400 strings of white beads (wampum), 300 strings of black beads, 50 pairs of stockings, 100 bars of lead, 1 keg of powder, 100 knives, 4 quarter-casks of wine, 40 jars, 60 splitting or cleaving knives, 60 blankets, 100 needles, 100 awls, and 1 clean pipe."

In their valley of the Wallkill, on a gentle rise, which now is the west side of the village of New Paltz, these French settlers built themselves a row of detached stone houses. Five of them survive to-day. They stand along a shady old street, apart from

Top—The Eltinge House
Lower—The Hasbrouck House

Top—The Freer House
Lower—The Bevier House

FOUR COLONIAL HOUSES AT NEW PALTZ

any apparent contact with the modern village or with life to-day. They are known as the Hasbrouck, Elting, Bevier, Dubois and Freer houses, and, in themselves and in their grouping, their setting and their detachment, they represent as charming an illusion of Hudson Valley colonial life as one can hope to find anywhere. One is fortunate if one finds the old street empty, for it would be disillusioning to see here any but children clattering their sabots on the stone pavements; or old men with bagged and be-buttoned trousers, and broad hats, and colorful shirts, and porcelain-bowled pipes dangling from bearded lips; or women with tight-laced though not quite waspish waists, their hips billowing with many petticoats, their shoulders spread with snowy kerchiefs.

The tenacity of their original character shown by this handful of old houses is highly representative of the men and women who built and first lived in them. Those French pioneers of New Paltz were almost, if not quite, as tenacious of their traditional habits as were the Dutch who soon surrounded them. It was probably the infiltration by marriage with the Dutch which broke down the French solidarity here, just as the Dutch social order succumbed, though even more slowly to the effect of English connections. The church records of New Paltz were kept in the French language for its first fifty years. During the next seventy years they were kept in the Dutch language. The English language influence overtook and conquered New Paltz only at the beginning of the nineteenth century.

New Paltz was not less individual in its form of government, which it established for itself, on its own plan, without relation to Dutch or English pattern or influence, and so maintained it until the state and federal reorganization after the end of the Revolutionary War. Control of all civic matters was in the hands of the Dusine or Twelve Men. They were elected annually and the posts had this hereditary factor, that no one was so elected to hold one of them unless he was a descendant, in either the male or female line, from one of the small group of original settlers. They were empowered to divide and allot the community land, to give title by word of mouth, to pass judicially on all matters which elsewhere would come under the jurisdiction of a court, and generally "to set in order and unity all common affairs."

Otherwise, it appears that the members of this little political *enclave* were not greatly different from their stout neighbors of their own generations. Eberlein reports a tradition which supports such a view, to the effect that "it was commonly said in the early days that when a young man of New Paltz went wooing, the young lady to whom he was paying his attentions never thought of enquiring whether he would get drunk, but simply whether he was *ugly* when drunk."

The tides of the river swing northward another fifty miles beyond Kingston, before they succumb to the lift of the land, at the point where our story ends, but which is historically unique as the point where the Dutch made their first known permanent settlement on this continent, within sight of the site of the city of Albany.

CHAPTER XII

ON TO THE TIDE'S END

The Catskill Mountains Look down on the Hudson—Beekman Lands—
Cruger's Island—Livingston Manor and the Livingston Family—A Monkey
Spoon—A Signer and a Chancellor—Clermont—Other Distinguished
Estates—De Zaagaartje and Saugerties—Oom Hans and His Tavern—The
Village of Catskill—*Rip Van Winkle*—The New Englanders Bring Whaling
to the River—The City of Hudson—Kinderhook—Martin Van Buren's
Lindenwald—The Original of *Ichabod Crane*—A Letter from Washington
Irving—The Island Sector—The Van Rensselaer Manors—Beverwyck and
Albany—Philip Schuyler's the Pastures—Alexander Hamilton's Wedding—
Fort Crailo—The Writing of *Yankee Doodle*—The Flats at Watervliet—
Troy—The Origin of "Uncle Sam"—Where the Salt Tides Meet the
Sweet Waters of Tear of the Clouds.

HE river, in the last third of its tidal length, from
old Kingston to the extinction of the tide's influence beyond older Albany, has a character all
its own. It is not, on the average, appreciably
narrower than it has been above the broad waters of Newburgh Bay except along its last dozen miles, and its occasional
slight bends maintain its general aspect of a series of lakes,
each of them longer here to be sure than below. But here a
series of islands split the surface of the waters, giving a new
variety to its lines. These islands multiply toward the end of
the tide, until they form a kind of chain, as it were an attenuated
archipelago; for the banks though often abrupt are, near the
water, rarely higher than one hundred feet. At a little distance
behind these green banks other occasional terraces rise higher,
so that there is no monotony of horizon-line.

The railroad on the west shore abandons the river altogether over this last stretch, swinging its way up the valleys between the folds of hills, unseen and unheard from the water. There is an increasing sense of a placid pleasant stream running through a broad smiling valley.

One especial natural factor, however, influences the picture along this stretch. It is the brooding serried jagged agglomeration known as the Catskill Mountains. They lie off to the west. At the nearest, their base line approaches no closer than five miles. But on this eastern side their flanks are comparatively precipitous, so that their peaks are little farther away from the river than is their base line. This mountain group extends about fifteen miles north and south and, as its highest summits rise over four thousand feet, they may be seen along all the last fifty miles of tidal Hudson. The Catskills were given their name by the Dutch, and it refers to the wildcats or catamounts which the first settlers on the river found there.

"Whoever has made a voyage up the Hudson," wrote Irving, "must remember the Kaatskill Mountains. They are a dismembered branch of the great Appalachian family, and are seen away to the west of the river, swelling up to a noble height, and lording it over the surrounding country. Every change of season, every change of weather, indeed every hour of the day, produces some change in the magical hues and shapes of these mountains, and they are regarded by all the good housewives far and near as perfect barometers. When the weather is fair and settled, they are clothed in blue and purple and print their bold outlines on the clear evening sky; but sometimes when the rest of the landscape is cloudless, they will gather a hood of gray vapors about their summits, which, in the last rays of the setting sun, will glow and light up like a crown of glory."

Writing, in another place, of the traditions of these great hills, he said:

"The Kaatsberg or Catskill Mountains have always been a region full of fable. The Indians considered them the abode of spirits, who influenced the weather, spreading sunshine or clouds over the landscape, and sending good or bad hunting seasons. They were ruled by an old squaw spirit, said to be their mother. She dwelt on the highest peak of the Catskills, and had charge of the doors of day and night, to open and shut them at the proper hour. She hung up the new moons in the skies, and cut up the old ones into stars. In times of drought, if properly propitiated, she would spin light summer clouds out of cobwebs and morning dew, and send them off from the crest of the mountain, flake after flake, like flakes of carded cotton, to float in the air, until, dissolved by the heat of the sun, they would fall in gentle showers, causing the grass to spring, the fruits to ripen, and the corn to grow an inch an hour. If displeased, however, she would brew up clouds black as ink, sitting in the midst of them like a bottle-bellied spider in the midst of its web, and when these clouds broke, woe betide the valleys."

Nearly all the east bank of the Hudson in sight from Kingston Landing was once the estate of the Beekman family whose immigrant ancestor came from the Netherlands to the Hudson in 1647. In 1698 Lord Bellamont, at the time royal provincial governor, wrote of this estate: "One Henry Beekman, a Lieut Coll, in the Militia, has a vast tract of land as large as the Midling county of England." Near the center of its original water-line is the village of Rhinecliff, the river and railway outlet of the larger and older village of Rhinebeck on the hill two miles east of this landing. About Rhinecliff are the estates of a number of families eminent in the American record. Just below this village is Ellerslie, home of the late Levi P. Morton, Vice-President of the United States. The picturesque ruins of one of the ancient Beekman houses stand on the hillside above the landing; and near it, happily still in excellent condition, is the old stone house known as Kip Tavern, perpetuating the name of a seventeenth-century family here. A distinguished white punctuation mark in the greenery on the bank next above Rhinecliff is Ferncliff, the estate of the descendants of John Jacob Astor.

Next above these Beekman lands were the northerly lands of Colonel Peter Schuyler, beginning at the Saw Kill, which enters the river inconspicuously midway of South Bay. But neither South Bay nor North Bay is so conspicuous as the rocky island once called Magdalen, now called Cruger's, which divides them, and derives its name from another old Hudson River family. One of the most interesting traditions of the island, or indeed of this sector of the river, is that of a remarkable tribal duel fought here by the Indians. Hasbrouck, a regional historian, repeats it in this way:

"Tradition relates, and has been supported by some evidence, that about the year 1700 an aboriginal battle was fought on Magdalen, now Cruger's Island, between fifty chosen warriors of each of the tribes composing the 'Six Nations,' namely the Oneidas, Onondagas, Mohawks, Cayugas, Senecas and the Tuscaroras. It was arranged that but one man from each tribe should enter the conflict at a time. At its close there were only a few of the Mohawks and Tuscaroras left, with the advantage in favor of the latter. The Mohawks fled in their canoes to the island about a mile north, then called Slipsteen, now Goat Island. There they lighted their camp fires and spread their blankets over sticks of wood and stones, expecting the visitors to fall upon them during the night. As they imagined, the victorious Tuscaroras came and proceeded to attack, as they supposed, their sleeping enemies. But they sprang from their hiding places behind the rocks, and in turn vanquished the Tuscaroras. The Mohawks thus went home victorious, and held the supremacy of the Six Nations, over which the dispute had arisen."

The large white house in the trees lining the shore of South Bay is Montgomery Place, which was the home of General

Richard Montgomery, who fell in the disastrous American attack on Quebec, December 31, 1775, and of his wife, the sister of Chancellor Livingston. Many years later, in the year 1818, his body was brought back from Canada for interment in Trinity Church. Its progress down the Hudson in funeral state is one of the events in the river's history to which the sentimental give a touch by recalling that "Mrs. Montgomery, then a grey haired widow sat alone on the porch" of this house while the funeral boat passed. It is a little difficult, however, to respond emotionally to this incident, for the Montgomerys had been married only two years when he died and the river "funeral" took place nearly half a century later.

Above North Bay the family names attaching to the estates remind that here was the great holding known as Livingston Manor. The first of this name on the Hudson was Robert Livingston, who arrived from Scotland via Massachusetts Bay, in 1674. The family had long been one of prominence on the other side of the Atlantic. Several of the men had been knighted, one of them was custodian of the Royal Palace of Linlithgow where Mary Queen of Scots was born, and two daughters of the family were maids of honor to that queen. Robert, the immigrant, was equal to these traditions of his race. He had not been long on the river before he saw where opportunity lay and followed that way. He held important public posts from his first years here, and in the year 1679 he attached himself to the Schuyler and other great river families by marriage with Alida Schuyler.

Perceiving that power lay with landholding, Livingston secured from the government a grant of one hundred and sixty thousand acres, which lay for ten miles along the river and thence east from it to the New England boundary-line. This vast estate was erected into a manor in 1715 with the extraordinary privilege of representation in the Colonial Assembly, enjoyed also by two other river manors, Van Rensselaerwyck and Cortlandt. From the time of the erection of the manor, until he retired from public life in 1725, this Livingston sat in the Assembly, and for seven years he presided there as speaker.

From this able man sprang a line of other characters even more distinguished in the public life of the nation. He was succeeded in the lordship of the manor by his eldest surviving son, Philip Livingston, who married Catharine Van Brugh. The hobby of this lord seems to have been to build churches on his manor, all of which he painted red, and one such, known as the Red Church, survives. When he died he was buried with two funerals of pomp; with one in New York City where he died, and with another at his residence on the manor, where he was buried. Sedgwick, in describing these funerals, said:

"In the City the lower rooms of most of the house on Broad street, where he resided, were thrown open to receive the assemblage. A pipe of wine was spiced for the occasion, and to each of the eight bearers, with a pair of gloves, mourning scarf and handkerchief, a monkey spoon was given. At the Manor the whole ceremony was repeated, another pipe of wine was spiced and besides the same presents to the bearers, a pair of black gloves and handkerchief were given to each of the tenants."

Of the monkey spoon the same author added:

"It would be desirable to know the origin of this custom now entirely obsolete. This spoon differed from the common spoon in having a circular and very shallow bowl, and took its name from the figure of an ape or monkey, which was carved *in solido* at the extremity of the handle."

Philip Livingston, second lord of the manor, was in turn succeeded by his eldest son, Robert Livingston. This third lord seems not to have been more distinguished than other children of his father. His brother, Peter Livingston, was a member of the Committee of One Hundred and also of the Provincial Congress, of which he was the first president. His brother, Philip Livingston, was also a member of the Committee of One Hundred, sat in the Continental Congress, and was a signer of the Declaration of Independence. His brother, William Livingston, became the eminent war governor of New Jersey. Sarah Van Brugh Livingston, daughter of Governor William Livingston, married John Jay, who became first Chief Justice of the Supreme Court of the United States. There is a tradition of a striking resemblance between her and Marie Antoinette, then queen of France, and that, when she and her husband were in Paris and entered the royal box at the opera, the entire audience rose, mistaking the American woman for their queen. Robert, the third lord, lived until after the Revolution, and so was the last lord of the manor.

Not less distinguished were the descendants of the first lord by his second surviving son, Robert Livingston. In admiration of a reputed act of bravery by this son, the first lord detached from the manor lands a tract of thirteen thousand acres on the Hudson, south of Roeliff Jansen Kill, and presented it to him. His son was Judge Robert Livingston of the New York Supreme Court, who married Margaret Beekman of Rhinebeck.

Their son, Robert R. Livingston, was one of the most distinguished characters in our national history. He was a member of the Provincial Congress and of the Continental Congress. He was one of the committee of five appointed to draft the Declaration of Independence, which he was prevented from signing by his enforced absence at a meeting of the Provincial Congress, and which his cousin, Philip Livingston, did sign; else the Livingston family of the Hudson might have shared the distinction of the Lee family on the Potomac in having two of its names attached to that document. Robert R. Livingston became first chancellor of the state of New York, and as such he administered the oath of office to George Washington on his inauguration as first president of the United States. In 1801 he went to France as our minister, by the appointment of President Thomas Jefferson; and there, in association with James Monroe, effected the purchase of Louisiana for our national domain. On his return to the Hudson he became the patron of Robert Fulton in the inauguration of a steam navigation service on the Hudson. With the overthrow of British political control and the establishment of the Republic, entail and its feudal privileges were abolished, and the Livingston manor lands were divided between the five sons of the third and last lord.

The first lord built a manor house in the north part of his estate, overlooking the Hudson near the village of Linlithgo, but in about the year 1800 it was taken down by his great-grandson, and it has never been replaced. No Livingston manor house, properly so-called, has been in existence for over a century and a quarter.

The Chancellor's brother, Edward Livingston, born at Clermont, was only a little less eminent. Many public services culminated in his succeeding Martin Van Buren as Secretary of State of the United States, and later he became the author of the Criminal Code of Louisiana. Victor Hugo is quoted as having said of him: "You will be remembered among the men of this age who have deserved most and best of mankind."

Among many houses of interest along this stretch of the river are Callendar House, Green Hill or the Pynes, Tivoli, Clermont, and Oak Hill, all eighteenth-century houses. Of them Clermont is of paramount interest, for it is the oldest of them all and links the story of the first division of the Livingston Manor with the most distinguished of all the descendants of the first lord. It will be remembered that he gave a large tract off the southeast corner of the original manor to his admired second son, Robert. That young man called his gift Clermont and from that time, 1728, until 1813, this estate was owned and dwelt on by only three Livingstons—father, son and grandson— and they were all named Robert. Though much altered from its original appearance by a stucco surface, verandas and an additional story, it has remained in the possession of the Livingstons.

Clermont House was built in 1730, and, unusual here at that time, it was built of stone with two full stories and with ceilings twelve feet high. It stood until October, 1777, when it was burned by the British on their up-river raid. The end walls remained intact, and in the new house, built on the original foundations, were incorporated these walls. At the time of the destruction of Clermont it was the home of Margaret Beekman Livingston, mother of the Chancellor, and after it was rebuilt she continued to live there until her death in the year 1800. Meantime, in 1783, the Chancellor built a home for himself on the banks of the river, just to the south of Clermont and within a stone's throw of it, and he called this home Arryl House. It was destroyed by fire a few years ago, and only fragments of its walls remain. There the Chancellor lived until after the death of his mother. It was in compliment to his distinguished patron that Robert Fulton named his steamboat the *Clermont,* and moored it overnight at Clermont Landing on its first voyage up, and again down, the Hudson.

From these lands of the Livingstons the lovely prospect of the Hudson is enhanced by the distant purple wall of the Catskill Mountains opposite. The traveler this way, in ascending the river beyond Cruger's Island, is diverted also by the sudden narrowing of the river's surface, for a long low point projects from the west shore and is extended beyond its own reach by a long dock. The navigable passage as left here is less than a quarter of a mile wide. A lighthouse ahead marks the channel westward into the mouth of Esopus Creek, whose upper waters wash the edges of Kingston. Just here above the Esopus about a half-mile inland from the river, which it overlooks from its own green tableland, sits the village of Saugerties, a community which dates its beginnings back to the first years of the eighteenth century when the Palatines had recently come to this neighborhood.

The village takes its name from an anonymous but very real character here in the early days. He has come down to us with no other identity than *"de zaagaartje"* (the sawmill man). His sawmill was at the mouth of Saw Creek just north of the present village. Those who first spoke of his mill as *"de zaag-aartje's"* gradually applied the name to the neighborhood, and it survives, anglicized, in the name of Saugerties.

Malden, on the river banks above it, is almost a twin for age, though not for size. Here the local-pride conscious will be apt to point out John Bigelow's home south of the village. This great naturalist must have been good company, but I would like to have been here in post-Revolutionary days when the tavern of Oom Hans Myer was in its heyday. Oom Hans was something of a personage in his humble way. Mention

has been made of the efforts of the British to control the river
by the plan of Burgoyne to fight his way south to Albany, and
how "Gentlemanly Johnny" was halted at Saratoga. His halt
there was only temporary, for eventually he reached Albany;
not to seize it, however, for he himself had been seized, but
as a paroled prisoner in an ambulance, with Oom Hans Myer
of Malden on the driver's box, reins and whip in hand. Oom
Hans had a way of associating with celebrities, for many of
them traveling the west shore in the days of his tavern stopped
with him, and among his frequenters we find the name of
Aaron Burr on his way to and from Albany on his law practise.

The banks of the river, in the succeeding ten miles, rise and
fall, recede and approach again, in a most beguiling way, let-
ting in vistas of the Catskills on the west and of lesser detached hills on the east, admitting the waters of Inbocht Bay
to double the river's width at one point, and narrowing beyond
to a mere half-mile, where Catskill Creek brings in the tribute
of its waters. At the creek's mouth is the village of Catskill,
presenting to the river voyager a mere bucolic suggestion of its
retiring self, reaching up the creek beyond an impressive avenue of vast old trees.

This village was the home of the best-known citizen of the
whole Hudson, beloved Rip Van Winkle; a celebrity, singularly,
who never was, yet who was made so real by the genius of
Irving that it is not easy to think or speak of him except in terms
of actuality.

"At the foot of these fairy mountains," wrote Irving, "the
voyager may have descried the light smoke curling up from
the village, whose shingle roofs gleam among the trees, just
where the blue tints of the upland melt away into the fresher
green of the nearer landscape. It is a little village of great

antiquity, having been founded by some of the Dutch colonists in the early times of the province, just about the beginning of the government of the good Peter Stuyvesant (may he rest in peace!) and there were some of the houses of the original settlers standing within a few years, built of small yellow bricks brought from Holland, having latticed windows and gable fronts, surmounted with weathercocks. . . . In that same village, and in one of these very houses (which, to tell the precise truth, were sadly timeworn and weather beaten) there lived many years since . . . a simple, good natured fellow named Rip Van Winkle."

It would seem as if there were no one who did not know the story of Rip, of his bibulous habits, of his shrewish wife who drove him out of their house, of his hunting trips into the near-by Catskill Mountains to escape from drab realities, of how on one such expedition he scrambled up to one of the highest parts of the mountains and there encountered the specters of the crew of the *Half Moon* playing at ninepins, drank with them, fell into a deep sleep which, when he woke, he found had lasted twenty years; and finally returned down the mountain to his native village to find himself more than a stranger, a myth even among the descendants of his own people.

Beyond the village of Catskill the river bends a little east of north and, where it resumes its direct northern course above Rogers Island, is the village of Athens, on the west shore, and opposite, on the east shore, the little city of Hudson. And when we peer deep into the past of the land where that city stands, we find that we have reached the original realm of those regents of the upper Hudson, the famous family of Van Rensselaers. They had two contiguous manors on the east shore of the Hudson, the Upper and the Lower. Hereabouts was the Lower Manor, and its manor house called Claverack was built here a short distance east of the river. Its river outlet was called

Claverack Landing, a name by which it was known for more than one hundred years.

The change came in 1783, and it was made by a group of men the like of whom had not before been seen hereabout, who had come hither for a reason that is only credible because it is well substantiated. The newcomers were four Quakers, and they were whalers, and they came to the upper Hudson, one hundred and twenty miles from the sea, to establish a whaling base!

The four Quakers had enriched themselves considerably, and they represented an additional twenty-six others, also well-to-do, also from the whaling industry on the coast of southeastern New England. During the Revolutionary War, however, the British cruisers had caused them considerable embarrassment and loss, and the association of thirty, on the advice of their four prospectors, decided to seek a new base in the seclusion of the upper Hudson at Claverack Landing, whose name they immediately changed to Hudson.

These pioneers came in their own vessels and began life here in portable houses which they had brought with them already framed at their former homes in Nantucket and Providence. They sent their ships down to the sea, not only into the South Atlantic for whales, but for general merchandising along the whole Atlantic coast and in the West Indies. The blockade of the river's mouth by the British during the second war with England put only a temporary damper on the activities of these Hudson River whalers, but when they resumed after this war they found they had competitors out of Poughkeepsie and Newburgh.

The ships from Hudson brought back enormous cargoes of sperm-oil and whale-bone, and the bonanza lasted until nearly the middle of the nineteenth century. The turn in fortune came from a variety of natural causes. As the supply of whale themselves grew scarcer, cheaper substitutes for their oil and bone appeared on the market. Perhaps the greatest single factor in the deterioration and disappearance of the Hudson whaling fleets was the universal adoption of natural crude oil, and its products, for light and lubrication.

The Lower manor house of the Eastern Manor of Van Rensselaerwyck is found in the hills east of the city of Hudson. It was built in 1685 by Hendrick Van Rensselaer. It is a modest house of simple lines, its two-feet thick brick walls quite unsuspected beneath their encasement of white clapboards. This house was secondary in importance to Fort Crailo on the Upper Eastern Manor, chief seat of this manorial administration. The house at Claverack was established as a convenience for the tenants thereabout who found it taxing and vexing, under pioneer conditions, to travel twenty-seven miles north to pay assessments and attend court.

In this sector the hinterland is richer in interesting old houses than is the river shore. Especially alluring is the valley of the Kinderhook, now sometimes called Stockport Creek, which comes to the great river four miles above the city of Hudson. The name Kinderhook appears on Adrian Block's map dated 1614-16. Of wide interest are a brick mansion and a little white schoolhouse here.

The mansion is called Lindenwald, and it is of interest because here Martin Van Buren, after his administration as president of the United States, lived until his death in 1862. Van Buren named the house Lindenwald. Previously it had been known as the Van Ness house after the builder, Peter Van Ness. He and his sons were eminent each in his own way. In the Van

Ness burying-ground, not far from the mansion, the tombstone over the builder's grave reminds that he had served in the colonial wars in the British invasion of Canada, was in command of a regiment at the capture of Burgoyne in the battle of Saratoga, was a member of the State Convention which adopted the Federal Constitution, and later served in several other eminent public capacities.

The builder had three sons, each of whom attained national prominence. One of them, John P. Van Ness, served in the Federal Congress and became mayor of the city of Washington, where he had a once-famous mansion on the site of the Pan American Building; another, Cornelius P. Van Ness, became chief justice of the supreme court of the state of Vermont, governor of that state, and United States minister to Spain; while a third, William P. Van Ness, read law in the office of Aaron Burr and, later, acted as Burr's second in the duel in which Alexander Hamilton was killed.

Washington Irving spent much time at Lindenwald, and it is accepted that he drew much of his characterization and at least two of his characters from this neighborhood. The original of Katrina Van Tassell, object of Ichabod Crane's affections, was, in real life, Katrina Van Alen, who lived in the quaint old Dutch brick dwelling known as the Van Alen house, near by, and which dates back to 1736. The original of Ichabod Crane, himself, was Jesse Merwin of Kinderhook. Though Ichabod is supposed to have taught school in Sleepy Hollow, Irving's friend, Jesse Merwin, actually taught school near Lindenwald in a schoolhouse on the site of the little white building now familiarly spoken of locally as "Ichabod Crane's school."

Nothing that Irving wrote is more representative of his style and personal charm, or more graphically suggestive of this old

Dutch neighborhood, than this letter, written in 1851 to his friend, the schoolmaster:

"You must excuse me, my good friend Merwin, for suffering your letter to remain so long unanswered; you can have no idea how many letters I have to answer, besides fagging with my pen at my own literary tasks, so that it is impossible for me to avoid being behind-hand in my correspondence. Your letter was indeed most welcome, calling up, as it did, recollections of pleasant scenes and pleasant days passed together in times long since at Judge Van Ness's, at Kinderhook. Your mention of the death of good old Dominie Van Nest recalls the apostolic zeal with which he took our little sinful community in hand, when he put up for a day or two at the Judge's; and the wholesome castigation he gave us all one Sunday, beginning with the two country belles who came fluttering into the school-house during the sermon, decked out in their city finery, and ending with the Judge himself on the stronghold of his own mansion. How soundly he gave it to us! How he peeled off every rag of self-righteousness with which we tried to cover ourselves, and laid the rod on the bare backs of our consciences! The good, plain-spoken, honest, old man! How I honored him for his simple, straightforward earnestness, his homely sincerity. He certainly handled us without mittens, but I trust we were all the better for it. How different he was from the brisk, dapper, self-sufficient little apostle who cantered up to the Judge's door a day or two after; who was so full of himself that he had no thought to bestow on our religious delinquencies: who did nothing but boast of his public trials of skill in argument with rival preachers of other denominations, and how he had driven them off the field and crowed over them. You must remember the bustling, self-confident little man with a tin trumpet in the handle of his riding-whip, with which I presume he blew the trumpet in Zion.

"Do you remember our fishing expedition in company with Congressman Van Allen to the little lake a few miles from Kinderhook, and John Moore, the vagabond admiral of the lake, who sat couched in a heap in the middle of his canoe in the centre of the water, with fishing-rods stretched out in every direction, like the long legs of a spider; and do you remember our piratical prank, when we made up for our bad luck in fishing by plundering his canoe of its fish when we found it adrift? And do you remember how John Moore came splashing along

THE VAN ALEN HOUSE, NEAR KINDERHOOK
Illustrating the brickwork

the marsh, on the opposite border of the lake, roaring at us; and how we finished our frolic by driving off and leaving the Congressman to John Moore's mercy, tickling ourselves with the idea of his being scalped, at least? Oh, well-a-day, friend Merwin; these were the days of our youth and folly; I trust we have grown wiser and better since then; we certainly have grown older. I don't think we could rob John Moore's fishing canoe now. By the way, that same John Moore, and the anecdote you told of him, gave me the idea of a vagabond character—Dirk Schuyler, in my Knickerbocker history of New York, which I was then writing.

"You tell me the old school building is torn down, and a nice one built in its place. I am sorry for it. I should have liked to see the old school-house once more, where, after my morning's literary task was over, I used to come and wait for you, occasionally, until school was dismissed; and you would promise to keep back the punishment of some little tough, broad-bottomed Dutch boy, until I should come, for my amusement—but never kept your promise. I don't think I should look with a friendly eye at the new school-house, however nice it may be.

"Since I saw you in New York I have had severe attacks of billious intermittent fever, which shook me terribly; but they cleared out my system, and I have ever since been in my usual excellent health—able to mount my horse and gallop about the country almost as briskly as when I was a youngster. Wishing you the enjoyment of the same inestimable blessing, and begging you to remember me to your daughter, who penned your letter, and to your son—whom, out of old kindness and companionship, you have named after me—I remain ever, my good friend, yours, very truly and cordially,

"WASHINGTON IRVING.

"Jesse Merwin, Esq."

Above the mouth of the Kinderhook the aspect of the river itself undergoes a marked change, though its valley retains the character it has already assumed in this upper third of its course. The scenery is mild and pleasing rather than arresting. Fields of grain, orchards and vineyards define its agricultural character. The river itself tapers by the most delicate degree. But it appears here to be much narrower than it actually is between its own banks, for the way is past, and sometimes between, that succession of long low islands.

It may not be easy to believe that the waters of the Atlantic Ocean exert their influence on these quiet and comparatively narrow waters. But a glance at the banks shows a dark earthen band at the water's edge, moist as mud, and it tells the story of a tide rising and falling even here, one hundred and fifty miles from the sea.

The first account of this portion of the river, written over three hundred years ago, is true to-day. Juet, in his chronicle of the voyage of the *Half Moon* in these waters in 1609, in the course of the log for September, noted:

"The Seventeenth, faire Sun-shining weather, and very hot. In the morning as soone as the Sun was up, we set sayle, and ran up six leagues higher, and found shoalds in the middle of the channell, and small Ilands, but seven fathoms water on both sides."

Hudson anchored among the islands and sent his mate and four men in a small boat to sound the river higher up. They returned after cruising north "eight or nine leagues" and reported "but seven foot of water, and unconstant soundings." Thereupon the *Half Moon* was turned back toward the sea, and so we know that Hudson never saw his river beyond these islands.

Here the lands on both sides, northward beyond the head of the tides and beyond the ken of this story, were the great patroonship of Rensselaerwyck, founded in 1630. Its northern boundary was beyond the point where the Mohawk empties into the Hudson. On the lands of Rensselaerwyck have risen the cities of Albany, Rensselaer, Cohoes and Troy and their contiguous communities in the river valley.

Emerging from the island area, the bends beyond throttle the vista of any long water. But the folds in the low hills define the unseen course, and where they open at their highest, on the horizon ahead, a searching eye discerns pale masses and outlines which are not the greens of either hillside fields or forests. Indefinite, vague and at first a little spotty, the vision articulates as one approaches, and so high does it rise on the crests and flanks of its own hilly pedestal that one is still miles away from it and can not see the waters that wash its base, when the realization comes clear that this is the city of Albany, the capital of New York.

Albany stands on ground associated with the first settlement on the river. Five years after the mate of the *Half Moon* made his "unconstant soundings" here, the Dutch came, in the year 1614, and built a fort, which they named Fort Nassau, on Castle Island, now indifferently called Rensselaer or Westerlo Island; and it had a garrison of ten or twelve men and mounted two pieces of cannon and eleven pederos. The fort's situation was found untenable and was abandoned after three years. But traders continued to sail hither, and in 1624 eighteen families came out from Holland and settled here and built Fort Orange on the site of present "Steamboat square." That was the beginning of the permanent settlement. At the head of the navigable water of the river, in contact with the vast fur-bearing regions north and west, the community at Fort Orange had a preferred position which manifested itself in its continually increasing size and importance. In 1652 there were one hundred houses about the fort, and it was declared a village and given the name of Beverwyck, in acknowledgment of the beaver's influence upon its vitality.

Beverwyck was as definitely Dutch in population and appearance as was New Amsterdam at the other end of the river. Its streets were narrow and short. Its houses were built of yellow brick with gable-end to the street, and the gables were often "stepped" to give easy access to the chimneys and to the inevitable metal weather-cock. The dress of the inhabitants was not less a reflection of the customs of the lowlands overseas. The women wore a plenitude of petticoats, a tight waist, short sleeves, a close-fitting bonnet, and for ornament the metal buttons which have ever been the adornment of a Dutch maiden's head. The men affected voluminous knickerbockers, a wide white collar, buckled shoes, bobbed hair, a broad-brimmed hat, a cape, and smoked the long drooping china-bowl pipe. The language and the mode of life were not less rigorously Dutch. But a significant fact is that Albany continued to bear its Dutch aspect longer than New York because it was less exposed to foreign influences. Long after the English took political control it kept its character and was the last important stronghold of Dutch life on the river.

Scarcely a vestige of that individualizing past remains except the Dutch patronyms of some of the contemporary English citizenry. One hunts in vain for an old Dutch church and finds a handsome new one which harbors, however, the pulpit of its ancestor. The old brick houses of patroons and burghers seem to have gone before "improvements" which have made the city a counterpart of the conventional American pattern. Among hundreds of street names there are not more than can be counted on the fingers of one hand that recall the streets and lanes of Beverwyck. But the hills of the Hudson endure, and Albany flings itself across them with a proud consciousness of its superb situation.

The one conspicuous historic survival that carries beyond the

Photograph by J. A. Glenn

THE SCHUYLER MANSION AT ALBANY

Photograph by J. A. Glenn

THE DRAWING ROOM IN THE SCHUYLER MANSION, ALBANY

Alexander Hamilton and Elizabeth Schuyler were married here before the fire

Revolution here is Schuyler house. It is a high, three-story mansion rising flush on a great rectangular basement. It was on an estate that once was called the Pastures, and then it commanded a superb view of the river valley to all horizons. It was built by General Philip Schuyler in 1762, and reflects the British colonial manner, of which there is not, perhaps, a finer example in America. Its tradition is in keeping with that distinction.

Philip Schuyler was the fourth in descent from the Schuyler ancestor who came from Holland to Beverwyck in 1650. His wife was Catherine Van Rensselaer, a descendant of the patroon, and his mother-in-law was Angelica Livingston of another manor farther down the river. He sat in the Provincial Assembly; in the Continental Congress of 1775, and again of 1779; he served as major-general of the Northern Department under Washington, from 1775 to 1777; and on the adoption of the Constitution he was the first United States senator from New York.

The Pastures was not only the scene of a distinguished domestic and social life, but here the Schuylers entertained all the eminent travelers who came to the head of tidewater Hudson during their lifetimes. Two among the many striking incidents in the history of this house are in connection with the name of General "Johnny" Burgoyne and Alexander Hamilton.

General Schuyler had participated in the battle of Saratoga and the surrender of Burgoyne who had ordered the destruction of his house there. Nevertheless, when Burgoyne and his staff were sent, as prisoners of war, to Albany, Schuyler invited them to be his guests at the Pastures. Burgoyne, when he returned to London, testified to this later in a speech which he made before the House of Commons, in these words:

"I expressed to General Schuyler my regret at the event which had happened [the burning of Schuyler's Saratoga house], and the reasons which had occasioned it. He desired me to think no more of it, saying that the reason justified it, according to the rules of war. . . .

"He did more: he sent his aide-de-camp to conduct me to Albany, in order, as he expressed it, to procure me better quarters than a stranger might be able to find. This gentleman conducted me to a very elegant house and, to my great surprise, presented me to Mrs. Schuyler and her family; and in General Schuyler's house I remained during my whole stay at Albany, with a table of more than twenty covers for me and my friends, and every other possible demonstration of hospitality."

Baroness Riedesel, wife of the Hessian general, both of the party, wrote:

"They loaded us with kindness, and they behaved in the same manner toward General Burgoyne, though he had ordered their splendid establishment to be burned, and without any necessity it was said; but all their actions proved that, in the sight of the misfortunes of others, they quickly forgot their own."

And the Marquis de Chastellux quotes Burgoyne as having been "affected to tears," as he acknowledged: "Indeed this is doing too much for a man who has ravaged their lands and burned their dwellings."

A gayer and more spectacular event there was the wedding of the general's daughter Elizabeth, the only one of his daughters to be married in the Pastures or, indeed, to be married with her father's consent. It took place in December, 1780. The groom on this occasion was a handsome young soldier of twenty-three years, a lieutenant-colonel and aide-de-camp of General Washington. His name was Alexander Hamilton. When, a year later, he resigned from Washington's staff, Hamilton resumed the study of law in Albany and he and his wife took up their home in the Schuyler house. Hamilton became as a son to Schuyler, and his widow's devotion to him endured unabated until she died in her ninety-seventh year.

One of the last of Albany's historic houses to vanish was the splendid mansion of the Van Rensselaers, which disappeared without being destroyed, for it was taken down with care and reerected in Williamstown, Massachusetts. The original splendid wall-paper and the woodwork of the great central hall, which measured twenty-three feet and six inches wide by forty-six feet and ten inches long, are preserved in a reproduction of this room in the American wing of the Metropolitan Museum.

This was the last of the manor houses of the Western Manor of Van Rensselaer. It must be remembered that the great tract of the patroon of Rensselaerwyck was divided into three contiguous Van Rensselaer manors. All the land of the western side of the Hudson was known as the Western Manor. The lands on the opposite side of the river, comprised of the Eastern Manor, were subdivided into what were known as the Upper Manor and the Lower Manor; and of the latter, as we have seen, the house of administration was at Claverack. The manor house of the Upper (Eastern) Manor was that called Fort Crailo, and it still stands on the banks of the river, across from Albany, in the community once known as Greenbush but now as the city of Rensselaer. Fort Crailo has come into the custody of the state and was recently "restored."

This is one of the oldest houses in the United States. The most venerable part of the structure was built in the year 1642 and was named after a Van Rensselaer place overseas in the Netherlands. Colonel Johannes Van Rensselaer more than doubled the original size of the house by his additions, forming the northwestern portion of the house when, in the year 1740, he brought the house to its present form. It was this gentleman's daughter Catherine, "beautiful Katrina" as she was called, who became the wife of Philip Schuyler and the mistress of the Pastures. Fort Crailo was owned and occupied by Van Rensselaers continuously until 1871, when it fell into the decay from which it has recently been rescued.

The entertainments here were scarcely less famous than those at the Western manor house, or at the Pastures. Commanders of passing troops were frequently the guests of the Van Rensselaers in residence at Fort Crailo during the French-Indian War and during the Revolutionary War. It was during that earlier war, in the year 1758, while General James Abercrombie and his staff made their headquarters here on their way to Ticonderoga and defeat at the hands of the Montcalm, that there happened here an incident which gives this place, and especially the old well in its garden, a peculiar national interest.

Abercrombie had on his staff a young surgeon whose name was Richard Shuckburgh and who was greatly amused by the primitive character of the raw Yankee recruits as they straggled in from the country roundabout, whose nondescript garments were suggestive of nothing at all and least of all of anything military. According to the tradition, Shuckburgh sat on the curb of Fort Crailo's old garden well and there scribbled the verses of *Yankee Doodle,* which later were made the rallying song of these same Yankees in the Revolution, and alone preserve their author's name.

Another place whose history reaches back into the earliest days of the colonies and again connects the two great colonial families of Van Rensselaer and Schuyler is the Flats, originally in Dutch *de Vlackte,* situated on the west bank of the Hudson between Albany and Troy, at the south end of Watervliet, opposite Breaker Island. There was a house here as early as the year 1664, for Richard Van Rensselaer lived here at least from that year until he returned to Holland in 1670. Two years later it was sold to Philip Pietersen Schuyler.

The Flats is occupied and is in good condition. It presents a simple aspect, rambling and roomy, but interesting rather than distinguished. Not much would be known of the past of this old place if it were not for a little girl who made her home here with the Schuylers, about 1760, and grew up to become one of Scotland's most admired writers. This was the famous Mrs. Grant of Laggan, in whose Memoirs live not only a picture of the old mansion and of life in it, and of its relation to life at other houses on the river, but one of the most valuable surviving pictures of authentic American colonial life at the head of tidal Hudson.

In full sight of this ancient house the city of Troy rises on the riverside hills. To some the fame of this city is associated with its educational institutions, to others with shirts and collars and cuffs. But that, in all its past or present, which most attaches Troy to national interest is the fact that here lived the prototype of our familiar "Uncle Sam." His name was Samuel Wilson, and he was familiarly known locally as Uncle Sam. He was a packer, and supplied meat to the army, during the war of 1812-14, through a contractor whose name was Elbert Anderson. His consignments to this contractor were marked "E. A.— U.S.," meaning Elbert Anderson, United States. One of the workmen, being asked by another of his fellows for an explanation of the letters "U. S.," said lightly that they stood for Uncle Sam Wilson. The joke took and soon passed current. Some of these workmen went into the army. They carried their facetious explanation with them. The term "Uncle Sam" soon spread through the army and, after the war, through the entire nation, and has endured; though few know that the original of it derived from "Uncle Sam" Wilson of Troy.

Troy looks down from its hillsides on a modest river. The character of the Hudson here has little to suggest the grandeur and the greatness past which its tides have swept up from the sea. Here their strength is all spent, here where the story of the Hudson's landings ends. In turning, they pause here to refresh themselves with the sweet waters of Tear of the Clouds.

THE END

INDEX

INDEX

INDEX

INDEX

Flick, A. C.
  quoted on loyalism, 108-9
Florida, 31
Floris, Count, 66
Font Hill, 210
Forrest, Edwin, 210
Fort Albany, 92
Fort Amsterdam, 80, 165, 168
Fort Arnold, 111
Fort Clinton, 111, 115, 116, 117, 245
Fort Constitution, 115, 246
Fort Crailo, 282, 291, 292
Fort Esopus, 264
Forth and Clyde Canal, 141
Fort Independence, 111
Fort James, 92, 168
Fort LaFayette
  British take, 122
Fort Lee, 111, 113, 186, 201, 202, 203
Fort Montgomery, 111, 115, 116, 245
Fort Nassau, 46, 287
Fort Orange, 73, 80, 264, 287
Fort Putnam, 111, 117, 245
Fort Schuyler, 261
Fort Stanwix, 261
Fort Washington, 36, 41, 111, 113, 176, 202, 203
Fort Webb, 117
Fort Wyllys, 117
Fox Hall, 85
France, 48, 89, 117, 252, 253, 275, 276
  Verrazzano's exploration for, 31-33
Francis I, King, 31
Franklin, Benjamin, 102
Fraunces, Phoebe, 173
Fraunces, Samuel, 172
  becomes Washington's steward, 173
  Fraunces's Tavern, 172, 193
  description of, quoted, 172-73
  Washington's dinner at, 135, 173
Frederycks, Kryn, 164
Freer house, the, 267
Frémont, John C., 224
French colonists and colonization, 89
Freneau, Philip, 102
Freylinghausen, Dominie, 103, 106
Friesland, 207
Frontenac, 254
Front Street, 162
Fulton, Robert, 23, 25, 142, 178, 262, 276, 278
  and his steamboat, *Clermont*, 141, 143
  describes significant details of trip, 144
  "Fulton's Folly," 143

Gallows Hill, 231, 233
Garrison, 244
Gastaldi, 33
Gates, General, 118, 249, 250
George III, King, 110
George Washington Bridge, 111, 201
German colonists and colonization, 89
Giant's Causeway, 203
Glen, Jacob Sanderz, 64
Goat Island, 272
Gomez, Estevan, 27, 31, 39, 242
  Estevan Gomez's Land, 33
Gomez the Jew, 98, 259
Goodwin, Maud Wilder, 26
Goshen, 151, 152
Gould family, 155
Governor's Island, 111
Gracie, Archibald, 180
Gracie house, the, 179
Grande Riviere, 27
Grant, Mrs., 82, 106, 293
  quoted, 87-88, 94, 99, 103-4
Great Britain, 78, 130, 133, 246
  salutes Washington and the Republic, 133
Great Dock Street, 172
Great Lakes, 137
Great River, 27, 79
Greenbush, 154, 291
Greene County, 84
Greene, General, 249
Green Hill, 277
Greenland, 34
Green Mountains, 22, 236
Greenwich Street, 165, 200
Greenwich Village, 168, 169
Grievous Point, 215
Groote Rivier, 27, 45, 231
Grymes, Lucy, 212

Hackensack (Town), 113, 151, 152
Hackensack River, 113, 185, 189, 190, 191, 204
Hague, The, 80, 166
Haldiman, Governor-General, 133
Hale, Nathan, 113
Half Moon, the, 23, 24, 46, 57, 146, 184, 211, 280, 286, 287
  Hudson sails in the, 34-39, 42, 43-44
Hall, E. H., 209
  quoted, 214
Hamilton, Alexander, 25, 128, 176, 181, 182, 199, 261, 283, 289, 290, 291
  account of duel with Burr, 200

INDEX

INDEX

Mayflower, the, 24
McLane, Captain, 190
M'Dongal, General, 257
Megapolensis, Dominie, 68
Mercer, General Hugh, 188
Merwin, Jesse, 283
   Irving's letter to, quoted, 284-85
Mesier's Dock, 192
Mexican War, 245
Middlebrook, 120
Mill House, 98, 259
"Millionaire's Row," 211
Minuit, Pieter, 49, 80, 164
   purchases Manhattan Island, 163
Mitman, Carl
   quoted, 196
Mohawk and Hudson Railroad, 154
Mohawk River, 33, 286
Mohawk Valley, 89
Molemacker, François, 164
Monmouth, 120
Monroe house, the, 180
Monroe, James, 180, 276
Montaigne River, 27
Montgomery family, 273
Montgomery Place, 272
Montgomery, Richard, 273
Moodna Creek, 20, 249
Moordener Creek, 20
Moore, John, 284, 285
Morgan family, 155
Morgan, John Pierpont, 246
Morris, George P., 157, 246
Morris, Robert, 112
Morris, Roger, 175, 176, 209, 210, 213
Morris Street, 162
Morristown, 113, 121
Morse, Samuel F. B., 262
Morton, Levi P., 157, 271
Mott's Tavern, 112
Mount Giulian, 131
Mount Morris, 174, 176, 177, 179, 209
   see also Jumel Mansion
Mount Saint Vincent Academy, 210
Mount Vernon, 108, 135, 193, 212, 213, 254
Murderers Creek, 21
Murray Hill, 112
Murray, Robert, 112
Myer, Oom Hans, 278, 279
Mystery of Marie Roget, The, Poe, 198

Nantucket, 281
Nassau River, 27

Neperhan Creek, 206, 207, 208, 211
Netherlands, 31, 34, 53, 55, 67, 76, 83, 99, 149, 179, 216, 264, 271, 291
Neuberg, 89
New Amsterdam, 25, 52, 57, 61, 63, 66, 70, 73, 74, 75, 79, 82, 86, 102, 164, 167, 168, 170, 171, 184, 186, 187, 191, 207, 208, 226, 227, 242, 288
   in 1650, 166
New Building, the, 250, 257
Newburgh, 22, 89, 108, 129, 130, 131, 133, 235, 248, 251, 252, 254, 257, 281
Newburgh Bay, 248, 269
Newburgh Letters, 250, 251
New Cæsarea, 185
New England, 47, 52, 71, 74, 107, 121, 122, 123, 139, 140, 141, 143, 144, 145, 146, 148, 150, 151, 152, 153, 154, 158, 185, 255, 273, 281
New England and Boston Gazette
   quoted, 105
New France, 46
New Hampshire, 22
New Jersey, 22, 83, 84, 120, 121, 124, 132, 173, 181, 182, 183, 185, 189, 192, 204, 275
New Netherland, 24, 28, 46, 47, 48, 49, 58, 68, 73, 77, 78, 79, 80, 82, 181, 184, 187, 206, 207, 264
   Dutch education in, 74-75
   population of, in 1664, 86
New Netherland, the, 47
New Paltz, 62, 266, 268
   survivals of old French dwellings at, 266-67
New Windsor, 119, 121, 129, 249, 251
New York Bay, 28, 36, 204
New York (City, County, Province), 18, 19, 22, 28, 57, 73, 79, 82, 83, 85, 86, 87, 89, 90, 91, 92, 94, 95, 96, 99, 100, 101, 102, 103, 105, 107, 108, 109, 110, 112, 114, 120, 121, 124, 129, 130, 132, 135, 165, 168, 169, 170, 171, 173, 174, 176, 177, 178, 181, 182, 183, 184, 186, 188, 189, 190, 191, 192, 198, 204, 208, 210, 212, 213, 222, 224, 225, 226, 228, 233, 244, 247, 255, 256, 259, 260, 261, 265, 274, 276, 285, 287, 288, 289
   British in, 121
   description of, in 1704, 96-97
   loyalism in, 108-9

INDEX

Potomac River, 20, 24, 141, 212, 254, 276

Poughkeepsie, 21, 22, 111, 114, 116, 151, 153, 154, 259, 260, 262, 263, 266, 281
  Vassar College at, 261

Powles' Hook, 111, 135, 182, 186, 188, 191, 192, 193

Prevost, Mrs. Theodosea, 124

Prime house, the, 179

Prince Maurice River, 27

Prince Street, 180

Principles of Action in Matter, Colden, 102

Providence, 281

Provincial Assembly, 86, 109, 110, 114

Provoost, Bishop, 174

Purchas
  His Pilgrims
    quoted, 31

Puritans, 47

Putnam County, 84

Putnam, Israel, 115, 233, 234, 256

Pynes, 277

Quassaic Creek, 20

Quebec, 133, 273

Queen's Head, 172

Queen Street, 135

Queen's, the, 172

Ranelagh, 171

Ranlagh Gardens, 105

Recruiting Officer, The, 105, 106

Red Hook, 151

Rensselaer (City or County), 83, 286, 291

Rensselaer Island, 287

Rensselaerwyck, 50, 53, 69, 83, 84, 206, 286, 291

Renwick, James, 146
  letter of, quoted, 145-46

Revolutionary War, 29, 106, 107, 109, 134, 136, 150, 161, 172, 174, 177, 182, 188, 195, 202, 210, 214, 217, 218, 220, 226, 231, 244, 245, 251, 252, 254, 255, 267, 275, 281, 289, 292

Rhinebeck, 117, 151, 271, 275

Rhinecliff, 271, 272

Rhine River, 89, 251

Rhode Island, 33, 130, 132

Ribero, 33

Riedesel, Baroness
  quoted, 290

Riker, Richard, 199

Rio de Gomez, 27, **33**

Rio de Guamas, 33

Rio San Antonio, 27, 33

Rittenhouse, David, 250

Riverby, 263

River of the Steep Hills, 27

Riverside Drive, 178

Rivington's Gazette, 202

Robinson house, the Beverley, 125, 128, 129, 213, 244
  Arnold's headquarters at, 244
  Washington visits, 120

Robinson, Beverley, 98, 112, 209, 210, 212

Robinson, Mrs. Beverley, 213

Robinson, John, 244

Rochambeau, Count de, 125, 132

Rockefeller family, 155

Rockefeller, John D., 224

Rockland County, 84, 119

Roe, E. P., 158, 246

Roeliff Jansen Kill, 20, 275

Rogers Island, 280

Rogers, Mary Cecelia, 198

Rombout, Catharyna, 255

Rome, 261

Rondout (Town), 57, 82

Rondout Creek, 116, 264

Rondout River, 21

Roosevelt family, 262

Roosevelt, Franklin Delano, 157, 262, 263

Roosevelt, Theodore, 157, 181

Rose, the, 111

Rumsey, James, 141

Ruprecht, Knech, 72

Russia, 51

Rutgers, Anthony, 209

Saint Lawrence River, 47, 236

Saint-Mark's-in-the-Bouwerie, 180-81

Saint Paul's Chapel, 172, 173, 181

Saint Peter's Church, 231, 233

Saint Philip's Church, 244

Salisbury, Captain Sylvester, 92

Salmagundi, Irving and Paulding 262

San Antonio, 242

Sandy Hook, 36

Santo Domingo, 176

Saratoga, 116, 117, 279, 283, 289, 290

Saugerties, 278

Saw Creek, 278

Saw Kill, 272

Saw Mill River, 20, 211

INDEX

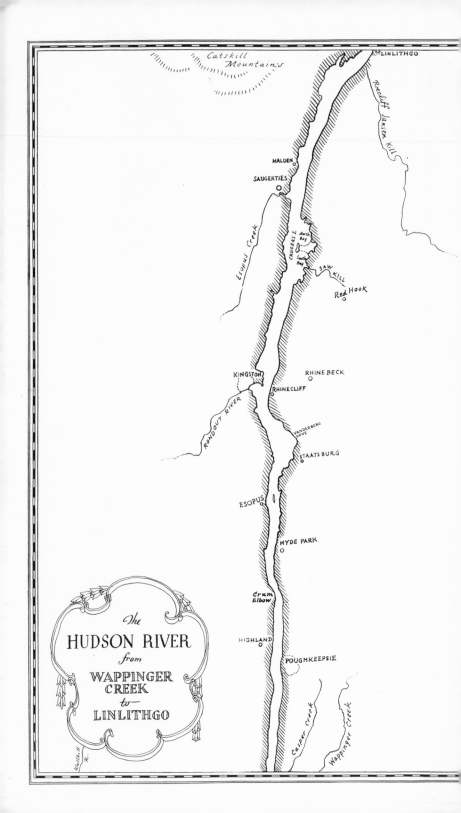